Kosher salt, not table salt

Use the right soy sauce

# FIVE NONNEGOTIABLE RULES

Keep your knife sharp!

Always grate your own cheese!

Mince garlic with a knife
(Unless I say otherwise)

RECIPETIN EATS
DINNER

*Dedicated to everyone who has ever made, read, watched, or eaten a* **RecipeTin Eats** *recipe.*

*You are the reason I love what I do.*

RECIPETIN EATS

# DINNER

NAGI MAEHASHI

Countryman Press

*An Imprint of W. W. Norton & Company*
*Celebrating a Century of Independent Publishing*

# CONTENTS

# Introduction

## On the day I launched my recipe website, I had just two visitors—my mum and myself. Last year, my website was viewed over 335 million times.

## Here's my story . . .

Eight years ago, I was a finance girl, tottering around the city in suits and stilettos, working long hours, and climbing the corporate ladder.

Today, I am the voice, cook, photographer, and videographer of ***RecipeTin Eats***, a website where I share recipes accompanied by photos and video tutorials. I also run a philanthropic division called **RecipeTin Meals**, where I have a team making meals for the vulnerable in our community.

And this book you are holding right now—this is my first ever cookbook. That you are reading a cookbook I wrote feels surreal! It's incredibly emotional. I'm so proud. And so happy!

How did a corporate lass end up in this position?
Here's my story . . .

Nikon

## Leaving corporate to start a food blog?

Everyone thought I was crazy when I ditched the security of an office job to start a food blog. And I often make playful jokes about it being a midlife crisis.

But here's the truth. It had always been my dream to build something of my own. And choosing to start a recipe website as my new venture was a considered, well-thought-out decision.

I did my research. I had a business plan. I tested the waters. I came up with ways to differentiate myself. I identified my strengths and weaknesses. I even prepared financial projections!

That might all sound very official and like I had a team of consultants to rely on, but nothing could be further from the truth. It was me, Dozer, and a secondhand $250 camera.

And I worked hard, harder than I ever have in my life, teaching myself food photography, learning how to build a website, how to navigate social media, how to monetize my website.

And of course, cooking. Cooking, cooking, cooking, to come up with recipes to share on my website!

## A really boring story of growth

On the day I launched my website in May 2014, I had two visitors. One was me. The other was my mum! However, in the last 12 months, there have been over 335 million views of my website and I have over 4.6 million followers on Instagram and Facebook.

I wish I had an amazing story to accompany what I realize is pretty big and rapid growth. But I don't. It's boring!

I simply focused on creating great recipes, written well, which work as promised, accompanied by good photos and, these days, a tutorial video. I did this quietly and consistently for years, steering clear of "clickbait" and not worrying about "going viral" like many other bloggers did.

As I built up my stable of recipes, I slowly gained the trust of readers, who then became regulars. And from there it was like a snowball effect. Word began to spread about *RecipeTin Eats* and that "cute dog of hers," both through word of mouth and through social media, and my website traffic grew.

And that, my friends, is the thoroughly unexciting way that I grew my readership—simply through publishing recipes that work. I told you it was a boring story!

However, it does bring me to something important that you should know about me . . .

## . . . I am irrationally obsessive about ensuring my recipes work!

Recipes that don't work are a pet peeve of mine. I hate wasting time, I hate wasting money, and I hate wasting food.

And the thought of you wasting your money because my recipes don't work? That feeds my fear.

If you are wondering if this obsession stems from a poor upbringing, you would be right.

But what you probably haven't guessed is that it's also fueled by messages I receive from readers. Like the reader in Ghana who told me meat was a once-a-month luxury and how much it meant knowing they could rely on my recipes. And the reader who asked me to help choose a recipe for what ended up being the last meal for her terminally ill husband.

Yup. Brings me to tears.

So yes, I am probably a little too obsessive about testing my recipes but I hope I never change. The record is 89 times, for My Perfect Vanilla Cake (page 304). Roast Duck was tested more than 30 times, but I wasn't comfortable enough with it so it was removed from the cookbook. Beef Wellington (page 252), the most iconic recipe in this book, was tested more than 35 times!

## This is what drives me

Having covered the serious side of what I do, fundamentally the thing that drives me and what I love the most about what I do, is creating and sharing recipes that taste so great it makes you do a happy dance.

It makes me smile when I see feedback from a reader, pumped because they nailed a cake that they thought was beyond them. I feel honored when people choose to make my turkey for their Christmas centerpiece.

I love hearing how people put together full-blown menus from my recipes for special occasions—starters, mains, sides, and dessert! Or how they won the local chilli contest, or how their brownies were the first to go at the school bake sale.

I've truly put my heart and soul into this cookbook. Literally, my blood, sweat, and tears.

I hope you enjoy it—and cook a lot of the recipes!

***Nagi xx***

# Dozer

Meet Dozer, my 10-year-old, abnormally large golden retriever.

I do the cooking. Dozer does the taste testing.

The problem is, he thinks everything tastes amazing!

He falls asleep in front of the oven when I'm slow-cooking roasts.

He hoovers up scraps better than any vacuum cleaner.

And he makes for the best hugs. Ever.

I love this damn dog so damn much.

DOZER

# RecipeTin Meals

## Because no one should go hungry.

***Nagi & Dozer***

RecipeTin Meals (RTM) is the philanthropic arm of RecipeTin, where we make homemade meals for distribution to the vulnerable in Sydney. RTM is a registered charity I started in 2021 during the pandemic, when there were increasing issues of hunger and food insecurity in the Sydney community.

Establishing a not-for-profit has been a secret dream of mine since I started RecipeTin and it's my proudest professional achievement to date. As of the time of writing, I have a team of three, headed by a professionally trained chef, working out of a commercial kitchen on the fringe of Sydney's city center.

We make meals five days a week (many recipes from my website!), which are then delivered to a wonderful organization called One Meal, who get the meals to those in need. I love that we've adopted a 100% "from scratch" policy—we even make our own stock!

With hundreds of people relying on us for meals every day, RTM is the top priority of my business.

I have an incredible team at RTM. That they work each day to make a genuine difference to the lives of Sydney's most vulnerable, and the extent to which they go, to ensure meals go out every day is unlike anything I saw in my corporate days. I am constantly grateful for their dedication, strength, and commitment.

They also happen to be the resident comedians! Most days they have me laughing so hard I have tears running down my face. Honestly, it's a wonder I can get any work done with those guys around!

To learn more about RecipeTin Meals and One Meal, please visit www.recipetineats.com/recipetin-meals/

*Left to right: Barl, Chef Jean-Baptiste, Chef Stephen*

*Me at the RTM kitchen, looking like I made all those meals*

# How to use this book

Bonus recipe!

BONUS RECIPE

PAGE 16

I know you know how to read a recipe, but I wanted to provide a recipe page "map" for those used to cooking from my website. Here is a bonus recipe (it is real, it works, and it's delicious!), pointing out the different elements on the page.

*Recipe symbols—great for those with these dietary preferences.*

*meat-free*

*gluten-free*

BONUS RECIPE

## CRISPY PARMESAN TOMATO RICE

*Rice is good. Crispy rice is very good. Parmesan crispy rice is insanely good!*

**SERVES: 2 I PREP 5 MINUTES I COOK 15 MINUTES**

This is a versatile recipe designed to make a meal out of leftover bits and bobs. Rice is mixed with sautéed veggies, tomato paste, parmesan, and egg for binding. Then you fry it up into a giant fritter of sorts until it's golden and crispy. It will break up into sections as you flip it, and that's exactly what's supposed to happen. Try serving it with a fried egg, and perhaps a splash of hot sauce!

*Introduction—this is the part where I tell you why your life is not complete until you've made this!*

4 tbsp extra-virgin olive oil

1 garlic clove,* finely minced

½ onion, finely chopped

1 small carrot,[1] peeled and finely chopped

1 small celery stalk,[1] finely diced

2 tbsp tomato paste

1½ packed cups cooked rice,[2] cold

1 egg

⅓ cup (1 oz) finely shredded parmesan*

¼ tsp kosher salt*

¼ tsp black pepper

2 tbsp green onion,* thinly sliced, then roughly chopped

*Sauté aromatics*—Heat 1 tablespoon of the oil in a large nonstick skillet over high heat. Add the garlic, onion, carrot, and celery and cook for 4 minutes or until the carrot is softened.

Add the tomato paste and stir for 20 seconds, then transfer to a large bowl.

*Add rice and egg*—Add the rice, egg, parmesan, salt, and pepper and stir until combined.

Roughly clean the pan with a paper towel, then return to the stove. Add the remaining oil and heat over medium–high.

*Crisp the rice*—Add the rice, spreading it out evenly. Cook for 4 minutes, pressing down lightly with a spatula every now and then, until very deep golden and crispy underneath. Flip in sections—it will break up into six or so big pieces—then cook the other side for about 2 minutes until golden and crispy.

*Serve*—Transfer to a plate, sprinkle with green onion, and serve immediately with leafy greens tossed with my Everyday Dressing (page 333).

**NOTES**

1. The carrot and celery can be substituted with other vegetables that can be diced and cooked, such as zucchini, mushroom, beans, and bell pepper. Or try proteins, such as bacon, ham, cooked meats—or even canned tuna!
2. Any type of cooked rice can be used in this recipe, including brown rice and white rice.

LEFTOVERS Fridge 2 days. Not suitable for freezing.

*Notes—you'd hardly expect me not to have notes! Look here to get extra info on techniques and ingredient swaps.*

*Leftovers—I can't bear food waste. Whenever a dish can be stored, I will tell you how and for how long.*

PAGE 17

1:00

*QR code—hover your phone's camera over the code to go to a section of my website where you can watch a how-to video for each recipe (along with extra helpful notes!)*

# EVERYDAY FOOD

The heart and soul of the food I make.

# VIETNAMESE BAKED CHICKEN

*One of my all-time favorite marinades!*

**SERVES: 4–6 I PREP: 10 MINUTES + 24 HOURS MARINATING I COOK: 1 HOUR**

This is the baked version of a popular Vietnamese chicken recipe on my website. It's got a sweet, caramelly Vietnamese glaze, and it's so delicious it's worthy of serving to guests. Just get the chicken marinating the night before then, the next day, pop it in the oven until the skin is bronzed and sticky. No stove splatter to deal with—yay!

---

3 lb bone-in, skin-on chicken thighs (about 6 pieces)

**LEMONGRASS MARINADE**

2 lemongrass*[1] stalks, white part only

4 garlic cloves,* finely grated

1/4 cup fresh lime juice

1/4 cup fish sauce

2 tbsp light soy sauce*[2]

1/4 tightly packed cup brown sugar

2 tbsp canola oil

**TO SERVE (OPTIONAL)**

Fresh cilantro, roughly chopped

1 long red chili pepper,* sliced

Finely sliced lime wedges

*Lemongrass*—Bash the lemongrass with a meat tenderizer, rolling pin, or similar, to make it burst open slightly. Slice diagonally into 1/4 inch thick pieces.

*Marinate chicken*—Mix the marinade ingredients in a large zip-top bag.* Add the chicken, then seal the bag, pressing out the air. Massage to disperse the marinade over the chicken. Place the bag in a bowl (for leak protection) and refrigerate for 24 hours.

Preheat the oven to 400°F. Line a baking tray with aluminum foil, then parchment paper (you'll thank me later!).

*Prepare for baking*—Remove the chicken from the marinade, brush off the lemongrass pieces, then spread out on the prepared tray. Discard the excess marinade.

*Bake and baste*—Bake for 30 minutes. Remove from the oven and baste the chicken by brushing the tray juices onto the skin. Bake for 10 minutes, baste again, and bake for a further 15 minutes. Remove from the oven.

*Serve*—Transfer the chicken to a serving platter and leave to rest for 5 minutes. Baste the skin generously one last time to make it shiny and golden, being sure to use the stickier brown juices on the tray to add color to the skin.[3] Pour the remaining tray juices all over the chicken (scrape the tray clean!). Sprinkle with cilantro and red chili pepper (if using), then serve with Fluffy Coconut Rice (page 337) and leafy greens tossed with Asian Sesame Dressing (page 333), with lime wedges on the side, if desired.

**NOTES**

1. If you can't get fresh lemongrass, use 1 tablespoon lemongrass paste.
2. All-purpose soy sauce can also be used. Do not use dark soy sauce or sweet soy sauce. Use gluten-free soy sauce or tamari to make this a gluten-free dish.
3. If the tray juices are watery, just pop the empty tray back in the oven while the chicken is resting and the tray juices will transform into a glaze in a few minutes.

LEFTOVERS Fridge 4 days, freezer 3 months. Raw, marinated chicken can be frozen for 3 months, thawed, then cooked as per the recipe (be extra generous with basting).

# GARLIC BUTTER SHRIMP

*The classic—done right.*

 **SERVES: 3–4 I PREP: 10 MINUTES + 20 MINUTES MARINATING I COOK: 10 MINUTES**

You know what the trick is to making really great garlic shrimp? Garlic. Butter. A splash of white wine. And turning the shrimp with tongs rather than trying to flip or toss with a spatula. This way, you can control the timing so every single shrimp is perfectly cooked. Because there are few things in this world sadder than overcooked shrimp!

---

1 lb peeled and deveined large raw shrimp*[1] with tails on (2 lb unpeeled whole shrimp)

3 tbsp extra-virgin olive oil

½ tsp kosher salt*

½ tsp black pepper

3 tsp finely minced garlic*

¼ cup chardonnay, or other dry white wine*[2]

Lemon wedges, to serve (optional)

Easy Crusty Artisan Bread (page 341), to serve[3]

**GARLIC BUTTER SAUCE**

3 tbsp unsalted butter, cut into ½ inch cubes

1 tbsp lemon juice

1 tbsp chopped parsley

*Marinate*—Toss the shrimp with 1 tablespoon of the olive oil and the salt and pepper, then set aside for 20 minutes.

*Cook shrimp*—Heat 1 tablespoon of the oil in a large nonstick skillet over high heat. Using tongs, place half the shrimp in the pan and sear each side for 45 seconds, then transfer to a plate. Add the last 1 tablespoon of oil, then sear the remaining shrimp for 45 seconds on each side.

Return the first batch of shrimp to the pan, then add the garlic. Toss gently for 30 seconds or until the garlic turns golden. Add the wine—it will steam dramatically!—and let it simmer, scraping the base of the pan with a wooden spoon, until the wine has mostly evaporated.

*Garlic butter sauce*—Add the butter and lemon juice and swirl in the pan. As soon as the butter has melted, add the parsley, then toss quickly to coat the shrimp. Tip the shrimp and sauce onto a serving plate.

*Serve*—Add the lemon wedges on the side (if using) and serve immediately with bread for mopping up that garlic-shrimp butter (seriously, the highlight!). For a refreshing side salad, serve with leafy greens drizzled with Lemon Dressing (page 333).

**NOTES**

1. Larger shrimp work better as they are meatier and there's less to turn (so annoying to turn a gazillion tiny shrimp!).
2. Deglazing the pan with wine adds extra depth of flavor to this dish. If you can't consume alcohol, substitute with nonalcoholic white wine (readily available at grocery stores these days) or low-sodium chicken broth* (yes really, chicken, not fish broth!).
3. For gluten-free, omit the bread or use a gluten-free variety.

LEFTOVERS Best served fresh, but leftover shrimp will keep for 3 days in the fridge.

# GREEK CHICKEN GYROS

*The marinade is incredible . . .*

 **SERVES: 4 | PREP: 25 MINUTES + 3–24 HOURS MARINATING | COOK: 10 MINUTES**

This recipe has been one of the biggest hits with my website readers since day one! I think it's because it's easy-as, yet 10 times better than greasy takeout gyros. The secret is the yogurt marinade for the chicken. Yogurt tenderizes the meat and pushes all those Greek flavorings we love, like garlic and oregano, deep into the meat. Serving is a cinch—pile everything on a platter and let everyone roll up their own gyros. (PS Please don't use low-fat yogurt!)

---

2 lb boneless, skinless chicken thighs[1]

2 tbsp olive oil

**MARINADE**

3 garlic cloves,* finely minced

3 tbsp Greek yogurt

3 tbsp lemon juice

1 tbsp white wine vinegar[2]

1 tbsp extra-virgin olive oil

1 1/2 tbsp dried oregano

1 tsp kosher salt*

1/4 tsp black pepper

**TZATZIKI**

2 x 6 inch cucumbers*

3/4 cup Greek yogurt

1 1/2 tsp lemon juice

1 1/2 tsp extra-virgin olive oil

1 tbsp finely chopped mint

1/4 tsp finely minced garlic*

1/2 tsp kosher salt*

Pinch of black pepper

**SALAD**

3 tomatoes,* deseeded and cut into 1/4 inch cubes

3 x 6 inch cucumbers,* cut into 1/4 inch cubes

1/2 red onion, finely chopped

1/4 cup roughly chopped parsley

1/8 tsp each kosher salt* and black pepper

**TO SERVE**

4 pita breads or Easy Flatbreads (page 342), warmed

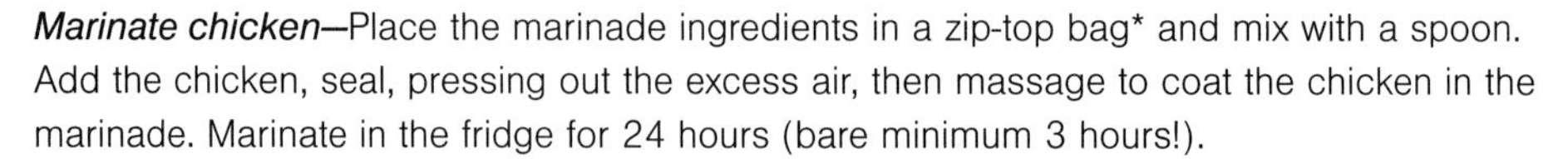

*Marinate chicken*—Place the marinade ingredients in a zip-top bag* and mix with a spoon. Add the chicken, seal, pressing out the excess air, then massage to coat the chicken in the marinade. Marinate in the fridge for 24 hours (bare minimum 3 hours!).

*Tzatziki*—Cut the cucumbers in half lengthwise. Use a teaspoon to scrape out the watery seeds. Save for another purpose.[3] Coarsely grate the cucumber using a box grater, then bundle the cucumber up in a dish towel and wring out any excess water as best you can (key step for great tzatziki!). Mix in a bowl with the remaining tzatziki ingredients, then set aside for 20 minutes to allow the flavors to meld. (Keeps for 3 days in the fridge.)

*Salad*—Mix the salad ingredients in a bowl, then set aside.

*Cook chicken*—Remove the chicken from the marinade 30 minutes prior to cooking and leave on the counter in a bowl. Discard the marinade. Heat 1 tablespoon of oil in a large nonstick skillet over medium-high heat. Cook half the chicken for 3–4 minutes on each side until deep golden brown (internal temperature 160°F[1]). Transfer to a plate and cover loosely with aluminum foil. Repeat with the remaining chicken. (Also excellent grilled! See Note 4.)

*Serve*—Once the chicken has rested for 5 minutes, slice thickly, then pile onto a platter. Place the salad, tzatziki, and pita or flatbreads on the side. To assemble a gyros roll, smear the flatbread with tzatziki, top with chicken, then salad. Roll up firmly and wrap with parchment paper or aluminum foil if you want to keep it secured. Devour!

**NOTES**

1. Chicken breast can also be used, but thigh is juicier. Breast should be cooked to 155°F and thighs to 160°F. To check the internal temperature, insert a cooking thermometer* into the middle of the thickest part of the chicken.
2. Can substitute with red wine vinegar or apple cider vinegar.
3. Throw into your green smoothie!
4. Grill: Heat the grill or flat plate on medium-high. No need to oil if your grill is well seasoned but, if not, then brush lightly with oil. Cook the first side for 4–5 minutes, then the second side for 3–4 minutes until deep golden brown.
5. To make this gluten-free, use gluten-free flatbreads, such as corn tortillas!*

LEFTOVERS Fridge 4 days. Raw chicken in the marinade can be frozen for up to 3 months. Thaw, then cook as per the recipe.

# CHEESY BAKED BROCCOLI FRITTERS

*Because nobody wants to PAN-FRY 24 fritters!!*

 **SERVES: 5–6 AS A MAIN (MAKES 24 FRITTERS) I PREP: 15 MINUTES I COOK: 35 MINUTES**

Who loves a good crispy vegetable fritter? Everybody! Who likes standing around forever, frying batch by batch on the stove? Nobody! These beautifully crispy oven-baked fritters are the cure to your fritter-frying nightmares. The fritters also have cooked rice added—a great way to use up leftovers while giving them a little more heft. You won't be able to stop munching them! (Obviously because of the broccoli, not the cheese.)

---

12 oz broccoli florets, cut into even-sized pieces (about 5 heaped cups)

Olive oil or canola oil spray

3 eggs

½ tsp garlic powder

½ tsp onion powder

¾ tsp Italian seasoning[1]

¾ tsp kosher salt*

½ tsp black pepper

2 cups cooked rice,[2] cooled

2 cups (7 oz) shredded* cheddar cheese

¾ cup finely sliced, then roughly chopped green onion*

½ cup panko bread crumbs*

**DIPPING SAUCE (CHOOSE ONE)**

Ketchup or plain yogurt

½ quantity Yogurt Sauce (see Tachin, page 251)

Instant Spicy Pink Sauce (page 221)

Tzatziki (see Greek Chicken Gyros, page 24)

*Prepare broccoli*—Boil the broccoli in a small pot of water for 6 minutes until the stalks are very tender. Drain, shake off the excess water well, then leave to steam-dry in the colander for 15 minutes. Chop so the stalks are pretty small, around ¼–½ inch pieces. The florets will kind of end up minced, which is fine.

Preheat the oven to 475°F. Lightly spray two large baking trays with oil, then line with parchment paper.

*Batter*—Mix the eggs, garlic and onion powders, Italian herbs, salt, and pepper in a large bowl using a wooden spoon. Add the broccoli, rice, cheese, green onion, and bread crumbs, then mix until well combined.[4]

*Form fritters*—Dollop 3-tablespoon mounds onto the baking trays (10–12 per tray, 20–24 in total). An ice cream scoop with a lever is super handy here! Flatten firmly to ½ inch thick using a spatula (and fingers if needed), then spray the surface with oil.

*Cook fritters*—Bake for 18 minutes, flip, then bake for a further 7 minutes until golden and crispy. The bottom tray may need a few extra minutes.

*Serve*—Serve the fritters with the dipping sauce of your choice. Enjoy!

**NOTES**

1. Italian seasoning is a store-bought dried herb mix.
2. Any type of cooked rice works here. Or try quinoa.
3. The mixture may seem a little crumbly but don't worry! The egg and cheese binds it as it bakes.

LEFTOVERS Fridge 3 days but will lose crispiness. To resurrect, bake for 8 minutes at 350°F.

# CRUNCHY BAKED CHICKEN TENDERS

*Anything you eat with your hands is a good thing!*

**SERVES: 3–4 I PREP: 20 MINUTES I COOK: 25 MINUTES**

Too often, baking breaded foods ends in minor disaster. The bread crumb isn't crunchy, it's soggy and unevenly browned. Just . . . yuck. This recipe is a game changer. The secret? Toast the panko bread crumbs until golden brown before crumbing. Yup, it's that easy. It works especially well with chicken tenders—which, let's face it, adults love as much as kids! Their natural shape makes them ideal for making chicken fingers that are perfectly crunchy and golden every time. Grab with your hands, dunk into sauce, and enjoy!

---

Canola oil spray

1½ cups panko bread crumbs*

1 lb chicken tenderloins[1]

¼ tsp kosher salt*

1 tsp finely chopped parsley (optional)

**BATTER**

1 egg

1 tbsp mayonnaise*[2]

1½ tbsp dijon mustard

2 tbsp all-purpose flour

½ tsp kosher salt*

¼ tsp black pepper

**DIPPING SAUCE OPTIONS**

Ketchup

Sweet chili sauce, store-bought

Sweet & Sour Sauce (page 327)

Honey Mustard Sauce (page 331)

½ quantity Yogurt Sauce (see Tachin, page 251)

Preheat the oven to 400°F. Place a wire rack[3] on a baking tray and spray with oil.

*Golden bread crumbs*—Spread the bread crumbs on a separate baking tray and spray with oil (spray vertically to avoid blowing the panko off the tray). Bake for 7 minutes or until golden, shaking the tray once. Transfer to a bowl.

*Batter*—Place the ingredients in a bowl and whisk with a fork until combined. Add the chicken and toss to coat.

*Crumb*—Pick up a piece of chicken with tongs and place it into the panko bowl. Sprinkle the surface with bread crumbs, then press with your fingers to adhere. Transfer to the prepared rack. Marvel at your clean fingers (!), then repeat with the remaining chicken.

*Bake*—Spray the breaded chicken generously with oil, then sprinkle with salt. Bake for 15 minutes for small to medium tenders, or 20 minutes for larger tenders.

*Serve*—Remove from the oven and serve immediately with your dipping sauce of choice. Sprinkle with parsley, if you're feeling fancy, and serve with a side of Creamy Mashed Potato (page 338) and leafy greens tossed with French Dressing (page 333), or with my signature Chinese Fried Rice (page 120).

**NOTES**

1. Boneless, skinless chicken breast can also be used, cut into ¾ inch thick slices lengthwise.
2. For a lighter version, the mayonnaise can be substituted with yogurt or sour cream.
3. A wire rack is not critical but it will make the underside of the chicken more crunchy because it is elevated off the tray.

LEFTOVERS Fridge 4 days, though the crumb won't stay crunchy. You can resurrect some crunch by baking for 5 minutes at 400°F.

# SWEDISH MEATBALLS

*The creamy gravy is to die for . . .*

**SERVES: 4 I PREP: 25 MINUTES I COOK: 25 MINUTES**

After cheap furniture, Swedish meatballs are probably the other thing we can thank IKEA for bringing to the masses! With the signature hint of nutmeg and allspice, these meatballs are smothered in a traditional creamy gravy that will have you wiping your plate clean. The best part: They're a whole lot easier to put together than flatpack furniture, that's for sure!

---

**MEATBALLS**

1 yellow onion, left whole, peeled

2 slices soft white sandwich bread,[1] crusts removed, cut into ½ inch cubes

Splash of milk, if needed

10 oz ground beef

10 oz ground pork (or use more beef instead)

1 egg

¼ tsp ground nutmeg, preferably freshly grated

¼ tsp ground allspice

¼ tsp black pepper

¾ tsp kosher salt*

1 tbsp canola oil

**CREAMY SWEDISH GRAVY**

3½ tbsp unsalted butter

3 tbsp all-purpose flour

2 cups low-sodium beef broth*[3]

½ cup heavy cream*

**TO SERVE**

1 tsp finely chopped chives (optional)

Lingonberry jam,[2] to serve (optional)

*Meatballs*—Grate the onion using a box grater in a large bowl. Add the bread and mix well—the onion juice should make the bread soggy (if not, add a tiny splash of milk). Set aside to soak for 1 minute.[4] Add the remaining meatball ingredients, except the oil. Mix well with your hands.

*Roll*—Scoop up 1 heaped tablespoon of the mixture and roll into a 1½ inch ball. An ice cream scoop with a lever will make short work of this! You should have 25–30 meatballs.

*Brown meatballs*—Heat the oil in a deep, medium nonstick skillet over medium–high heat. Add half the meatballs and cook until they are browned all over, but still raw inside, about 3 minutes. Transfer to a plate, then brown the remaining meatballs (add more oil if needed) and add to the plate with the first batch.

If there is a lot of residual oil, pour off the excess and discard. Lower the heat to medium.

*Creamy Swedish gravy*—Melt the butter in the same skillet until foamy. Add the flour and stir it in for 1 minute. While stirring constantly, slowly pour in about one-fourth of the beef broth—it will thicken quickly into a paste. Gradually pour in the remaining beef broth, stirring as you go. This technique should make the sauce virtually lump-free but, if not, switch to a whisk.

*Simmer*—Turn the heat up to medium–high and bring the sauce to a simmer. Add the meatballs and tip in any juices pooled on the plate. Cook for 8–10 minutes or until the liquid thickens into a thin gravy, stirring occasionally. Stir in the cream, simmer for a further 2 minutes, then remove from the stove.

*Serve*—Sprinkle with chives (if using). Serve with Creamy Mashed Potato (page 338) or Creamy Mashed Cauliflower (Puree) (page 338) and steamed broccolini.

**NOTES**

1. Use everyday soft white sandwich bread, not fancy artisan bread like crusty sourdough (it's too dense!).
2. A staple in Scandinavian countries, this tart/sweet jam is served with various dishes, including Swedish meatballs. Find it at IKEA and continental grocers. Purely optional—I don't use it!
3. Beef broth can be substituted with chicken broth* but the gravy will have a slightly milder flavor and the color will be paler.
4. The bread-soaked-in-onion is a technique loved by website readers all over the world, which makes meatballs tastier and more tender.

LEFTOVERS Fridge 4 days. Not suitable for freezing.

# HOUSE SPECIAL GLAZED MEATLOAF

*You never knew meatloaf could be soooo gooood.*

**SERVES: 8 PEOPLE (OR 1 DOZER*) I PREP: 15 MINUTES I COOK: 1 HOUR 15 MINUTES**

Meatloaf gets a bad name because it's often done so badly. But when it's tender, juicy, beautifully glazed, and packed with flavor—as it should be—it's up there with the best tastes of home. My tips for a great one? Soak the bread crumbs in grated onion, which makes the meatloaf extra tender and flavorful—a proven technique I use regularly. Also, using a loaf pan holds all the juices in as it bakes and stops it drying out. And finally, beef bouillon cubes rather than salt is the path to more flavor! The hardest decision will be how much to have for dinner tonight, and how much to save for sandwiches tomorrow. The easiest solution—make two. Ha!

---

Olive oil spray

**MEATLOAF**

1 cup panko bread crumbs*

1 large yellow onion, left whole, peeled

2 lb ground beef, preferably not lean

2 eggs

3 garlic cloves,* finely minced

1 tsp Worcestershire sauce

1/4 cup ketchup

1/4 cup finely chopped Italian parsley or 2 tsp dried parsley (optional)

1 tsp dried thyme

2 beef bouillon cubes,* crumbled

1 tsp black pepper

**GLAZE**

1/2 cup ketchup, plus extra to serve

2 tbsp apple cider vinegar

1 lightly packed tbsp brown sugar

**GARNISH**

1/2 tsp finely chopped parsley (optional)

Preheat the oven to 350°F. Spray a 9 x 5 x 2½ inch loaf pan[1] with oil.

*Glaze*—Mix the glaze ingredients in a small bowl.

*Meatloaf*—Place the bread crumbs in a very large bowl. Grate the onion into the bowl using a box grater. Mix to wet the bread crumbs with the onion juice. Add the remaining meatloaf ingredients, then mix well using your hands. Form into a loaf shape, pinching together, then smoothing over creases.[2] Transfer to the loaf pan. Brush generously with half the glaze.

*Bake*—Bake for 45 minutes. Remove from the oven and pour off the excess fat pooling in the loaf pan. Brush/dab with the remaining glaze, then spray with oil. Bake for a further 30 minutes or until the edges of the meatloaf are brown and the glaze is caramelized.

*Stand and slice*—Remove the meatloaf from the oven. Stand for 10 minutes before turning it out and cutting into thick slices,[3] sprinkled with parsley (if using).

*Serve*—Divide the slices among serving plates and serve with ketchup, Creamy Mashed Potato (page 338), and a green salad or steamed vegetables tossed with Italian Dressing (page 333).

**NOTES**

1. If your loaf pan is a different size, that's totally fine. Your meatloaf will just be taller or flatter.
2. Seal the creases well before placing in the oven, as they tend to open up during baking.
3. You may get a bit of crumbling on the edges of the first couple of slices. This is normal and indicative of the tenderness of the meatloaf. Zero crumble indicates firmly packed, harder meatloaf, which isn't as enjoyable!

LEFTOVERS Fridge 4 days, freezer 3 months.

# SIMPLE, VERY TASTY CAULIFLOWER CHEESE STEAKS

*Also known as "An Easy Way to Make Cauliflower Irresistible."*

 **SERVES: 2 | PREP: 10 MINUTES | COOK: 30 MINUTES**

Here's a cauliflower steak recipe that won't have you running for the hills. Not when there's cheese, garlic, spices, and a crunchy parmesan crumb involved! It's as good as simple meatless mains get. I like to use sharp cheddar cheese for the eye-catching orange shade it gives the cauliflower. But you can use your favorite melty cheese or whatever you have on hand.

---

1 large head of cauliflower, cut into 1 inch thick steaks[1]

4 tsp extra-virgin olive oil

3/4 cup (3 oz) shredded* sharp cheddar cheese[2]

1/2 tsp finely chopped parsley

**SEASONING**

1/2 tsp smoked paprika

1/2 tsp garlic powder

1/4 tsp ground coriander

1/4 tsp kosher salt*

1/8 tsp black pepper

**PARMESAN CRUMB**

1 tightly packed tbsp finely grated parmesan*

2 tbsp panko bread crumbs*[3]

1/8 tsp kosher salt*

1 tbsp extra-virgin olive oil

2 tsp finely chopped Italian parsley

Preheat the oven to 475°F. Line a baking tray with parchment paper.

*Season cauliflower*—Combine the seasoning ingredients in a bowl. Place the cauliflower steaks on the prepared tray, then drizzle one side of each steak with 1 teaspoon of oil. Sprinkle evenly with half the seasoning (use your fingers). Turn the cauliflower and repeat.

*Roast*—Put the tray in the oven and roast the cauliflower for 15 minutes. Flip, then roast for a further 10 minutes. Remove from the oven—the cauliflower should be just about cooked. Turn the oven down to 400°F. Cover with the sharp cheddar cheese, then bake for a further 5 minutes until the cheese is melted.

*Parmesan crumb*—While the cauliflower is roasting, mix the parmesan, bread crumbs, and salt in a bowl. Heat the oil in a small nonstick skillet over medium heat. Add the bread crumb mixture and stir for 1 minute until just golden (the parmesan will clump, that's normal!). Transfer to a bowl, then let it cool. Crumble with your fingers, then stir in the parsley.

*Serve*—Transfer the cauliflower to serving plates. Sprinkle with the parmesan crumb and parsley (if using). Enjoy with a side of leafy greens or a garden salad tossed with my Everyday Salad Dressing (page 333).

**NOTES**

1. To cut the cauliflower steaks, remove the outer leaves and trim the excess stalk off the cauliflower. Cut right down through the middle, then cut a 1 inch thick slice from one half, keeping the core intact (the base keeps the steak together). Repeat with the other half so you have two steaks. (The recipe video is helpful here! Scan the QR code.) Reserve the leftover cauliflower for another purpose.
2. Sharp cheddar cheese has that beautiful orange color you see in the photo. But it can be substituted with your favorite melting cheese, such as colby or gruyere. If you use mozzarella, mix in 2 tablespoons of grated parmesan for flavor. For this recipe, store-bought pre-grated parmesan can be used (the sandy type, not the shredded type).
3. Ordinary bread crumbs also work well. The crumb clumps even more so you get crunchy balls!

LEFTOVERS Fridge 3 days, though best made fresh as cauliflower goes a bit soggy. Not suitable for freezing.

# SUN-DRIED TOMATO PESTO PASTA SALAD

*My current favorite pasta salad. (But I do have a thing about new toys.)*

 **SERVES: 6–8 | PREP: 20 MINUTES | COOK: 10 MINUTES**

A great pasta salad is all about the right mix of ingredients and this one ain't short on flavor! Here, the blend of salty antipasto bits, fresh basil, juicy tomato, and pops of creamy feta hits all the right notes. You could settle for a regular vinaigrette to bring it together, but lately I'm loving a serious flavor double-down in the form of sun-dried tomato pesto tossed through instead! This recipe makes a heap—so it's a good one to take to gatherings, for lunches on the go, or for dinner tonight and an excellent side for tomorrow.

---

2 tsp kosher salt*

1 lb fusilli pasta, or other short pasta of choice (penne, macaroni, bow ties)

7 oz Danish feta,[1] crumbled

½ red onion, finely sliced[2]

½ lb cherry tomatoes, halved

1 x 6 inch cucumber,* halved lengthwise, finely sliced ½ inch thick[2]

2 tightly packed cups baby arugula

3 lightly packed cups basil leaves, roughly torn

1 cup (5 oz) drained sliced kalamata olives

1 cup (6 oz) red pepper strips (from a jar), drained and cut into 1¼ inch pieces

2½ cups (12 oz) artichokes (from a jar), drained and cut into 1 inch pieces

**SUN-DRIED TOMATO PESTO**

½ cup pasta cooking water[3]

2 x 8 oz jars sun-dried tomato strips in oil (including the oil)

3 tbsp extra-virgin olive oil

½ tightly packed cup (2 oz) finely grated parmesan*

1 tsp finely grated garlic* (1 large clove)

½ tsp kosher salt*

⅓ cup pine nuts,* toasted

*Cook pasta*—Bring 5¼ quarts of water to a boil with the salt. Add the pasta and cook as per the package directions plus 2 minutes to make it very soft.[4] Just before draining, scoop out ½ cup of the pasta cooking water and set aside—we need this for the pesto.[3] Drain the pasta, briefly rinse with cold tap water, then shake off the excess water well. Leave in the colander to dry and cool to room temperature.

*Pesto*—Place all the pesto ingredients, except the pine nuts, in a food processor. Use all the oil from the jar of sun-dried tomatoes and don't forget the pasta cooking water! (It's fine if it's still hot.) Blitz for 15 seconds on low until the sun-dried tomatoes are smooth, scraping the sides as needed. Add the pine nuts and blitz again until they are very finely chopped.

*Assemble*—Set aside one-fourth of the feta for topping. Place the pasta and all the sun-dried tomato pesto in a very large bowl. Toss well, then add the remaining salad ingredients and toss again.

*Serve*—Tumble into a large serving bowl. Crumble the remaining feta on top and serve!

**NOTES**

1. Use Danish feta or other creamy feta, rather than the hard crumbly Greek feta, so it gets a bit melty. Goat cheese makes an excellent substitute.
2. A mandoline* will make finely slicing the onion and cucumber a total breeze. Otherwise, it's time to show off your knife skills!
3. Using a bit of the pasta cooking water is a good way to loosen the pesto to make the pasta salad juicier without using more oil. It's better than just plain water because the starch in the cooking water emulsifies the pesto, creating a creamier pesto.
4. Hot tip for cold pasta salads—overcook the pasta so it's on the soft side. Why? Because pasta goes firm when it's cool. This will ensure your pasta isn't too firm.

LEFTOVERS Fridge for up to 3 days. In fact, the flavor is even better the next day! Toss well and serve at room temperature. Not suitable for freezing.

# BIZARRELY GOOD WINGS

*The name is appropriate.*

 **SERVES: 6 AS A STARTER, 3–4 AS A MAIN | PREP: 10 MINUTES | COOK: 40 MINUTES**

Cumin? Parmesan? Sesame oil? Chives? Is she mad? Hear me out, friends! This unlikely combination of ingredients just works. Think of them as modern Asian-style, garlicky, spiced, chili-flecked wings given a good salty smack with some parmesan. Bizarre ingredients . . . bizarre cooking method . . . but bizarrely addictive! Just wait, you'll be picking at the little parmesan, chili, and garlic bits on the tray . . . seriously possibly the best part.

---

Olive oil spray

**SEASONING**

3 tsp smoked paprika

1 1/2 tsp ground cumin

1 1/2 tsp garlic powder

1 1/2 tsp onion powder

1 1/2 tsp kosher salt*

3/4 tsp ground coriander

**WINGS**

2 1/2 lb chicken drummettes and wingettes[1]

1 1/2 tbsp extra-virgin olive oil

1 tightly packed cup (4 oz) finely shredded parmesan*

2 tbsp finely chopped chives

2 tsp white sesame seeds

**CHILI GARLIC CRUMB**

2 tbsp sesame oil*

1 each long red and green chili pepper,* deseeded and finely chopped

2 tsp finely minced garlic cloves*

Preheat the oven to 475°F. Line a baking tray with aluminum foil, then parchment paper. Set a wire rack[2] on the tray and spray well with oil.

*Season wings*—Mix the seasoning ingredients in a small bowl. Place the wings in a large bowl, drizzle with olive oil, then sprinkle with the seasoning. Toss with a rubber spatula.

*Bake*—Spread the wings out on the rack (they can be fairly snug). Bake for 30 minutes, rotating the tray halfway through cooking, until the wings are golden brown.

*Parmesan toss*—Put the wings into a clean large bowl and scrape in all the drippings on the tray. Add the parmesan, then toss to coat. Remove the rack from the tray, then spread the wings out on the tray. Scrape the leftover parmesan in the bowl over the wings. Bake the wings for another 5 minutes until the parmesan has melted.

*Chili garlic crumb*—Meanwhile, in a small skillet, heat the sesame oil over medium heat. Add the chili pepper and garlic and cook for 2 minutes until soft.

*Serve*—Return the wings to the bowl. Add the chili garlic crumb, chives, and sesame seeds. Toss, then transfer to a serving bowl, being sure to scrape over all the little crunchy bits on the tray!

**NOTES**

1. To get the quantity required, you can buy 3 lb whole wings and break them down yourself. Discard the wing tips or reserve them for homemade Chicken Broth (page 349). In my case, they go straight into Dozer's* mouth.
2. A rack will allow the wings to brown better on the underside but is not critical.

LEFTOVERS Fridge 4 days, though the crispy bits won't be crispy any longer! Not suitable for freezing.

# CRISPY KOREAN PANCAKES

*Ohhhhh, they're just so good! I can't stop eating these.*

**SERVES: 2 (MAKES 3 PANCAKES) I PREP: 20 MINUTES I COOK: 15 MINUTES**

Fun to make, delicious to eat! Cold club soda is the trick here for these addictively crispy Korean pancakes. I've made them vegetarian—because if anyone can get me excited about a meat-free dinner, it's the Koreans! But you can absolutely add animal protein if you wish. Either drape finely sliced raw meat across the surface or add quick-cooking seafood like calamari and chopped shrimp. The dipping sauce is a must. Don't even think about downgrading to plain soy sauce!

---

1/3 cup canola oil[1]

1 small zucchini,[2] cut into 2 x 1/4 inch matchsticks

1 small carrot,[2] peeled, grated using a box grater

1/4 cup finely sliced green beans[2]

2 green onions,*[2] stems, cut into 5 inch lengths (you need 9 pieces)

1 1/2 tsp deseeded and finely minced long red chili pepper* (optional)

**DIPPING SAUCE**

1 tbsp light soy sauce* (or all-purpose soy sauce)

1 tbsp rice vinegar

1 tbsp water

1/2 tsp sugar

1/2 tsp sesame oil*

1/2 tsp red pepper flakes, preferably Korean (optional)

1/2 tsp white sesame seeds

**PANCAKE BATTER**

1 cup all-purpose flour

1 tbsp cornstarch

1/2 tsp each garlic powder and onion powder

3/4 tsp kosher salt*

1 cup + 1 tbsp fridge-cold club soda[3]

Preheat the oven to 250°F. Place a wire rack on a baking tray. This is to keep the cooked pancakes warm and crispy.

*Dipping sauce*—Mix the ingredients in a small jar until the sugar dissolves. Transfer to a small sauce dish.

*Batter*—Whisk together the flour, cornstarch, garlic powder, onion powder, and salt in a medium bowl. Mix in the club soda with a whisk just until barely incorporated—some small flour lumps are fine.[4] The batter should be thin enough so it can spread into a thinnish pancake (loosen with more water if needed).

*Make pancakes*—Heat 2 tablespoons of oil in a medium nonstick skillet over medium-high heat until you see wisps of smoke. Ladle in one-third of the batter (the oil should sizzle!) and swirl to spread into a 7 inch wide, fairly thin pancake. Sprinkle the surface with about 1/3 cup (combined) zucchini, carrot, and beans. Press three green onions on the surface, then drizzle over a little batter (to help adhere when flipped). Sprinkle with 1/2 teaspoon of finely minced red chili pepper (if using), then immediately reduce the heat to medium.

Cook for 2 1/2 minutes, lifting the pancake once and tilting the pan to spread oil under it, until the underside has deep golden, crispy patches. Flip and cook the other side for 1 1/2 minutes, pressing down lightly (this side won't go crispy).[5]

Transfer the pancake to the rack, green onions facing up, then place in the oven to keep warm. Cook the remaining pancakes (makes three in total), heating 2 tablespoons of oil for each pancake.

*Serve*—Cut each pancake into 9 or 12 pieces. Serve with the dipping sauce.

**NOTES**

1. If you skimp on the oil you will deprive yourself of crispiness. Don't do it. Nobody wants a soggy Korean pancake!
2. Substitute with finely sliced vegetables of choice, such as cabbage, asparagus, bell pepper, spinach, or kale.*
3. Cold club soda makes the pancake crispier. Fridge-cold tap or sparkling water can be substituted but the pancakes won't stay crispy for as long.
4. Overmixing the batter causes dense pancakes. Small flour lumps will cook out.
5. Korean pancakes are crispy on the underside and edges, but the surface is not that crispy.

LEFTOVERS Fridge 3 days but, sadly, will lose crispiness.

# ONE-POT BAKED GREEK CHICKEN & LEMON RICE

*The one that started it all.*

 **SERVES: 5 I PREP: 15 MINUTES + 12–24 HOURS MARINATING I COOK: 1 HOUR**

When I first published this recipe on my website all those years ago, I couldn't believe how bonkers people went over it on social media. Why all the fuss? It's because it's one of those small-effort-big-reward winner recipes that everybody adores. It's quick to prepare, foolproof, and all baked in one pan. The chicken is garlicky and juicy and goes perfectly with fluffy lemon rice. It's the best chicken and rice of your life—other people's words, not mine!

2 lb skin-on, bone-in chicken thighs[1] (about 5 pieces)

1/2 tbsp extra-virgin olive oil

**MARINADE**

1 tbsp lemon zest (2 lemons)

1/4 cup lemon juice

1 tbsp dried oregano

4 garlic cloves,* finely minced

1/2 tsp kosher salt*

**LEMON RICE**

1 tbsp extra-virgin olive oil

1 small yellow onion, finely diced

1 cup long-grain rice,[2] uncooked

1 1/2 cups low-sodium chicken broth*

3/4 cup water

1 tbsp dried oregano

3/4 tsp kosher salt*

1/4 tsp black pepper

**GARNISH (OPTIONAL)**

Oregano leaves

Lemon slices, pan-fried to slightly char

*Marinade*—Place the chicken and marinade ingredients in a zip-top bag,* then place in the fridge for 12–24 hours.[3]

Preheat the oven to 350°F.

*Brown chicken*—Using a 10–11 inch wide cast-iron pan with a lid (or other ovenproof skillet),[4] heat 1/2 tablespoon of oil over medium-high heat. Remove the chicken from the marinade (reserve the marinade) and cook, skin-side down, for 3–4 minutes or until golden brown. Turn and cook the flesh side for 1 minute, then transfer to a plate. (It will still be raw inside.)

Discard the fat in the pan and wipe out any loose black bits in the skillet using a paper towel.

*Lemon rice*—Return the pan to the stove and heat 1 tablespoon of oil over medium-high heat. Cook the onion for 3 minutes until translucent, then add the remaining rice ingredients and the reserved marinade.

*Bake*—Once the liquid starts bubbling, let it simmer for 30 seconds, then place the chicken on top (it will be partially submerged). Pour in any juices from the chicken plate, cover with a lid,[5] then transfer to the oven.

Bake for 35 minutes, then remove the lid and bake for a further 10 minutes, or until all the liquid is absorbed and the rice is tender (45 minutes total).

*Rest and serve*—Remove from the oven and leave to rest for 10 minutes. Transfer the chicken to a plate, then use a fork to fluff the rice. Divide the rice and chicken among serving plates, topped with oregano and lemon slices (if using). For a side salad, try your favorite garden salad drizzled with Mediterranean Dressing (page 333).

**NOTES**

1. Bone-in chicken thighs are best as they stay juicy. However, to use boneless thighs or breast, add them after the rice has been in the oven for 20 minutes.
2. Long-grain white rice works best for lovely fluffy rice. White basmati, medium-grain, and short-grain rice also work. Not suitable for brown rice, jasmine, paella, or risotto rice.
3. In the event of a dinner emergency, 20 minutes of marinating time will suffice!
4. If you don't have an ovenproof pan, transfer everything to a baking dish after the liquid starts bubbling and cover with aluminum foil. Expect to add 5–10 minutes to the bake time before the liquid is all absorbed.
5. If you don't have a matching lid for your skillet (which I don't), use any pot lid the same size as, or larger than, the skillet. Otherwise, cover with aluminum foil.

LEFTOVERS Fridge 4 days, freezer 3 months.

# BEEF BIRYANI

*No exaggeration—it's biryani. But fast!*

 **SERVES: 5–6 I PREP: 20 MINUTES I COOK: 20 MINUTES**

Biryani is one of my absolute favorite Indian dishes. The fluffy, scented rice, the chunks of tender, curried meat hiding beneath. It's pure magic. The only problem is, it's a long slog to make from scratch! This ground beef version I came up with is everything we love about biryani, but much faster to make. It's based around a biryani-style qeema—a homestyle Indian curried ground beef dish. Don't be put off by the long list of ingredients. The recipe has a nice flow to it and is so easy that anyone can follow it!

**BIRYANI RICE**

1¾ cups basmati rice[1]

2⅔ cups low-sodium chicken broth*

7 whole cloves

1 star anise

3 dried bay leaves*

¼ tsp ground cardamom

1 tsp kosher salt*

2 tbsp ghee,* melted (or unsalted butter)

**BIRYANI BEEF**

1½ tbsp canola oil

3 garlic cloves,* finely minced

2 tsp finely minced ginger*

1 small yellow onion, finely diced

1 lb ground beef

¼ tsp ground cinnamon

½ tsp cayenne pepper[2]

¾ tsp ground turmeric

1½ tsp ground coriander

2 tsp garam masala*

1 tsp kosher salt*

¼ cup tomato passata*

½ cup water

**MINTED YOGURT**

¾ cup plain yogurt

½ tightly packed cup mint leaves

2 tsp fresh lemon juice

¼ tsp kosher salt*

**LAYERING**

1 lightly packed tsp saffron threads[3]

2 tbsp boiling water

½ cup crispy fried shallots*

½ cup roughly chopped cilantro

*Biryani rice*—Place all the ingredients, except the ghee, in a large saucepan and bring to a simmer over medium-high heat. Place the lid on, then immediately turn the heat down to low. Cook for 12 minutes (no stirring or peeking!). Check to ensure all the liquid is absorbed, then remove from the stove and leave to rest for 10 minutes with the lid on. Fluff the rice gently with a rubber spatula, then stir the ghee through. Cover and keep warm.

*Biryani beef*—Heat the oil in a large nonstick skillet over high heat. Cook the garlic, ginger, and onion for 1½ minutes until the onion edges are tinged with gold. Add the beef and cook, breaking it up as you go, until it changes from red to brown. Add all the spices and salt, then continue to cook for 1 minute. Add the passata and water, then cook for 2 minutes—the beef should be juicy but not watery.

*Minted yogurt*—Set aside ½ cup of yogurt then place the remaining ingredients in a jar just large enough to fit the head of an immersion blender. Blitz until the mint is very finely chopped. Gently stir in the reserved yogurt, then transfer to a small serving bowl.

*Saffron drizzle*—Grind the saffron into a powder in a mortar and pestle,[3] then mix in the boiling water. Drizzle the saffron water randomly across the surface of the rice. No need to mix.

*Assemble*—Spread half the hot rice on a serving platter or in a bowl—you'll get a lovely jumble of white and yellow rice, the signature biryani look! Spread half the beef, then sprinkle with half the crispy shallots and half the cilantro. Cover with remaining rice, then top with the remaining beef, crispy shallots, and cilantro.

*Serve*—Serve with the minted yogurt on the side. Enjoy!

**NOTES**

1. This recipe is only suited to basmati rice, which is the traditional rice used in biryani. No need to rinse the rice if purchased in packages at grocery stores. If you're concerned about cleanliness, rinse and drain the rice well and reduce the chicken broth by ¼ cup.
2. The spice level of this dish is very mild—just a warm hum. Feel free to reduce or increase the cayenne pepper to your taste.
3. Grinding the saffron threads gets more flavor and color out of them—a good tip for this very expensive spice! But this isn't a critical step. Substitute with ⅛ teaspoon imitation saffron powder.

LEFTOVERS Fridge 3 days. Not suitable for freezing.

# CHICKEN SHAWARMA

*The smell when this is cooking is outrageous. OUTRAGEOUS!*

 **SERVES: 4 I PREP: 15 MINUTES + 12–24 HOURS MARINATING I COOK: 15 MINUTES**

This recipe will be very familiar to my friends, because I make it for them a lot! They're all hopelessly addicted—and you will be too, with one bite of the juicy, charred chicken, slathered with the richly spiced Middle Eastern marinade. This is excellent food for feeding a crowd, yet easy enough for a weeknight family dinner. I love this kind of food where you simply marinate a meat, grill it up, and pile it all onto platters with sides, letting everyone put together their own dinner. Less work for me!

2 lb skinless, boneless chicken thighs[1]

2 tbsp olive oil

**MARINADE**

1 tbsp each ground coriander, cumin, and cardamom

1 tsp cayenne pepper (omit or reduce for less spice)

2 tsp smoked paprika (or use regular)

2 tsp kosher salt*

½ tsp black pepper

1 tsp finely minced garlic*

2 tbsp fresh lemon juice

3 tbsp extra-virgin olive oil

**YOGURT SAUCE**

1 cup full-fat Greek yogurt

¼ tsp finely minced garlic*

1 tsp ground cumin

2 tsp fresh lemon juice

⅛ tsp each kosher salt* and black pepper

**TO SERVE**

3 cups finely sliced lettuce (romaine or iceberg)

2 tomatoes, halved, then sliced

Lemon slices

4 flatbreads, such as Lebanese, pita bread, or Easy Flatbreads (page 342)

¼ cup roughly chopped fresh cilantro

Chili sauce or hot sauce—I like sriracha* (optional)

*Marinate chicken*—Combine the marinade ingredients in a large bowl. Add the chicken and use tongs to make sure each piece is coated in the marinade. Cover and marinate for 12–24 hours in the fridge.

*Yogurt sauce*—Place the ingredients in a bowl and mix. Cover and put in the fridge until required (it will last for 3 days).

*Cook chicken*—Heat 1 tablespoon of oil in a large nonstick skillet over medium-high heat. Place half the chicken in the pan and cook for 3–4 minutes on each side until deep golden brown (the internal temperature of thighs should be 165°F). Transfer to a plate and cover loosely with aluminum foil. Repeat with the remaining chicken. (See Note 2 for grill option.)

*Serve*—Once the chicken has rested for 5 minutes, slice thickly,[3] then pile onto a platter. Put the lettuce, tomato, yogurt sauce, lemon, and flatbreads on the side. To make a shawarma roll, smear the flatbread with yogurt sauce, top with lettuce, tomato, then chicken. Sprinkle with cilantro. Add a splash of hot sauce, if desired. Roll up firmly, wrap with parchment paper if you want to keep it secured, then devour!

**NOTES**

1. I like thighs best as they are beautifully juicy. However, chicken breasts will also work. It's best to cut them in half horizontally to form thin steaks before marinating. Cook for 2 minutes on each side to an internal temperature of 150°F.
2. Grill: Heat the grill or flat plate on medium-high. No need to oil if your grill is well seasoned but, if not, then brush lightly with oil. Cook the first side for 4–5 minutes, then the second side for 3–4 minutes until deep golden brown.
3. If your chicken thighs are not that large, slicing is optional.
4. To make this gluten-free, use gluten-free flatbreads. Corn tortillas* are an excellent option!

LEFTOVERS Fridge 4 days. Not suitable for freezing, however, uncooked chicken in the marinade can be frozen for 3 months. Thaw, then cook as per the recipe.

# BUTTER CHICKEN

*Extravagantly flavored fall-apart chicken—my kind of food!*

 **SERVES: 5 I PREP: 15 MINUTES + 3–24 HOURS MARINATING I COOK: 25 MINUTES**

Butter chicken is by far the most loved curry recipe on my website! It's easy to see why. We all can't get enough of that silky and buttery sauce tinged with tomato and soft spices and, because it's not at all spicy, it's one that everyone can enjoy. Happily, butter chicken is also a total breeze to make at home. The only thing you'll be chopping is the chicken, and it's pretty much impossible to mess up. Give this a go and I promise it'll be on regular rotation.

---

1½ lb boneless, skinless chicken thighs,[1] cut into 1 inch pieces

2 tbsp ghee* (or unsalted butter)

1 cup tomato passata*[2]

1 cup heavy cream*[3]

1 tbsp sugar

1¼ tsp kosher salt*

**MARINADE**

½ tsp ground red chili*

1 tsp ground turmeric

1 tsp ground cumin

2 tsp garam masala*

1 tbsp freshly grated ginger*

2 garlic cloves,* finely minced

1 tbsp lemon juice

½ cup plain yogurt

**GARNISH (OPTIONAL)**

Cilantro

*Optional blitz*—For an extra-smooth sauce, combine the marinade ingredients in a food processor and blend until smooth. I do this when I'm making it for guests!

*Marinate chicken*—Mix the marinade ingredients with the chicken in a bowl. Cover and refrigerate for a minimum of 3 hours and up to 24 hours.

*Cook chicken*—Melt and heat the ghee over high heat in a large nonstick skillet. Take the chicken out of the marinade, but do not wipe the excess marinade off the chicken, and reserve the marinade dregs left in the bowl. Place the chicken in the pan and cook for around 3 minutes, stirring, or until the chicken is white all over (it won't go brown).

*Make sauce*—Add the tomato passata, cream, sugar, and salt. Also scrape in any remaining marinade left in the bowl. Stir to combine, then turn the heat down to low and simmer for 20 minutes. Do a taste test to see if it needs more salt.

*Serve*—Garnish with cilantro (if using). Serve over Basmati Rice (page 336) with Naan (page 50) and/or No-fry Pappadums[4] on the side for slopping! Add a side of cucumber chunks tossed with the Minted Yogurt Sauce in the Beef Biryani recipe (page 44).

**NOTES**

1. Chicken thighs work best as they stay tender and juicy. However, chicken breast will also work.
2. Substitute with canned crushed tomatoes, preferably pureed smooth with an immersion blender (blend in the can but cover the sides of the mouth of the can with your hand!).
3. If you use low-fat cream the sauce will lack the creamy mouthfeel that you know and love about butter chicken!
4. No-fry Pappadums: Place store-bought raw pappadums in the microwave around the edge of the turntable. Microwave for about 45 seconds to 1 minute on High, or until they puff up. Transfer to a bowl and repeat as desired. They will crisp up when they cool!

LEFTOVERS Fridge 4 days. Not suitable for freezing.

# NAAN

*Years in the making in pursuit of the best. Turns out, no kneading required!*

**MAKES: 6 NAAN (6 INCHES DIAMETER) I PREP: 20 MINUTES + 2 HOURS RISING I COOK: 10 MINUTES**

So many naan recipes are nothing more than a basic flatbread. They lack the signature puffiness, chew, and elasticity that proper naan should have. The greatest challenge to making authentic naan is that most people don't have a raging hot tandoor burning in their kitchen (err . . . that would be me, for one!) After rolling out more naans than anyone should in a lifetime, I think I've finally cracked the recipe. For something made in a regular skillet, I think this is a truly worthy homemade naan incredibly close to the restaurant breads. And my website readers agree!

1 tsp instant/rapid rise yeast[1]

½ cup warm tap water[2] (about 105°F)

1 tbsp sugar

2 tbsp whole or low-fat milk

1½ tbsp whisked egg,*[3] at room temperature (about ½ egg)

1¾ cups bread flour or all-purpose flour,[4] plus extra for dusting

½ tsp kosher salt*

2 tbsp ghee,* melted (or unsalted butter), plus an extra 2 tbsp to serve

**FINISHES (OPTIONAL)**

Nigella seeds

Finely chopped cilantro, to garnish

*Bloom yeast*—Mix the yeast with the warm water and sugar in a small bowl. Cover with plastic wrap, then leave for 10 minutes until foamy.

*Dough*—Whisk the milk and egg together. Sift the flour into a separate bowl, then add the salt. Make a well in the flour, then add the yeast mixture and the milk and egg mixture. Mix together with a spatula. Once the flour is mostly incorporated, switch to using your hands and bring it together into a ball inside the bowl. No kneading required.

*Dough rise 1*—Cover the bowl with plastic wrap, then leave in a warm place for 1–1½ hours until it doubles in size.[5]

*Cut dough*—Turn the dough out onto a lightly floured surface. Cut into six equal pieces, then shape into smooth balls by stretching the surface and tucking it underneath.

*Dough rise 2*—Place the balls on a lightly floured tray. Dust the surface with flour and cover loosely with a lightweight dish towel. Put in a warm place[5] to rise for 15 minutes until it increases in size by about 50 percent.

*Roll*—Place the dough balls on a lightly floured work surface and flatten with your hand. Roll out into ⅛ inch thick, 6 inch diameter rounds.

*Cook*—Rub a cast-iron skillet[6] with a very light coating of ghee using ½ teaspoon melted ghee on a paper towel (unless the pan is already well seasoned). Set over high heat until you see wisps of smoke. Place a naan dough in the pan and cook for 1–1½ minutes until the underside is deep golden/slightly charred—the surface should get bubbly. Flip, then cook the other side for 1 minute until the bubbles become deep golden brown. Transfer to a plate, and repeat with the remaining ghee and naan, taking care to regulate the heat of the pan so it doesn't get too hot.

*Serve*—Brush the freshly cooked naan with ghee or melted butter (see Note 7 for garlic butter option). Sprinkle with nigella seeds and cilantro (if using) and serve hot!

**NOTES**

1. This yeast normally does not need to be activated in warm water but it's a very specific step for this recipe because it yields a softer naan than adding the instant yeast directly into the dough. Dry active yeast works too, but the naan is marginally less pillowy. If using active yeast, just follow the recipe as written, using the same yeast quantity.
2. If you don't have an instant read thermometer,* use the bath test. If it's warm enough to want to have a cozy bubble bath in it, it will be around the correct temperature. If it's too cold to have a bubble bath, then it's not warm enough!
3. I wouldn't ask you to measure this exact amount of egg if it didn't matter . . . but it matters!
4. Higher-protein bread flour yields a slightly fluffier, softer naan. But don't make a special trip to buy it—all-purpose flour is almost as good!
5. Ambient temperature for dough rising—minimum 75°F, up to 85°F. The warmer it is, the faster the dough will rise.
6. Do not use a nonstick skillet as the high heat may ruin the nonstick coating. If you don't have a cast-iron skillet, use your grill or any other pan.
7. Garlic butter: Add ¼ teaspoon finely minced garlic* into the butter, then melt.
8. Make ahead: After dough rise 1, cover and store the dough in the fridge (do not punch down). It will deflate in the fridge. When ready to cook, remove from the fridge, cut into six pieces, and proceed with the recipe. Dough rise 2 will take 30 minutes+ longer as you're starting with cold dough.

LEFTOVERS Fridge 3 days. Warm before serving.

# EFFORTLESS

My very best ultra-low-effort dinner recipes!

# MISO-GLAZED EGGPLANT

*One of my favorite ways with eggplant. And it's completely effortless!*

**SERVES: 4 | PREP: 7 MINUTES | COOK: 1 HOUR**

There's a good reason miso is a staple of Japanese food. It's packed with umami (read: savory flavor!), which means it's a brilliant shortcut to add a ton of taste with very few other ingredients. Here, I'm using miso to slather on eggplant before baking. It sets into a beautiful golden glaze, which fills the slits that open up as the eggplant cooks. As for eating it? Smoosh it all up so the sweet glaze mixes with the creamy flesh. Eat with chopsticks, to be vaguely authentic, but there's no shame in using a spoon!

---

**MISO GLAZE**

3 tbsp red miso[1] (or dashi miso or shiro miso)

1½ tbsp mirin*

2 tsp cooking sake*

1½ tsp sugar

**EGGPLANT**

2 x 14 oz eggplants[2] (about 9 inches long)

2 tbsp canola oil

Canola oil spray (optional)

**TO SERVE**

Sesame seeds

Finely sliced green onion*

Chopped cilantro (optional)

Preheat the oven to 400°F.

*Miso glaze*—Mix the ingredients in a bowl until smooth.

*Prepare eggplant*—Cut the eggplants in half lengthwise and place them flesh-side up. Using a small knife, cut 1 inch diamonds into the flesh, almost through to the skin. Don't cut through the skin (though if you do a bit, it's okay!)

*Roast*—Place the eggplant on a baking tray, then brush the surface with oil. Roast for 30 minutes. Remove from the oven and brush with two-thirds of the miso glaze. Bake for a further 15 minutes, then brush with the remaining miso glaze. Bake for a further 10–15 minutes or until the eggplant is soft all the way through (cook time will depend on the eggplant size; use a butter knife to check if it's soft).

*Caramelize*—Flick the oven broiler on high with the shelf 10 inches from the heat source. Spray the surface of the eggplant with canola oil, if you want better caramelization! Broil for 3–6 minutes, or until the surface is caramelized. Don't walk away—it can burn easily!

*Serve*—Transfer to serving plates, sprinkle with sesame seeds and sliced green onion, and serve straight away. Ideal served over soba noodles and chunks of smashed cucumber drizzled with Ginger Dressing (page 333), and a sprinkle of chopped cilantro.

**NOTES**

1. This recipe will work with most types of miso, but do not use saikyo miso or sweet miso (too sweet).
2. Asian/Japanese eggplants (the thinner, smaller ones) can also be used. Do not score, and reduce baking time to around 30 minutes in total, brushing with glaze and finishing under the broiler as per the recipe.

LEFTOVERS Fridge 2 days, though best made fresh as cooked eggplant does get a bit saggy and soft!

# FRIED CABBAGE WITH NOODLES & BACON

*Shockingly good and super quick!*

**SERVES: 4 I PREP: 6 MINUTES I COOK: 6 MINUTES**

Cabbage and noodles sounds like an unlikely winner, but this dish knocks out absolutely everyone who tries it! (I think the added bacon and parmesan might have a small hand in this.) A good finishing hit of black pepper and squeeze of lemon really brings the dish to life. I love this sort of weekday dish that packs a heap of veggies but doesn't skimp on flavor. Try it and thank me later!

---

2 tsp kosher salt*

3 cups short-cut angel hair pasta[1]

**NOODLE FRY-UP**

1 tbsp extra-virgin olive oil

8 oz bacon, chopped into 1 x 1/2 inch pieces (or so)

2 garlic cloves,* finely minced

1 yellow onion, halved and sliced 1/4 inch thick

5 heaped tightly packed cups (14 oz) sliced green cabbage (1/4 inch thick)

1 tbsp unsalted butter

1/3 tightly packed cup (1 oz) finely grated parmesan,*[2] plus extra to serve

1 1/2 tsp coarsely ground black pepper (or 1/2 tsp finely ground)[3]

3/4 tsp kosher salt*

1 tbsp fresh lemon juice

*Cook pasta*—In a small pot bring 12 cups of water to a boil with the salt. Add the pasta and cook as per the package directions (usually 2–3 minutes). Drain in a colander, then set aside until required.

*Sauté onion and bacon*—Heat the oil in a large nonstick skillet over high heat. Add the bacon and cook for 30 seconds. Add the garlic and onion, then cook for 3 minutes until the bacon is golden and the onion is translucent.

*Noodle fry-up*—Add the cabbage and butter. Cook for 2 minutes until the cabbage is wilted. Add the pasta, parmesan, pepper, and salt. Toss for 1 minute. Add the lemon juice and toss to coat.

*Serve*—Divide among bowls, then sprinkle with the extra parmesan and enjoy!

**NOTES**

1. Short-cut angel hair pasta ("broken angel hair") is thin spaghetti broken into around 1 inch lengths. Fairly accessible these days in the pasta aisle. Can't find it? Get normal angel hair pasta, egg vermicelli pasta, or the thinnest spaghetti you can find and break it yourself (it's fun!). Use leftover broken pasta to make the Moroccan Harira Soup on page 164.
2. It's okay! Store-bought pre-grated parmesan is just fine here! As long as it's from the fridge section, not the dried pasta aisle (that's not real cheese).
3. The dish is mildly spicy, from the pepper. You can reduce or omit, to taste.

LEFTOVERS Fridge 4 days. Not suitable for freezing.

# MUSSELS IN WHITE WINE

*One of the world's most underrated quick meals!*

 **SERVES: 4–5 AS A STARTER, 2 AS A MAIN | PREP: 10 MINUTES | COOK: 7 MINUTES**

Cooking mussels in white wine is a classic preparation made in kitchens all around the world, though the French claim it to be theirs. And we're happy to let them stake their claim, because when we serve this up to friends, we can tell them, "It's French, darling." (Skip trying to pronounce the French name though—*moules marinière*—it might affect your credibility. It does mine!) Crusty bread for dunking into the broth is essential. It's the best part!

---

3½ tbsp unsalted butter

½ yellow onion, finely sliced

3 garlic cloves, finely sliced

1 cup finely sliced celery (about 1½ stems)

2 lb fresh mussels*[1]

½ cup chardonnay, or other dry white wine*[2]

½ lightly packed cup parsley leaves

*Make sauce*—In a large pot, melt the butter over medium–high heat until foamy. Add the onion, garlic, and celery, then cook for 1½ minutes. The celery should still have a bit of a bite to it, and not be completely soft.

*Cook mussels*—Add the mussels, wine, and parsley. Turn the heat to high. Once the liquid starts bubbling, cover with a lid and cook for 3 minutes, shaking the pot every minute.

*Remove lid*—Opened mussels indicate they are cooked. Mussels that remain closed do not need to be discarded, it does not mean they are off! Just pry them open with a butter knife.

*Serve*—Tip the mussels into a large bowl. Serve with a side of leafy greens with French Dressing (page 333) and don't forget Easy Crusty Artisan Bread (page 341) for dunking!

**NOTES**

1. See page 360 in the Glossary for my guide to buying and cleaning mussels.
2. Substitute with nonalcoholic white wine, which is fairly readily available these days, even in supermarkets.

LEFTOVERS Fridge 2 days. Not suitable for freezing.

mussels

# THE ASIAN GLAZED SALMON

*. . . that Kath makes "all the time."*

**SERVES: 2 | PREP: 5 MINUTES + 30 MINUTES OR UP TO OVERNIGHT MARINATING | COOK: 10 MINUTES**

My friend Kath insisted that this be included in the cookbook, declaring it to be a recipe she makes "all the time" because she always has the ingredients on hand, and it's so quick and easy. Plus, of course, it's a hit with everyone. Think juicy salmon slathered in a savory, gingery, slightly sweet Asian glaze. You know it's good!

---

2 x 6 oz salmon fillets, skinless[1]

Canola oil spray

**MARINADE GLAZE**

1 tsp finely minced ginger*

1 garlic clove,* finely minced

1 tbsp soy sauce,* light or all-purpose[2]

2 tbsp oyster sauce

2 tbsp sweet chili sauce[3]

**GARNISHES (OPTIONAL)**

Sesame seeds

Finely sliced green onion*

*Marinade glaze*—Combine the ingredients in a shallow bowl. Add the salmon and turn to coat. Cover and marinate for 30 minutes or up to overnight.

*Prepare salmon*—Heat the oven broiler to high. Place the shelf 6–8 inches from the heat source.[4]

Line a baking tray with aluminum foil, then place the salmon on the tray, skin-side down (if it's got skin). Dab or brush some glaze onto the surface of the salmon. Discard the remaining glaze (don't pour it over the salmon as any glaze pooled around the salmon will burn).

*Grill salmon*—Place the salmon under the broiler for 7 minutes. Remove, then spray the surface with oil. Broil for another 1–3 minutes until the surface is beautifully caramelized and the salmon is cooked (the flesh should flake easily). The internal temperature should be 120°F for medium-rare (recommended) or 140°F for medium[5].

*Serve*—Transfer the salmon to serving plates and leave to rest for 3 minutes. Serve the salmon sprinkled with the sesame seeds and green onion (if using). Serve with a side of White Rice (page 335) and kale and shredded carrot tossed with Asian Sesame Dressing (page 333).

**NOTES**

1. It doesn't matter if the skin is on, just eat the flesh off the skin.
2. Light or all-purpose soy sauce can be used. Do not use dark soy sauce (too intense) or sweet soy sauce.
3. I just use store-bought sweet chili sauce.
4. If your broiler is separate and the shelf can't be positioned the specified distance from the heat source, lower the heat to medium and monitor closely during the final caramelization part.
5. Insert a cooking thermometer* into the middle of the thickest part of the salmon. 120°F is the default doneness for salmon served at restaurants, which is medium-rare for optimum juiciness. The internal temperature will rise to 125°F while resting. For medium, target an internal temperature of 140°F, which will rise to 145°F after resting. It will still be juicy, but juicier if medium-rare! If you don't have a cooking thermometer, you can tell the salmon is cooked when the flesh flakes easily.

LEFTOVERS Fridge 3 days, but best served fresh.

# TERIYAKI BEEF BOWLS

*A three-ingredient sauce and hidden veggies. It's a life essential!*

**SERVES: 4–5 I PREP: 8 MINUTES I COOK: 12 MINUTES**

I think my mum will frown when she sees this recipe, because you will never see teriyaki ground beef in Japan. But when it's this delicious and easy to make, I say it's time to open your mind! It's packed with good vegetables and I serve it all over rice so it's a one-bowl meal. Who knows, maybe I'm onto something and it will be the next big thing in the Japanese food scene! *[I really want to insert a laughing emoji here, but my publisher won't let me!]*

---

1 tbsp canola oil

2 garlic cloves,* finely minced

1 yellow onion, finely chopped

1 carrot, peeled and grated using a box grater

1 zucchini, grated using a box grater

1 lb ground beef

**TERIYAKI SAUCE**

3 tbsp light or all-purpose soy sauce*[1]

3 tbsp mirin*[2]

3 tbsp cooking sake*[2]

½ tsp sugar

**TO SERVE**

White Rice (page 335) or other faux or real rice of choice (pages 334–37)

Sesame seeds (optional)

Finely sliced green onion* (optional)

*Teriyaki sauce*—Mix the ingredients in a small bowl.

*Cook vegetables*—Heat the oil in a very large nonstick skillet over high heat. Add the garlic and onion, then stir for 2 minutes until the onion is translucent. Add the carrot and zucchini, then cook for a further 3 minutes until the water leaches out of the vegetables and it mostly evaporates.

*Cook beef*—Add the beef and cook, breaking it up as you go, until it changes from red to light brown. Add the teriyaki sauce and cook for 4 minutes until the sauce evaporates and the beef is a little caramelized.

*Serve*—Serve the teriyaki beef over rice, sprinkled with sesame seeds and green onion (if using), and a side of steamed vegetables tossed with Asian Sesame Dressing (page 333).

**NOTES**

1. Mum would say it has to be a Japanese soy sauce (our family uses Kikkoman). Mind you, she won't "approve" of this recipe anyway, because it's not authentic. Ha! I say any all-purpose soy sauce will be fine. Light soy sauce will also work. Do not use dark soy sauce or sweet soy sauce, though.
2. Mirin and cooking sake are key ingredients in teriyaki sauce and contain small amounts of alcohol. So if you can't consume alcohol for health or religious reasons, unfortunately you'll need to give this recipe a miss! Note that the high heat cooking in this recipe, where all the liquid is virtually evaporated, leaves little residual alcohol in the finished dish.

LEFTOVERS Fridge 4 days, freezer 3 months. Reheat with a slosh of water to juice the beef up again.

# SPICY SICHUAN PORK NOODLES

*My pick of the chapter. It's that good—and so quick!*

**SERVES: 2 I PREP: 10 MINUTES I COOK: 8 MINUTES**

This is how you get your spicy Chinese noodle fix—fast! I've turned the famous Sichuan stir-fried pork with green beans dish into hellishly tasty noodles. The simple three-ingredient sauce here is one of my little secrets. It's got it all—great savory flavor, some balancing sweetness, and you can make it as spicy as you want. The trick is to get your green beans nicely blistered in the pan and a good bit of caramelization on your noodles. That's what makes this dish taste like it came straight from a restaurant wok!

**MY SECRET SPICY ASIAN SAUCE**

1½ tbsp oyster sauce

1½ tbsp kecap manis*

4 tsp sambal oelek*[1]

**NOODLES**

9 oz fresh lo mein noodles[2]

2 tbsp vegetable oil

2 cups (7 oz) green beans, ends trimmed and cut in half[3]

½ yellow onion, finely diced

1 garlic clove,* finely minced

2 tsp finely minced ginger*[4] (optional)

7 oz ground pork[5]

*Spicy Asian sauce*—Mix the ingredients in a small bowl.

*Cook noodles*—Cook the noodles according to the package directions. Drain, then rinse briefly under tap water. Leave in the colander until ready to use.

*Char beans*—Heat 1 tablespoon of the oil in a large cast-iron skillet[6] over high heat until it is almost smoking. Add the green beans, spreading them out in a single layer. Leave to cook for 2 minutes, stirring only every 30 seconds, until lightly charred and just cooked through. Put the beans into a bowl and set aside.

*Cook pork*—Cool the skillet for 15 seconds, then place it back over high heat. Heat the remaining 1 tablespoon of oil, then cook the onion, garlic, and ginger (if using) for 30 seconds. Add the ground pork and cook, breaking it up with a wooden spoon until it mostly changes from pink to white, about 1 minute. Add 1 tablespoon of the sauce and continue cooking the pork for another 1 minute until it is nicely browned.

Add the noodles, green beans, and remaining sauce. Toss for 2 minutes with two wooden spoons, ensuring that the noodles get some nice caramelization.

*Serve*—Divide between two bowls and devour!

**NOTES**

1. Reduce the sambal oelek to 1 teaspoon for barely-there spicy, or increase to 6 teaspoons for very spicy!
2. This recipe will work with any medium thickness or thin noodles, dried or fresh. For fresh, use the amount as per the recipe. For dried, use 6 oz and prepare as per the package directions. You can also use two instant noodle or ramen packages, discarding the seasoning packages as we're making our own sauce!
3. Green beans can be substituted with asparagus or broccolini, cut vertically into green bean–sized sticks.
4. Ginger is optional. It brings something extra to the dish but the dish is still terrific without it.
5. Pork works best here, but you can also use ground beef, chicken, or turkey.
6. A cast-iron or other heavy-based skillet is best here so you can get a nice char on the beans and caramelize the noodles. It makes this dish! Do not use a nonstick skillet. High-heat cooking like this will ruin the nonstick coating.

LEFTOVERS Fridge 3 days. Not suitable for freezing.

# CRISPY SKIN FISH WITH BEAN RAGU

*Make once. Make forever.*

 **SERVES: 2 I PREP: 10 MINUTES I COOK: 10 MINUTES**

This is THE fish recipe that will save you on those days when you've got a beautiful piece of fish and want something quick on the side to complete your meal. The bean ragu does triple duty as a starch and vegetable side dish, as well as a sauce for the fish. I've made a crispy-skinned barramundi here because, well, crispy skin! But you can simply pan-fry any piece of fish, whether it has skin or not. See page 139 for directions.

---

2 x 6 oz cod, snapper, or other fish[1] fillets (no thicker than 3/4 inch at the thickest point[2]), skin on, pin-boned

1/2 tsp kosher salt*

1/4 tsp black pepper

2 tbsp canola oil

Sea salt flakes, to serve (optional)

**BEAN RAGU**

2 tbsp extra-virgin olive oil

1/2 yellow onion, finely diced

1/4 cup each diced carrot, celery, and fennel (1/4 inch cubes)

2 garlic cloves,* minced

1/4 tsp kosher salt*

1/4 tsp black pepper

2 tsp tomato paste

15 oz can white cannellini beans, including all the liquid in the can

3/4 cup low-sodium chicken broth*

1 tightly packed cup roughly chopped kale leaves*

2 tsp dill leaves, roughly chopped

*Prepare fish*—Pat the fish skin dry with paper towels. If time permits, leave the fish in the fridge, uncovered, skin-side up, for 1 hour (for crispy skin insurance).

Using a sharp knife, make three slits lengthwise on the skin—1 1/2 inches long, 1/2 inch apart, 1/8 inch deep. This helps prevent the skin from curling up—some fish types are greater offenders than others!

*Bean ragu*—Heat the oil in a medium saucepan over medium-high heat. Add the onion, carrot, celery, fennel, garlic, salt, and pepper. Cook for 4 minutes, stirring every now and then. Add the tomato paste, cannellini beans (including all the liquid in the can), and the chicken broth. Stir, then once it starts bubbling, cover with a lid and reduce the heat to medium-low. Simmer for 5 minutes. Stir in the kale, then simmer for a further 1 minute until wilted. Remove the pan from the stove and keep warm until required.

*Cook fish*—Meanwhile, sprinkle the skin and flesh of the fish with the salt and pepper. Heat the oil in a large nonstick skillet over medium-high heat until you see the first small wisps of smoke. Place one fillet in the pan, skin-side down, then use your fingers or a spatula to press down lightly on the fish for 10 seconds to allow the skin to seal flat against the hot skillet surface. Repeat with the other fillet (or do both at the same time!). Cook for 3–4 minutes until the skin is crispy and golden (lift up to check). Turn and cook the flesh side for 1 1/2 minutes, or until the flesh flakes easily and the internal temperature registers 130°F.[3]

*Rest*—Transfer the fish to a rack, skin-side up, to rest for 3 minutes.

*Serve*—Stir the dill into the bean ragu, then divide between two shallow bowls. Place the fish on top, skin-side up. Sprinkle with salt flakes (if using) and eat immediately!

**NOTES**

1. Salmon, trout, striped bass, and black bass will all work well for this recipe.
2. If your fish fillet is thicker than 3/4 inch at the thickest point, do not flip the fish at the 3 minute mark. Leave it skin-side down and transfer to a 325°F oven to finish cooking it until the internal temperature registers 130°F. As a guide, a 3/4 inch thick, 6 oz barramundi fillet will take around 10 minutes to cook.
3. See Note 3 of Baked Fish with Lemon Cream Sauce on page 68.
4. For gluten free, be sure to use gluten-free chicken broth (or make your own—see page 349). If using homemade, add an extra 1/8 teaspoon of salt into the bean ragu.

LEFTOVERS Fridge 3 days. Not suitable for freezing.

# BAKED FISH WITH LEMON CREAM SAUCE

*It makes its own sauce!*

 **SERVES: 4 I PREP: 5 MINUTES I COOK: 10 MINUTES**

This is the single most popular fish recipe on my website because it's an incredibly delicious way to cook fish that's completely effortless. You simply put fillets in a baking dish, pour the sauce over, then bake. And out comes a beautifully tender, semi-poached fish with a creamy lemon sauce. Add a simple garden salad with a bread roll for sauce-mopping, and that's dinner done!

---

4 x 6 oz skinless white fish fillets,[1] about 3/4 inch thick

1/2 tsp kosher salt*

1/4 tsp black pepper

1 1/2 tbsp very finely minced shallots*

**LEMON CREAM SAUCE**

3 1/2 tbsp unsalted butter

1/4 cup heavy cream*

1 garlic clove,* finely minced

1 tbsp dijon mustard

1 1/2 tbsp lemon juice

1/4 tsp kosher salt*

1/4 tsp black pepper

**TO SERVE**

2 teaspoons finely chopped parsley

4 lemon slices or wedges

Preheat the oven to 400°F.

*Lemon cream sauce*—Place all the ingredients in a heatproof jar or bowl. Microwave on High in two 30-second bursts, stirring in between, until melted and smooth.

*Season fish*—Place the fish in a 13 x 9 inch baking dish.[2] Sprinkle both sides of the fish with salt and pepper, then arrange the fish so there is space between each fillet. Sprinkle the fish with the shallot, then pour the sauce over the top.

*Cook fish*—Bake for 10–12 minutes until the fish is cooked, with an internal temperature of 130°F,[3] or the flesh flakes easily. (Thicker fillets around 1 inch will take about 17 minutes.)

*Rest*—Remove the fish from the oven and transfer the fish to serving plates. (Leave the sauce in the dish for now.) Rest for 5 minutes.

*Serve*—Spoon the sauce over the fish and serve sprinkled with parsley and lemon slices over Creamy Mashed Potato (page 338) and arugula tossed with my Everyday Salad Dressing (page 333).

**NOTES**

1. This recipe works best with 3/4 inch thick white fish fillets, which cook quickly in the oven. Cod, halibut, and striped bass all work well.
2. Use a baking dish large enough so there is space between the fillets. If the fish is crammed in too snugly then the sauce won't reduce and thicken.
3. Insert a cooking thermometer* into the middle of the thickest part of the fish—130°F is the internal temperature for white fish when it just reaches the point of being fully cooked, which means it is at optimum juiciness! The internal temperature will rise to 135°F while resting. If you don't have a cooking thermometer, you can tell the fish is cooked when the flesh flakes easily.

LEFTOVERS Fridge 3 days, but best served fresh.

# SOUTHERN PORK & BEANS

*Southerners know how to make beans irresistible! (Dozer agrees.)*

 **SERVES: 6 AS A MAIN, 10 AS A SIDE | PREP: 15 MINUTES | COOK: 1 HOUR 20 MINUTES**

Pork and beans are a rib-sticking staple. It comes in cans, but of course homemade leaves that stuff for dead! I especially love the Southern-style versions of pork and beans in a rich, barbecue-like sauce. I dial down the sweetness a bit and add bits of tender pork shoulder to turn it into a low-effort meal. Serve with cornbread and a side of slaw for the real-deal experience!

---

1 lb skinless, boneless pork shoulder, excess fat trimmed, cut into 3/4 inch cubes

1/2 tsp garlic powder

1/2 tsp smoked paprika (or ordinary paprika)

1/2 tsp kosher salt*

1/4 tsp black pepper

2 tbsp canola oil

**BEANS**

6 oz bacon, cut into 1/4 x 1/2 inch pieces

1 yellow onion, finely chopped

3 garlic cloves,* minced

3 x 15 oz cans kidney beans, drained

1 cup ketchup

1 cup tomato passata*

1/3 cup molasses*[1]

3 tbsp apple cider vinegar

1 1/4 cups water

2 tsp mustard powder

1 tbsp Worcestershire sauce

1/2 tsp cayenne pepper (adjust spiciness to taste)

1/4 tsp kosher salt*

1/4 tsp black pepper

Preheat the oven to 350°F.

*Prepare pork*—Place the pork in a bowl, sprinkle with the garlic powder, paprika, salt, and pepper and toss to coat.

*Cook pork*—Heat the oil in a 9½–11 inch heavy-based pot over high heat. Add half the pork and cook until light golden all over, about 4 minutes. Don't worry if it's still raw inside. Transfer the pork to a bowl using a slotted spoon. Repeat with the remaining pork.

*Cook bacon and add beans*—Add the bacon to the same pot. Cook for 1 minute, reduce the heat to medium-high, then add the onion and garlic. Cook for 3 minutes or until the onion is translucent and the bacon is light golden. Add the remaining ingredients and stir to combine.

*Simmer pork and beans*—Return the pork to the pot along with any juices accumulated in the bowl. Bring to a simmer, place a lid on, then transfer to the oven[2] for 1 hour or until the pork pieces are tender.

*Serve*—Ladle into bowls and serve with cornbread or bread for slopping and mopping. Goes especially well with Cornbread Muffins (page 342).

**NOTES**

1. Substitute with ⅔ cup brown sugar.
2. This recipe can also be cooked on the stove over a very low heat, but it will need to be stirred regularly to ensure the base doesn't burn. Frankly, the oven is easier!

LEFTOVERS Fridge 4 days, freezer 3 months.

# ONE-TRAY MOROCCAN BAKED CHICKEN WITH CHICKPEAS

*Spiced chicken, stewy-crispy chickpeas. BIG flavors!*

 **SERVES: 5 | PREP: 10 MINUTES + 24 HOURS MARINATING (MINIMUM 4 HOURS) | COOK: 65 MINUTES**

This is a favorite one-pan dinner that has got a whole lot going on. There's juicy chicken infused with heady Moroccan spices. A rubble of golden chickpeas—some a bit crispy, some a bit stewy. Pops of fresh tomatoes burst in your mouth. And of course, a tasty sauce that just makes itself—my favorite kind! Don't skip the fennel. Not only does it add to your daily veggie quota, it's the secret ingredient that makes the sauce extra tasty.

5 x 8 oz (or so) skin-on, bone-in chicken thighs

½ lb cherry tomatoes

1 medium–large fennel bulb, top trimmed, halved and cut into ½ inch wedges[1]

1 tbsp extra-virgin olive oil

⅛ tsp each kosher salt* and black pepper

**MARINADE**

1 tbsp baharat spice mix[2]

1 tsp each ground cumin and smoked paprika[3]

1 tsp kosher salt*

½ tsp black pepper

2 garlic cloves,* finely minced

2 tbsp fresh lemon juice

3 tbsp extra-virgin olive oil

**GOLDEN CHICKPEAS**

2 x 15 oz cans chickpeas, drained

1 tbsp extra-virgin olive oil

1¼ tsp each ground turmeric and ground ginger

½ tsp ground cumin

¼ tsp each kosher salt* and black pepper

**TO SERVE**

¼ cup cilantro, roughly torn

*Marinate chicken*—Mix the marinade ingredients in a large zip-top bag.* Add the chicken, seal the bag, pressing out the excess air, then massage to coat. Marinate for 24 hours in the fridge (or 4 hours at the very least).[4]

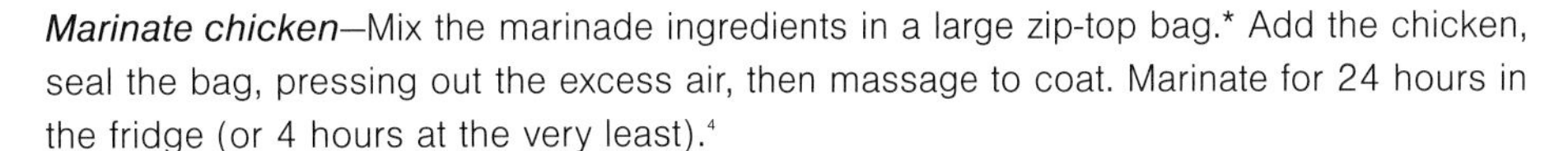

Preheat the oven to 400°F.

*Golden chickpeas*—Toss all the ingredients in a bowl to combine.

*Vegetables*—Toss the cherry tomatoes and fennel with the olive oil, salt, and pepper in a separate bowl.

*Bake chicken*—Place the chicken on a large baking tray (18 x 13 inches), skin-side up, and dab on the residual marinade. Surround with the chickpeas, pick the fennel out of the bowl, and randomly place it around the chicken. Bake for 35 minutes.

Remove the tray from the oven. Mix the chickpeas and fennel to coat in the juices on the tray, then dab the juice onto the chicken skin with a basting brush. Scatter the tomatoes around the chicken. Bake for a further 30 minutes until the chicken is golden. Remove from the oven and leave to rest for 5 minutes.

*Serve*—Dab the tray juices onto the chicken skin once more, then serve sprinkled with cilantro. Be sure to use the tray juices as the sauce!

**NOTES**

1. Cut the fennel into wedges so the core holds the wedges together. Don't get too hung up about fennel size—you just want enough to scatter randomly across the tray without covering all the chickpeas.
2. This Middle Eastern spice mix is fairly commonly found these days in the general spice aisle of major grocery stores. If you can't find it, use any Moroccan spice mix.
3. Use ordinary paprika if you don't have smoked.
4. In the event of a dinner emergency, the marinating time can be skipped altogether because there's enough tasty sauce to compensate.

LEFTOVERS Fridge 4 days. Not suitable for freezing.

# ONE-POT SAUSAGE MEATBALL PASTA

*You will love the meatball hack!*

**SERVES: 4–5 I PREP: 15 MINUTES I COOK: 35 MINUTES**

Anyone who knows me knows I hate rolling meatballs—hence why I love these sausage meatballs. Just cut sausages up into pieces and voila, instant meatballs! Here I cook them in a bright tomato sauce with rigatoni. Think a big, bubbly pasta bake—only you've done it all on the stove in one pot in less time than it'd take to roll up proper meatballs!

---

1 ½ tbsp extra-virgin olive oil

1 lb good-quality thin beef or pork sausages,[1] cut into ¾ inch pieces (mini meatballs!)

1 yellow onion, finely chopped

2 garlic cloves,* minced

1 carrot, peeled and finely diced

1 celery stalk, finely diced

1 bay leaf*

1 tsp dried rosemary

3 tbsp tomato paste

28 oz can crushed tomatoes

2 cups low-sodium chicken broth*

1 ½ cups water

¾ tsp kosher salt*

½ tsp black pepper

10 oz rigatoni (or penne, ziti, or macaroni)

1 ½ cups (5 oz) shredded* colby cheese[2]

1 tsp finely chopped parsley, to serve (optional)

*Brown meatballs*—Heat the oil over high heat in a large heavy-based pot. Add the sausage "meatballs" and cook for 4–5 minutes, stirring regularly, until golden brown. Transfer to a bowl.

*Sauté aromatics*—Turn the heat down to medium–high. Discard all but 2 tablespoons of the fat in the pot, then return to the stove. Cook the onion, garlic, carrot, celery, bay leaf, and rosemary for 3 minutes or until the onion is translucent.

*Make sauce*—Add the tomato paste and cook for 1 minute. Add the crushed tomatoes, broth, water, salt, pepper, sausage meatballs, and the rigatoni. Stir, let it come up to a simmer, then place the lid on and turn the heat down to medium–low so it is simmering gently.

Cook for 20 minutes, stirring every now and then so the base doesn't catch. Take the pot off the stove, remove the lid and check to ensure the pasta is just about cooked. It should still be soupier than you want. Stir well for 10 seconds—the sauce will reduce quickly. It should still be quite saucy—more gets absorbed in the next step.

*Cheese it!*—Working quickly, smooth the surface, then sprinkle with the cheese. Put the lid back on, then leave the pot on the turned-off stove for 3 minutes or until the cheese melts.

*Serve*—Serve immediately, sprinkled with parsley, if desired. I like to serve this with a handful of arugula drizzled with Balsamic Dressing (page 333).

**NOTES**

1. Any sausages will work well in this recipe as long as they are the thin ones around ¾ inch wide. The really fat sausages work too, but you get fewer meatballs. Be sure to choose good-quality sausages as they are part of the flavor base in this dish. There is a time and place for the really economical ones (Aussie fundraising sausage sizzle approved!) but they are laden with fillers, so now is not the time! Opt for sausages where you can see fat specks, or check the ingredients to see how much of the sausage is not meat (aim for 90%+ meat). Beef sausages brown more than pork and chicken, but any of these are fine. Just get your favorite!
2. Any melting cheese will work here—colby seems to always be in my fridge these days.

LEFTOVERS Fridge 4 days, freezer 3 months. Fully thaw, then microwave to reheat.

# MAGIC BAKED CHICKEN FRIED RICE

*Just put it all in a pan—even the uncooked rice—and bake!*

**SERVES: 4 AS A MAIN | PREP: 10 MINUTES | COOK: 45 MINUTES**

Sometimes after a long day, even I don't have the energy to deal with the hassle of chopping vegetables, pulling out woks, and smoking out my kitchen–let alone remembering to cook rice the day before! So I published a "dump and bake" fried rice on my website–albeit with some trepidation–convinced it would be slammed as an abomination. To my total surprise, the recipe was a smash hit and had 100,000 views in 24 hours! Truth is, it's delicious–the flavor is fantastic, the rice is fluffy and moist. The most asked question I get is, "How can I add chicken to this?" Well, here's how!

---

**BAKED FRIED RICE**

1½ cups long-grain white rice,[1] uncooked

1½ cups low-sodium chicken broth*

1½ tbsp light soy sauce*[2]

1 tbsp Shaoxing cooking wine*[3]

2 garlic cloves,* finely minced[4]

¼ tsp white pepper

2 cups frozen diced vegetables (carrots, peas, and corn mix), still frozen

¾ cup chopped bacon or ham (I use store-bought chopped bacon)

**MARINATED CHICKEN**

1 lb boneless, skinless chicken thighs, cut into ½ inch pieces

1 tbsp oyster sauce

1 tbsp Shaoxing cooking wine*

1 tbsp light soy sauce*

2 tsp sesame oil*

1 garlic clove,* finely minced

**TO FINISH**

2 eggs, scrambled[5] (optional)

2 tsp sesame oil*

1 green onion,* finely sliced

Preheat the oven to 400°F.

*Bake covered*—Place all the baked fried rice ingredients, except the vegetables and bacon, in a 13 x 9 inch metal pan (not ceramic or glass). Shake to spread the rice evenly, ensuring all the rice is submerged under the broth. Sprinkle the vegetables evenly across the surface, then sprinkle the bacon on top. Cover with aluminum foil and bake for 25 minutes.

*Marinate chicken*—Meanwhile, place the marinated chicken ingredients in a bowl and mix well to combine. Set aside to marinate while the rice cooks.

*Bake uncovered*—Remove the aluminum foil (reserve the foil), then spread the chicken in a single layer across the surface of the rice. Bake, uncovered, for 20 minutes.

*Rest and serve*—Remove from the oven, cover with the reserved aluminum foil, and rest for 10 minutes. Use a rubber paddle to turn the rice over and gently break it up. Add the scrambled egg (if using). Drizzle with sesame oil and sprinkle with the green onion. Gently toss the fried rice to mix it together, then serve!

**NOTES**

1. Basmati and medium-grain white rice can also be used. Not suitable for risotto rice, paella rice, brown rice, or sushi rice.
2. Or all-purpose soy sauce. Do not substitute with dark soy sauce.
3. Or mirin* or dry sherry. If you can't consume alcohol, omit and add ¼ cup low-sodium chicken broth and cook for 1 minute longer.
4. I just use a garlic crusher in this recipe for convenience.
5. I tried all sorts of ways to bake the egg in the oven along with the rice! But it just didn't work, or got unnecessarily fiddly. Really, it's just easiest to cook it on the stove. Whisk the eggs, then scramble them in a nonstick skillet over medium–high heat with a teaspoon of oil until just cooked. Transfer to a bowl, then add to the rice as directed.

LEFTOVERS Fridge 3 days, freezer 3 months.

# GARLIC BREAD PIZZA

*What I make in a pizza emergency.*

**SERVES: 4 I PREP: 10 MINUTES I COOK: 20 MINUTES**

Pizza, meet garlic bread. Garlic bread, meet pizza. It's the love child that was absolutely meant to be! The quick homemade pizza sauce makes all the difference here. Don't resort to store-bought.

---

1 supermarket Italian bread, split in half lengthwise

**GARLIC BUTTER**

3½ tbsp unsalted butter

2 garlic cloves, crushed using garlic crusher[2]

1 tbsp finely chopped parsley (optional)

¼ tsp kosher salt*

**PIZZA SAUCE**

1 cup tomato passata*

1 tbsp tomato paste

1 tsp kosher salt*

2 tsp superfine sugar

**TOPPINGS[3]**

½ red onion, finely sliced

1½ cups (5 oz) shredded* mozzarella

6 white mushrooms, sliced ¼ inch thick (2 cups)

3 oz finely sliced salami, cut into ½ x ¼ inch strips

Preheat oven to 400°F. If you don't have a baking tray long enough for the pide or Italian bread, take out an oven shelf and cover with aluminum foil.

*Garlic butter*—Melt the butter with the garlic and stir in the parsley (if using) and salt.

*Pizza sauce*—Mix the ingredients together in a small bowl.

*Garlic bread*—Place the bread cut face down on the tray. Lightly brush with a bit of melted garlic butter (reserve most of the butter for the cut side). Bake for 5 minutes. Flip, brush the cut side with the remaining garlic butter (scoop up all the garlic bits!), then bake for 5 minutes.

*Toppings*—Spread with the pizza sauce right to the edge, then sprinkle with onion followed by cheese. Top with the mushrooms, then sprinkle with salami.

*Bake and serve*—Bake for 10 minutes or until the cheese on the edges is golden. Cut into slices and devour!

**NOTES**

1. Here in Australia I use pide, a popular Turkish flat-ish bread that is around 18 inches long, 6 inches wide and 1 inch thick. What's sold as "Italian bread' in American supermarkets is also ideal as it is similar in both size and texture. I don't mean a crusty, French-style baguettes, I'm referring to the soft squishy loaves that are labeled "Italian bread."
2. Or very finely minced using a knife.
3. Obviously feel free to use your own toppings of choice. You're only limited by your imagination!

LEFTOVERS Fridge 3 days, but best eaten fresh.

# ITALIAN BEEF RICE PILAF

*Beefy, tomatoey, and juicy!*

 **SERVES: 5 | PREP: 10 MINUTES | COOK: 40 MINUTES**

Everything you love about risotto and bolognese, all in one pot! Never mind authenticity, the nonnas of Italy would love it too—if only they'd thought of it first (wink).

---

2 tbsp olive oil

2 garlic cloves,* minced

1 yellow onion, finely chopped

1 large carrot, peeled and diced into 1/4 inch cubes

1 celery stalk, diced into 1/4 inch cubes

1 1/2 tsp fennel seeds[1]

1/2 tsp dried red pepper flakes

1 lb ground beef[2]

1 1/4 tsp kosher salt*

1 1/2 cups long-grain white rice[3]

14 oz can crushed tomato

2 1/2 cups low-sodium beef broth*

1 bay leaf*

2 tsp Worcestershire sauce

2 tomatoes, cut into 8 wedges, then halved

**TO SERVE**

1/4 cup roughly chopped parsley (optional)

Parmesan,* finely grated (*not* optional!)

*Sauté aromatics*—Heat the oil in a large pot over high heat. Add the garlic, onion, carrot, celery, fennel seeds, and red pepper flakes. Cook for 5 minutes until the onion is translucent.

*Brown beef*—Add the beef and ½ teaspoon salt. Cook, breaking it up as you go, until it changes from pink to brown.

*Cook pilaf*—Add the rice and stir to coat in the oil. Add the remaining ingredients, stir, then once it comes to a simmer, cover with a lid (do not stir again) and turn the heat down to low.

Cook for 22 minutes or until the rice is tender (there should still be a layer of liquid). Remove from the stove and rest, covered, for 5 minutes—the rice will soften further.

*Serve*—Remove the lid. Add the chopped parsley (if using) and gently stir, then serve, sprinkled with as much parmesan as you desire!

**NOTES**

1. This is the secret ingredient that adds a special touch to this otherwise simple dish. Don't be tempted to skip it!
2. Ground pork or lamb would also work well in this recipe.
3. Medium-grain rice, jasmine, and basmati rice can be substituted. Please don't use brown rice, sushi or other short-grain rice, wild rice (or any other "gourmet" rices for that matter), quinoa, or cauliflower rice! You can't use risotto rice either because it's not actually a risotto!

LEFTOVERS Fridge 3 days. Not suitable for freezing.

# BAKED CREAMY FETA ORZO

*Very high returns for very little effort.*

**SERVES: 5 | PREP: 5 MINUTES | COOK: 40 MINUTES**

Think risotto but with pasta, all baked in one dish! Don't skip the feta—some of it melts to make a creamy sauce and some remains as soft little salty nuggets. They're definitely the party-starters in this dish!

---

**ROASTED TOMATOES**

1 lb cherry tomatoes[1]

½ red onion, finely sliced

2 garlic cloves,* finely minced

1 tsp dried oregano[2]

½ tsp kosher salt*

¼ tsp black pepper

3 tbsp extra-virgin olive oil

**CREAMY ORZO**

2½ cups orzo

4 cups low-sodium vegetable or chicken broth,* hot[3]

1 cup boiling water[3]

½ tsp kosher salt*

7 oz Danish feta,[4] crumbled

2 lightly packed cups basil leaves, finely sliced

Preheat the oven to 400°F.

*Roasted tomatoes*—Toss the ingredients in a 13 x 9 inch baking dish, then roast for 25 minutes.

*Orzo*—Add the orzo, broth, water, and salt to the baking dish. Stir, then shake the pan to spread the orzo out evenly.

*Bake*—Cover with aluminum foil, then return to the oven for 20 minutes or until the orzo is tender.

*Finish*—Remove from the oven. It will seem like there's too much liquid, but have faith! Stir briefly to loosen the orzo. Add three-fourths of the feta, then stir until it is partially melted—some can remain as soft lumps. It should be quite creamy like risotto. If it's too thick, add a splash of hot water.

*Serve*—Stir in the basil leaves, crumble the reserved feta on top, then serve immediately!

**NOTES**

1. You can also use standard tomatoes cut into chunks, sliced zucchini, or small broccoli florets.
2. Or other dried herbs of choice (thyme is lovely too).
3. If you start with cold liquids, the orzo won't cook through evenly. I use a saucepan over high heat to heat the broth and water.
4. This is the creamy type of feta. Firm Greek feta won't melt into the sauce but will still make a great-tasting dish! Goat cheese can also be used. But don't talk to me about low-fat cheese!

LEFTOVERS Fridge 3 days. Not suitable for freezing.

# 3-MINUTE DOUBLE SMASH BURGERS

*Wait—you've never had a smash burger?*

**SERVES: 2 I PREP: 5 MINUTES I COOK: 10 MINUTES**

Smashing ground beef into a wafer-like patty not only cooks it faster, it's an express ticket to flavor. Crispy, charred burger edges PLUS dinner in 10 minutes flat? It's why it's a total thing!

PS I'm greedy so I made these double burgers. You don't have to be greedy.

---

Oil spray

1 lb ground beef,[1] 15–20% fat

½ tsp each kosher salt* and black pepper

2 tbsp canola oil

4 slices Swiss cheese (or other cheese of choice)

**BURGER**[2]

2 brioche buns, split

2 tbsp salted butter

Ketchup

1½ cups shredded iceberg lettuce

1 tomato, cut into ¼ inch slices

¼ red onion, very finely sliced

Pickles of choice, sliced

Mustard

Locate a smashing tool. A heavy skillet or pot is best—something sturdy enough to press down hard to flatten the beef. Spray the base lightly with oil.

*Beef balls*—Loosely shape four mounds with the ground beef—no need to roll balls, just gather and press the beef together. Sprinkle the top of the mounds with half the salt and pepper.

Preheat your oven broiler to medium–high, then lightly toast the cut surface of the buns for 3 minutes.

Open the windows! Then heat a large cast-iron skillet[3] over high heat until it is screaming hot and smoking.

*Smash 'em!*—Add half the oil, then place two of the beef mounds, salted-side down, in the skillet. Smash them down really hard by pressing on them with the second pan (or your chosen smashing tool), to form thin patties around ¼ inch thick. The edges will split and be craggy, which is exactly what you want as they go crispy. It's the best!

*Cook 90 seconds*—Sprinkle the surface of the patties with half the remaining salt and pepper, then leave the patties to cook undisturbed for 90 seconds—they will shrink and get thicker. Flip the patties, place a slice of cheese on each, then cook for another 90 seconds.

*Rest and repeat*—Transfer to a plate, then repeat with remaining two mounds.

*Assemble and serve*—Butter the buns and assemble as you wish. Here's my order—bun, ketchup, lettuce, tomato, onion, burger with cheese, pickle, mustard, lid. Eat and be happy!

**NOTES**

1. Great with chuck or standard ground beef from grocery stores. But for a truly top-shelf burger, ask your butcher for a 50/50 chuck/brisket blend with 20% fat.
2. Don't let anyone (including me) tell you what you should or should not have on your burger! These are just suggestions.
3. You need to use a cast-iron skillet for this. Do not use a nonstick skillet or you will destroy the coating. If you don't have a skillet large enough to fit four burgers (I don't), cook two at a time (it's okay if they jam up against each other a bit). They cook so quickly you can assemble the first burger as you cook the other patties.

LEFTOVERS Fridge 4 days, freezer 3 months.

# STICKY CHICKEN DRUMSTICKS

*With my secret five-ingredient glaze.*

**SERVES: 4–5 I PREP: 5 MINUTES I COOK: 1 HOUR**

The secret to sticky, drool-worthy, napkin-staining glazed chicken drumsticks is simple: Who bastes wins. The more you baste, the better!

4–5 corn cobs, halved

1 tbsp butter, melted, plus extra to serve

Pinch of kosher salt*

8–10 drumsticks (about 3 lb)

1 tsp finely chopped parsley (optional)

**GLAZE**

½ cup ketchup

⅓ cup sweet chili sauce

3 tbsp soy sauce,*[1] light or all-purpose

3 tbsp apple cider vinegar[2]

2 garlic cloves, crushed using a garlic crusher[3]

Preheat the oven to 400°F. Line a large baking tray with aluminum foil, then parchment paper.

*Toss*—Toss the corn in the butter with pinch of salt.

*Glaze*—Mix the ingredients in a medium bowl.

*Glaze drumsticks*—Dunk the drumsticks into the glaze one by one, then spread them out on the tray. Spoon one-third of the glaze over the drumsticks, coating the meaty end.

*Bake*—Bake for 25 minutes. Flip the drumsticks, then spoon half the remaining sauce over the meaty end of the drumsticks.

Bake 10 minutes. Remove the tray from the oven. Place the corn cobs on the tray standing on their ends so they are upright (i.e. not lying on the side on the kernels). Spoon the remaining sauce over the drumsticks.

Bake for a further 25 minutes, basting twice more with the juices on the tray, until the chicken is glazed and sticky. When basting, either use a brush to dab the jammy tray juices generously onto the chicken (avoid the watery parts), or use a spoon.

*Rest and serve*—Remove the tray from the oven and leave for 5 minutes. Baste one more time (why not!), then serve with the corn on the side with extra butter, and parsley if you like.

**NOTES**

1. Do not substitute with dark or sweet soy sauce! They are too intense.
2. Or any other clear vinegar.
3. Or finely minced with a knife.

LEFTOVERS Fridge 4 days. Not suitable for freezing.

# GREEN SPAGHETTI

*Green power!*

**SERVES: 4 | PREP: 7 MINUTES | COOK: 10 MINUTES**

Here's a fast, brilliant way to up your veggie intake in an eye-catching bowl of spinach-pesto spaghetti. Unlike basil, baby spinach is available year-round, it's cheaper and requires no prep other than ripping open a bag. For a different take, swap the spinach for kale* or Swiss chard, and the pine nuts for almonds or walnuts!

---

1 lb spaghetti, or other pasta of choice

2 tsp kosher salt*

Extra parmesan,* shaved or shredded, to serve

Baby spinach, to serve

Pine nuts, toasted,* to serve

**SPINACH PESTO**

4 tightly packed cups baby spinach leaves

1 tsp finely minced garlic*

½ cup pine nuts,* toasted[1]

½ tightly packed cup (2 oz) finely shredded parmesan*

1¼ tsp kosher salt*

¼ tsp black pepper

1 tsp lemon zest

3 tbsp fresh lemon juice

⅓ cup extra-virgin olive oil

*Spinach pesto*—Place all the ingredients, except the oil, in a food processor—jam that spinach in, there's a LOT of it! Blitz until the spinach is chopped into little pesto-sized bits. Scrape the sides down as needed. With the motor running on low, pour in the oil in a thin stream. Pesto, done!

*Spaghetti*—Cook the spaghetti in boiling water with the salt as per the package directions. Just before draining, scoop out 1 cup of the pasta cooking water. Drain the spaghetti, then return to the empty pot.

*Toss and serve*—Add the pesto to the pot with ½ cup of the pasta cooking water. Toss well, using the extra water as needed to loosen. Serve immediately while hot, or let it cool and serve at room temperature like you would a pasta salad. Either way, garnish with parmesan, baby spinach, and pine nuts.

**NOTES**

1. Walnuts, almonds, and pumpkin seeds are also great with baby spinach. Toast pumpkin seeds as you do pine nuts. For walnuts and almonds, toast in a 350°F oven for 10 minutes, shaking the pan once or twice, or until they smell nutty. Cool slightly, then roughly chop.

LEFTOVERS Fridge 2 days. Serve warm or at room temperature.

# CHORIZO POTATO STEW-SOUP

*There's chorizo in it. That's all you need to know!*

 **SERVES: 4–5 | PREP: 10 MINUTES | COOK: 25 MINUTES**

Is it a stew? A soup? All I know is that something so easy has no business being this tasty. Deeply smoky with chorizo and paprika, this hearty little flavor rocket also involves barely any chopping!

---

- 1 tbsp olive oil, plus extra to serve
- 1 lb chorizo,[1] sliced ¼ inch thick
- 2 rosemary sprigs[2]
- 3 garlic cloves,* finely minced
- 1 red onion, cut into ¾ inch squares
- 1 red bell pepper, cut into ¾ inch squares
- 1 tbsp smoked paprika[3]
- 14 oz baby potatoes, cut into ½ inch cubes
- 2 x 14 oz cans crushed tomatoes
- 2½ cups low-sodium chicken broth*
- ½ tsp kosher salt*
- ½ tsp black pepper

*Cook chorizo*—Heat the oil in a large pot over high heat. Cook the chorizo with the rosemary until golden, about 5 minutes.

*Cook vegetables*—Add the garlic, onion, and bell pepper. Cook for 2 minutes or until the onion is softened (but not floppy). Add the paprika and cook for 1 minute. Add the potato and stir to coat in the tasty flavors.

*Simmer*—Add the tomatoes, broth, salt, and pepper. Bring to a simmer, then lower the heat slightly to medium so it's bubbling. Cover with a lid, then cook for 20 minutes or until the potato is soft and the sauce has thickened.

*Serve*—Ladle into bowls, drizzle with olive oil, and serve with Easy Crusty Artisan Bread (page 341) on the side for dunking!

**NOTES**

1. Other smoked sausages like kielbasa will also work great here.
2. Substitute with 1 teaspoon dried rosemary leaves.
3. Adds a great smoky flavor to the dish but can be substituted with ordinary paprika. Avoid hot paprika unless you want it spicy!

LEFTOVERS Fridge 4 days, freezer 3 months.

# STIR-FRIES & NOODLES

**Toss with enthusiasm!**

# CHARLIE—MY ALL-PURPOSE STIR-FRY SAUCE

*Keeps for weeks. Infinite possibilities!*

**MAKES: 1½ CUPS, ENOUGH FOR 16 SERVES I PREP: 5 MINUTES I COOK: NONE**

Here's my Swiss army knife of stir-fry sauces! It's a classic Chinese brown sauce that has enough flavor to use just as is, but is also neutral enough as a base you can build on with other added flavors.

"Brown sauce" sounded a bit ick, so I ended up always calling it "Charlie"—as in "Charlie Brown," ha! Charlie is my trusty side-kick for so many different quick stir-fries. Keep a stash of this stuff on hand in your fridge like I do. It'll save you time and again when you need to whip up a weeknight dinner in a flash!

---

½ cup light soy sauce*[1]

½ cup oyster sauce

¼ cup Shaoxing cooking wine*[2]

¼ cup cornstarch

1 tbsp sugar

2 tbsp sesame oil*

1 tsp white pepper (or more!)

Place all the ingredients in a jar and shake well to combine. Store Charlie in the fridge and shake well before use. See page 96 for how to use—just add water!

To use, mix 3 tablespoons of Charlie with ⅓ cup water to make a stir-fry or stir-fried noodles for 2 people. See next page for my **Stir-Fry Formula**!

Makes 1½ cups of sauce, enough to make 16 servings of stir-fries or noodles.

**NOTES**

1. Can be substituted with all-purpose soy sauce, though the sauce will be darker in color.
2. Can be substituted with low-sodium chicken broth,* though this will reduce the shelf life of the sauce to 1 week.

LEFTOVERS Fridge 6+ weeks (subject to the shelf life of the ingredients used). Shake the jar every couple of days to prevent the cornstarch from settling and hardening on the base of the jar. Not suitable for freezing.

# STIR-FRY FORMULA

Here lies the answer to the world's most important question, *What should I make for dinner tonight?* A STIR-FRY, using whatever you've got! Delicious, healthy, and takes minutes. You're welcome!

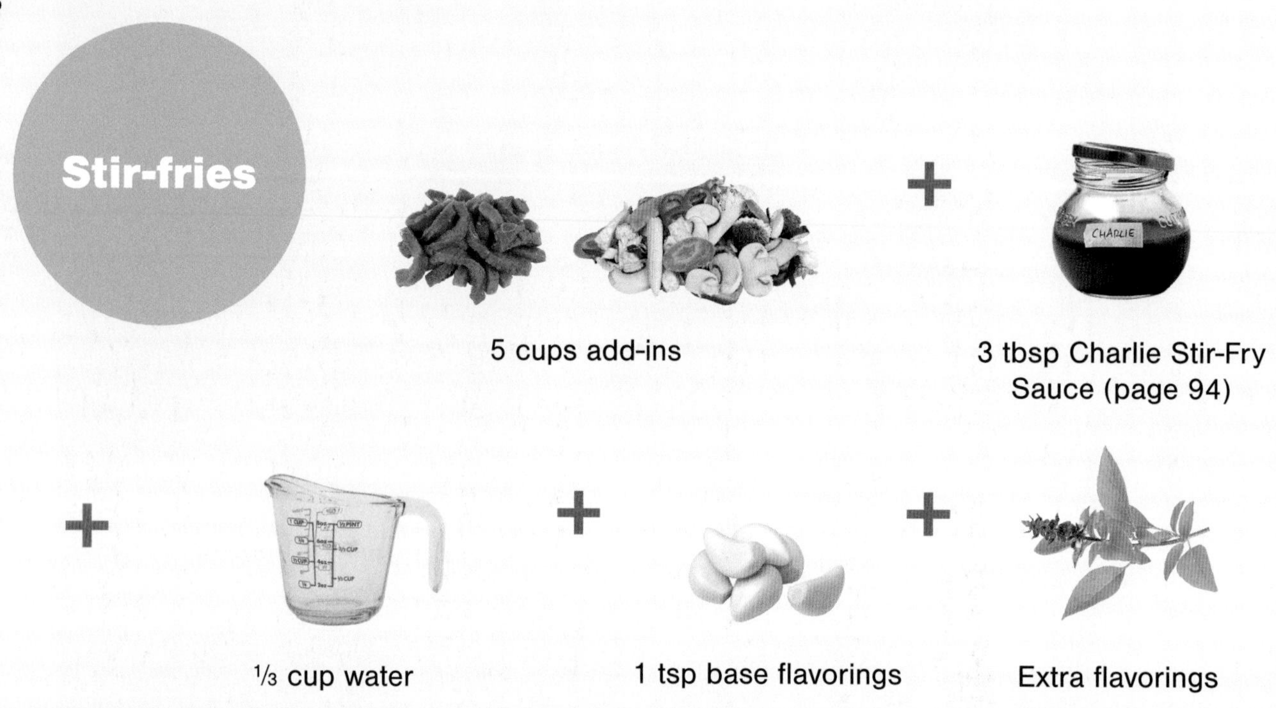


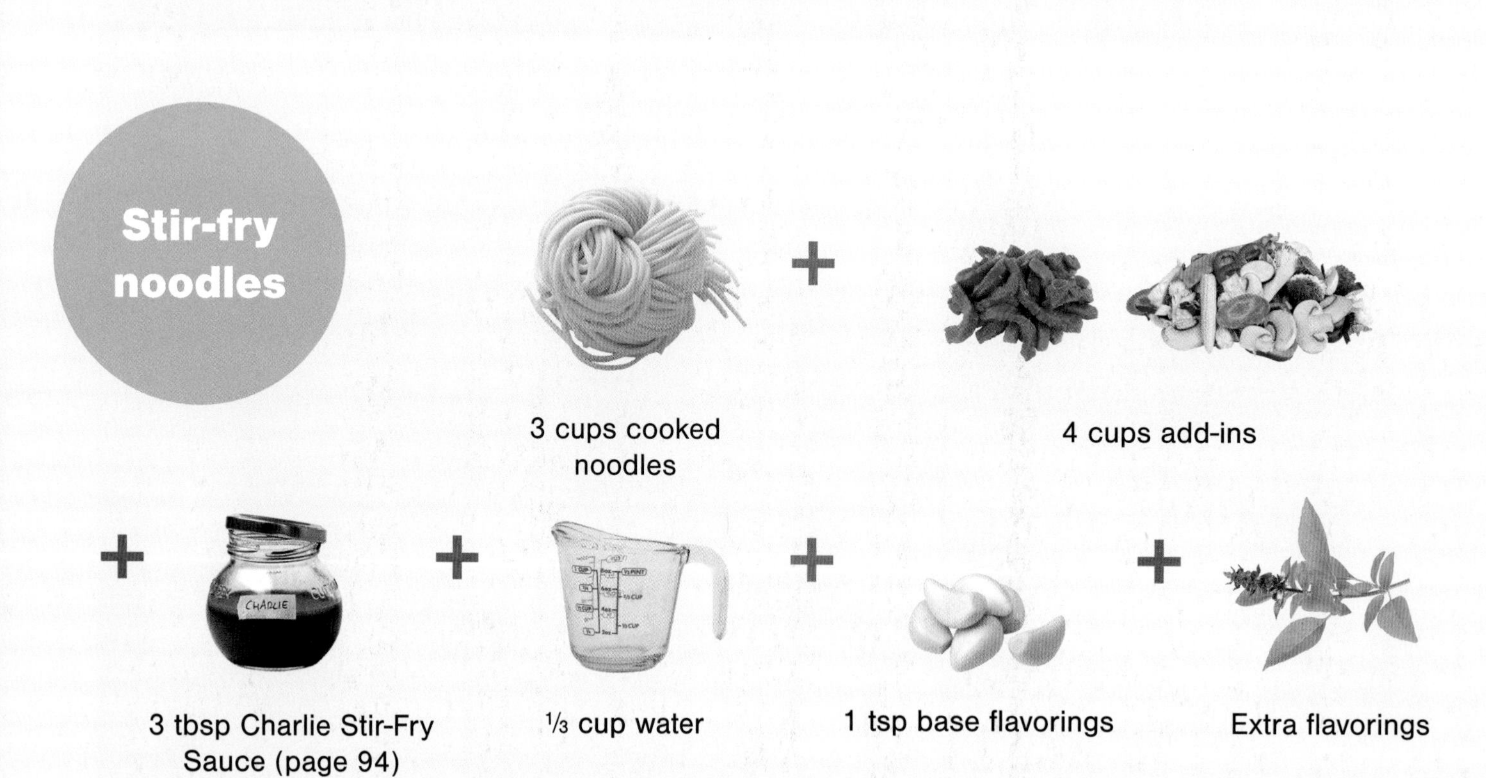

# BUILD YOUR OWN STIR-FRIES AND NOODLES

**SERVES 2 | PREP: 5 MINUTES | COOK: 5 MINUTES**

Be sure to have all your ingredients measured out and ready to toss into the pan because, once you start cooking, things move fast! See page 98 for my Easy Everyday Chicken Stir-Fry made using my Stir-Fry Formula.

---

2 tbsp canola oil

**BASE FLAVORINGS**

1 garlic clove,* finely minced[1]

1 tsp+ finely minced ginger*

Fresh chili peppers,* finely minced

**STIR-FRIES**

5 cups add-ins (raw proteins[2] and vegetables[3])

3 tbsp Charlie Stir-Fry Sauce (page 94)

1/3 cup water

**STIR-FRIED NOODLES**

4 cups add-ins (raw proteins[2] and vegetables[3])

3 cups cooked noodles[4] of choice (7 oz fresh or 3 oz dried)

3 tbsp Charlie Stir-Fry Sauce (page 94)

1/3 cup water

**ADDITIONAL FLAVORINGS**

Sriracha,* chili bean paste, or other spicy addition

Sweet chili sauce

Sesame oil*

Substitute the water with pineapple juice or orange juice

Thai basil,* garlic chives,* or cilantro

Chinese five spice*

*Sauté aromatics*—Heat the oil in a large skillet or wok over high heat. Add your choice of base flavorings and stir for 10 seconds until light golden.

*Stir-fry*—Add the stir-fry add-ins in order of the time they take to cook, starting with the ingredients that take the longest (e.g. onion, proteins, carrot first, leaving leafy greens like cabbage and Asian greens until the end). Stir constantly or they will become watery.

*Noodle option*—Add the noodles (if using).

*Add Charlie Stir-Fry Sauce*—Add Charlie, water, any additional flavorings you're using, and leafy greens.

*Reduce sauce*—Gently toss to combine and cook for around 1 minute. The sauce will become a thick, glossy sauce that coats your stir-fry.

*Serve*—Serve immediately! Serve stir-fries over rice (pages 334–37). The noodles can be divided between bowls and served as is.

**NOTES**

1. Always mince garlic with a knife for stir-fries, rather than using a garlic press, which makes the garlic paste-like so it burns, spits, and sticks to the wok!
2. Protein suggestions: Finely sliced chicken (see page 98 for how to tenderize!), pork, beef, medium whole shrimp, or even ground meat.
3. Vegetable suggestions: Sliced onion (I almost always use), carrot, bell pepper, zucchini, Asian greens (separate stems from leaves, put stems in first as they take longer to cook), cabbage, mushrooms, bean sprouts, broccoli and cauliflower (steam before use), baby corn* (canned or fresh), bamboo shoots (canned).
4. Noodle options: 7 oz fresh noodles (from the fridge), such as lo mein noodles; 4 oz dried noodles (egg, wheat, or rice noodles); 2 large or 3 small ramen cakes. (Note that these are the weights straight out of the package.) Prepare them as per the package directions. Fresh noodles are my favorite—best flavor and texture.

# EASY EVERYDAY CHICKEN STIR-FRY

*Just like you get from Chinese restaurants!*

**SERVES: 2 I PREP: 10 MINUTES + 20 MINUTES CHICKEN TENDERIZING (OPTIONAL) I COOK: 5 MINUTES**

This is a typical chicken stir-fry that I make all the time using my Charlie Stir-Fry Sauce. I've "velveted" (tenderized) the chicken breast here, for that real-deal Chinese restaurant texture and juiciness to the meat. It's a total game changer if you've never tried it! However, this step is entirely optional. The veggies I've chosen are things I typically have in the fridge that I like to use because they take the same length of time to cook, so you can throw them all in at the same time. But you can change them up as you like. Just be mindful of cooking times when selecting and slicing your veggies, and try to pick a variety of colors.

---

**TENDERIZED CHICKEN**

6 oz boneless, skinless chicken breast, cut into 1/4 inch thin strips

1/2 tsp baking soda*

1/2 tsp light or all-purpose soy sauce*[1]

**SAUCE OPTION 1**[2]

3 tbsp Charlie Stir-Fry Sauce (page 94)

**SAUCE OPTION 2**[2]

1 tbsp light soy sauce*

1 tbsp oyster sauce

2 tsp Shaoxing cooking wine*

1 tsp cornstarch

1/2 tsp sugar

1 tsp sesame oil*

Pinch of white pepper

**STIR-FRY**

2 tbsp canola oil

1/2 yellow onion, cut into thin wedges

1 large garlic clove,* finely minced

1 cup snow peas, trimmed

1/2 red bell pepper, deseeded and cut into 1/4 inch wide strips

1 small carrot, peeled and finely sliced

1/3 cup water

*Tenderize chicken*—Place the chicken in a bowl and sprinkle with the baking soda. Toss with your fingers to coat, then set aside for 20 minutes.[3] Rinse in a colander under tap water for 5 seconds, shake off the excess water, then pat the chicken dry with paper towels.

*Season chicken*—Place the chicken in a bowl and toss with the soy sauce.

*Stir-fry sauce*—If making the sauce from scratch (option 2), mix the sauce ingredients in a small bowl until lump-free. If using my Charlie Stir-Fry Sauce, just give the jar a shake and measure out 3 tablespoons.

*Stir-fry*—Heat the oil in a wok or large nonstick skillet over medium–high heat. Add the onion and stir for 15 seconds. Add the chicken and cook, stirring constantly, for 1 minute or until it mostly changes from pink to white. Add the garlic and toss for 15 seconds.

*Add vegetables*—Add the snow peas, bell pepper, and carrot and toss for 1 minute.

*Sauce*—Add the stir-fry sauce and water. Toss for 1 minute until the sauce thickens into a glossy sauce that coats the ingredients.

*Serve*—Pour onto a plate and serve with rice (pages 334–37). Marvel at the deliciously tender chicken!

**NOTES**

1. Any soy sauce is fine here—it's just to flavor the chicken a little. Light or all-purpose is better because the chicken will stay white. If you use dark soy sauce, the chicken will be darker brown.
2. If you don't have the Charlie Stir-Fry Sauce on hand, make the sauce by mixing together the Sauce Option 2 ingredients. If you can't consume alcohol, the Shaoxing cooking wine can be omitted, but substitute the water with low-sodium chicken broth.*
3. This tenderizes the chicken breast so it's soft and velvety, just like you get at Chinese restaurants. There are a few different methods to tenderize chicken, but I find this is the most straightforward way for home cooking. There's no need to tenderize chicken thighs, if you use those instead.

LEFTOVERS Fridge 4 days, though stir-fries are always best made fresh because the sauce goes watery due to water leaching out of the vegetables. Not suitable for freezing.

# VIETNAMESE SHAKING BEEF

*Dinner on the table in 3 minutes flat!*

 **SERVES: 2 | PREP: 5 MINUTES + 24–48 HOURS MARINATING | COOK: 3 MINUTES**

Called *bo luc lac* in Vietnamese, this marinated beef stir-fry has a richly dark sauce that's garlicky, sweet, and salty with a frisky black pepper bite. The dish is often known in English as "shaking beef"—a reference to the energetic wok-shaking needed to brown those meat cubes well! I use rump steak for this stir-fry, tenderized with a sprinkle of baking soda. You will be floored by how this little technique turns economical cuts of beef into something that tastes more akin to premium rib-eye!

---

10 oz beef top sirloin steak,[1] cut into 1 inch cubes

2 tbsp canola oil

1 lime, cut into cheeks or wedges, to serve (optional)

**BEEF MARINADE**

4 tsp oyster sauce

2 tsp superfine sugar

2 tsp fish sauce

1 tsp finely grated garlic*

2 tsp kecap manis*

½ tsp freshly ground black pepper

½ tsp baking soda*[2]

1 tsp canola oil

**LIME PEPPER DIPPING SAUCE**

1½ tsp lime juice

1 tsp freshly ground black pepper

⅛ tsp fish sauce

*Marinate beef*—Mix the beef marinade ingredients together in a bowl, then add the beef and mix to coat. Cover and refrigerate for 24 hours (up to 48 hours).

Drain the beef in a colander set over a bowl, reserving the marinade. Measure out 2 teaspoons of the marinade and set aside.

*Dipping sauce*—Mix the ingredients together and set aside.

*Cook beef*—In a wok (or large nonstick skillet), heat the oil over high heat. Once smoking, add the beef. Toss for 2½ minutes using two wooden spoons. Add the reserved 2 teaspoons of marinade, then (in the spirit of the dish name!) shake that wok good for another 30 seconds until the beef is caramelized on the outside (3 minutes' total cooking time!).

*Rest and serve*—Immediately tip the beef out onto a serving plate. Rest for 3 minutes, then place the lime cheeks on the side with the lime pepper dipping sauce and serve. It's terrific served with Fluffy Coconut Rice (page 337) along with smashed cucumber chunks and green onion tossed with Ginger Dressing (page 333).

**NOTES**

1. Or New York strip or rib-eye tenderloin can also be used but won't have as good a beefy flavor.
2. This is used to tenderize the beef so even an economical piece of beef will be beautifully tender all the way through.

LEFTOVERS Fridge 4 days though best made fresh. Not suitable for freezing.

# CHILI GARLIC GINGER SHRIMP

*Tastes like Thai chili jam, but so much easier to make!*

**SERVES: 4 I PREP: 10 MINUTES I COOK: 7 MINUTES**

I just love the sweet, fragrant, and deeply savory taste of Thai chili jam. The idea for this recipe comes from the stir-fries tossed through with chili jam that you often see at modern Thai restaurants. This is a faster version, but still has the same big, gutsy flavors with a chili tickle—just perfect with sweet, plump shrimp.

---

1½ tbsp canola oil

1 lb peeled and deveined raw shrimp,* tails intact (2 lb unpeeled shrimp)

1 tsp sesame oil*

3 garlic cloves,* finely minced

2 tsp finely minced ginger*

1 tsp dried red pepper flakes[1]

½ cup water

3 tbsp sriracha*[1]

2 tsp light soy sauce*[2]

3 packed tbsp brown sugar (or granulated sugar)

**GARNISHES (OPTIONAL)**

White sesame seeds

Red chili pepper,* deseeded and finely sliced

Green onion,* finely sliced

*Sear shrimp*—Heat the oil in a large nonstick skillet over high heat. Add half the shrimp and sear each side for 45 seconds until light golden, then transfer to a bowl—they will still be raw inside. Repeat with the remaining shrimp.

*Cool pan*—Remove the pan from the stove to cool down slightly. Turn the heat down to medium.

*Make sauce*—Return the pan to the stove and heat the sesame oil. Add the garlic, ginger, and red pepper flakes and cook for 20 seconds or until the garlic turns golden. Add the water, then the sriracha, soy sauce, and sugar. Stir, increase the heat to medium-high, then let the sauce simmer for 3 minutes or until it starts to thicken to a thin, syrupy consistency.

*Coat shrimp*—Return the shrimp to the pan and toss to coat in the sauce. Cook for a further 1 minute until the shrimp are cooked and the sauce has thickened and is coating the shrimp.

*Serve*—Transfer the shrimp and all the sauce to a serving plate. Sprinkle with sesame seeds, red chili pepper, and green onion (if using). Serve with rice (pages 334–37) or Chinese Fried Rice (page 120) to soak up the awesome sauce! Team with your favorite garden salad given an Asian spin by tossing with Asian Sesame Dressing (page 333).

**NOTES**

1. This dish has a decent amount of spiciness but is not blow-your-head-off spicy! Reduce the red pepper flakes and sriracha for less spice. You can always add a bit extra at the end if you think you can handle more!
2. Can be substituted with all-purpose soy sauce. Do not use dark soy sauce.

LEFTOVERS Fridge 2 days though best made fresh. Not suitable for freezing.

# CASHEW CHICKEN

*The soft crunch of cashews is everything!*

**SERVES: 4 WITH RICE | PREP: 8 MINUTES + 10 MINUTES (OR OVERNIGHT) MARINATING | COOK: 7 MINUTES**

This is one of the first classic Chinese stir-fries I learned to make and still remains one of my favorites. There's something about the crunch of the cashews amongst the tender chicken and juicy bell pepper squares that reels me in every time. You can use my Charlie Stir-Fry Sauce for this recipe if you have some on hand (sauce option 1).

---

1 lb boneless, skinless chicken thighs, cut into 1 inch pieces

2 tbsp canola oil

2 garlic cloves,* finely minced

½ yellow onion, chopped into ¾ inch squares

1 green bell pepper, deseeded and chopped into 1 inch squares

⅓ cup water

¾ cup roasted unsalted cashews

**SAUCE OPTION 1**

½ cup Charlie Stir-Fry Sauce (page 94)

**SAUCE OPTION 2**

1 tbsp cornstarch

3 tbsp light soy sauce*[1]

1½ tbsp Shaoxing cooking wine*[2]

3 tbsp oyster sauce

2 tsp sesame oil*

Pinch of white pepper

*Sauce*—If making the sauce from scratch (option 2), mix the cornstarch and soy sauce until there are no lumps, then add the remaining sauce ingredients and mix to combine. If using my Charlie Stir-Fry Sauce, just give the jar a shake and measure out 8 tablespoons.

*Marinate chicken*—Place the chicken in a bowl, add 2 tablespoons of the sauce, then mix to coat. Set aside for 10 minutes (even overnight!).

*Stir-fry*—Heat the oil in a wok or large nonstick skillet over high heat. Add the garlic and onion and cook for 1 minute. Add the chicken and cook for 2 minutes, then add the bell pepper and cook for a further 1 minute. Add the sauce and water, bring to a simmer, and cook, stirring, for 1 minute or until the sauce thickens. Stir through the cashews, then remove from the stove.

*Serve*—Serve immediately with rice (pages 334–37)!

**NOTES**

1. Can be substituted with all-purpose soy sauce. Do not use dark soy sauce.
2. Substitute with dry sherry or mirin.* If you cannot consume alcohol, leave this out and use low-sodium chicken broth* instead of water.

LEFTOVERS Fridge 4 days though best made fresh. Not suitable for freezing.

# CRISPY CHINESE EGGPLANT

*Crispy on the outside, melting on the inside, with a candied sweet–savory coating.*

SERVES: 4 AS A MAIN | PREP: 15 MINUTES + 30 MINUTES SALTING | COOK: 30 MINUTES

**Crispy-shelled fried eggplant coated in a sweet, sticky sauce is a signature dish at one of Sydney's top new-wave Chinese restaurants. It's so good I order it every time I go, and for years have dreamed about replicating it at home. This cookbook has finally given me the excuse to do so! I'm chuffed with the result and think it's every bit as good as the restaurant's—dare I say, possibly better? This dish takes a bit of effort but is absolutely worth making. It's truly epic!**

**EGGPLANT**

14 oz eggplant, cut into 1¼ inch cubes (about 28 pieces)

¾ tsp kosher salt*

4 cups canola oil

**CRISPY BATTER**

½ cup all-purpose flour

1 cup cornstarch

¾ tsp baking powder*

¾ tsp kosher salt*

1 cup cold club soda[1]

**CANDIED SAUCE**

½ cup superfine sugar

½ cup brown sugar

2½ tbsp water

2 tbsp cooking sake*

3 tsp tamarind puree*

2 tsp ketchup

2 tbsp light soy sauce*

1½ tsp glucose syrup[2]

¼ tsp Chinese five spice*

¾ tsp finely grated ginger*

¾ tsp finely grated garlic*

1 tsp red miso[3]

2 tsp white sesame seeds

**TO SERVE**

½ tsp white sesame seeds

1 long red chili pepper,* deseeded and finely sliced

1 green onion,* finely sliced on a long angle and curled[4]

*Sweat eggplant*—Place the eggplant in a colander, sprinkle with the salt, then toss. Leave for 30 minutes to sweat. No need to pat the moisture off.

*Chill dry batter ingredients*—Place the flour, cornstarch, baking powder, and salt in a bowl. Whisk, then put in the fridge to chill.[5]

*Candied sauce*—Place all the ingredients in a medium saucepan, mix to combine, then simmer on medium heat for 5 minutes. Reduce the heat to low, then simmer for a further 10 minutes, stirring regularly toward the end as it thickens, until it is a thick, syrupy consistency. To check it is ready, drop ⅛ teaspoon into a bowl of cold water. After 20 seconds you should be able to roll it into a ball-like pliable dough. Cover and keep warm until ready to use.

*Heat oil*—Fill a 9½ inch heavy-based pot with 1½ inches of oil. Heat to 390°F[6] over high heat.

*Finish batter*—When the oil is near the target temperature, add the cold club soda to the chilled dry ingredients, then do the minimum of whisks to just combine—some lumps are fine.

*Fry 1*—Dip a piece of eggplant into the batter, then place in the oil. Repeat with another six pieces and fry for 3 minutes until golden. Transfer to a paper towel–lined tray. Repeat with the remaining eggplant, ensuring the oil is back at 390°F before cooking the next batch.

*Fry 2*[7]—Line a large bowl with paper towels. Keep the oil temperature at 390°F.[6] Add half the eggplant (you can crowd the pot for this frying step) and fry for 2 minutes until it changes from golden to very deep golden in color and crispy. Transfer to the bowl. Repeat with the remaining eggplant.

*Coat eggplant*—Remove the paper towels from the mixing bowl, leaving the eggplant in the bowl, and pour the warm candied sauce over. Toss immediately before the sauce sets.

*Serve*—Pile the eggplant in a tall mound on a parchment paper–lined plate.[8] Sprinkle with sesame seeds, then the chili, and green onion. Serve with a side of Chinese Fried Rice (page 120) and finely shredded green cabbage dressed with Ginger Dressing (page 333).

**NOTES**

1. Not to be confused with sparkling mineral water. We need the full-on manmade fizzy bubbles in club soda ice-cold from the fridge, which makes our batter light, crispy, and remarkably ungreasy.
2. Makes the sauce harden into a candied coating on the crispy eggplant batter rather than making it soggy. Substitute with corn syrup.
3. Any type of miso will work here—red, white (shiro), dashi miso, or even saikyo miso.
4. To make green onion curls as pictured, place in a bowl of cold water in the fridge for 3 minutes until they start to curl.
5. Cold batter is the secret to a light and crispy coating. This is one of the steps that helps achieve that. If it's really hot in your kitchen, place the batter bowl inside another bowl containing ice to keep it cold.
6. Best checked with an instant read thermometer.* If you don't have one, see Oil temperature testing in the Glossary (page 361).
7. Fast becoming the worst-kept Asian frying secret, a double-fry is THE secret to an ultra-crispy batter coating that is not greasy!
8. Paper is needed otherwise the sticky coating on the eggplant will adhere to the plate and rip the crunchy coating off when you try to pick it up!

LEFTOVERS Fridge 3 days though best made fresh. However, fried but unsauced eggplant can be recrisped in a 400°F oven for 8 minutes, flipping after 5 minutes, before tossing in the sauce.

# SESAME GINGER GARLIC STIR-FRIED VEGETABLES

*You can eat a LOT of veggies when they're smothered in a great sauce!*

 **SERVES: 4 | PREP: 10 MINUTES | COOK: 7 MINUTES**

Ginger and garlic are brilliant together with vegetables. This stir-fry is a big pan of feel-good, colorful vegetables smothered in a tasty sauce that goes heavy on both of them. If you're cleaning out your vegetable crisper, this dish is a great destination for random leftover odds and ends. Just remember to add the vegetables in the order of the time it takes to cook them, starting with the vegetables that take the longest.

---

2 tbsp canola oil

2 cups (4 oz) small broccoli florets[1]

½ yellow onion, cut into ½ inch wedges

1 tsp finely minced garlic*

1 tsp finely minced ginger*

1 cup shiitake* or other mushrooms, sliced ¼ inch thick

1 small carrot, peeled, cut into 1½ inch lengths, then finely sliced

½ red bell pepper, deseeded and sliced ½ inch thick

¾ cup (3 oz) baby corn,* cut in half lengthwise

2 tsp sesame oil*

**GARLIC GINGER SAUCE**

3 tsp cornstarch

¾ cup water

1 tbsp hoisin sauce

2 tbsp light soy sauce*[2]

1 tbsp Shaoxing cooking wine*[3]

1 tsp finely grated ginger*

1½ tsp finely grated garlic*

**TO SERVE**

1 tsp white sesame seeds

*Sauce*—Mix the cornstarch in a jar with a small splash of the water until lump-free. Add the remaining water and sauce ingredients and mix to combine. Set aside.

*Stir-fry*—Heat the oil in a large nonstick skilelt over medium heat. Add the broccoli and stir for 1 minute—try not to let it brown. Add the onion, garlic, and ginger, then cook for 1 minute. Turn the heat up to high, then add the mushrooms, carrot, bell pepper, and baby corn. Cook for 2 minutes or until the mushroom has a bit of golden color on it.

*Sauce it!*—Give the sauce a quick mix, then pour it all into the pan. Stir for 1–1½ minutes or until the sauce thickens and becomes glossy, coating all the vegetables. Stir in the sesame oil.

*Serve*—Transfer all the vegetables and sauce to a serving platter, sprinkle with sesame seeds, and serve with rice (see pages 334–37)!

**NOTES**

1. Cut the broccoli florets quite small, about 1½ inches long and 1 inch wide. This way, you can cook them in the pan instead of cooking them separately beforehand.
2. Can be substituted with all-purpose soy sauce. Do not use dark soy sauce.
3. Substitute with dry sherry or mirin.* If you cannot consume alcohol, leave this out and use low-sodium chicken broth* instead of water.

LEFTOVERS Fridge 3 days though best made fresh as water leaches out of the vegetables, which thins the sauce. Not suitable for freezing.

# CRISPY SALT & PEPPER TOFU

*Pan-roasted crispiness finished with a secret seasoning.*

**SERVES: 3 AS A MAIN WITH RICE | PREP: 10 MINUTES + 30 MINUTES TOFU PRESSING | COOK: 10 MINUTES**

At Chinese restaurants, the tofu is normally deep-fried for this dish. However, I find that pan-frying it is very nearly as good if you follow my technique of tossing the cornstarch-coated tofu with a spatula in the pan, adding a little extra oil as you go. Finish the dish by tossing the golden-brown tofu nuggets with a crispy medley of fried garlic, chili pepper, and green onion. Finish with a flurry of my secret finger-licking Chinese spice mix seasoning—this stuff makes the dish!

---

1 lb firm or hard tofu[1]

2½ tbsp cornstarch, plus more if needed

3 tbsp canola oil

2 large garlic cloves,* finely minced

1 green onion,* stem, white and green parts separated, finely minced

1 each long red and green chili pepper,* deseeded and finely minced

**SECRET SALT AND PEPPER SPICE MIX**

1 tsp table salt*[2] (not kosher salt)

½ tsp finely ground white pepper

½ tsp Chinese five spice*

¼ tsp ground fennel seeds

¼ tsp superfine sugar

*Press tofu*—Cut the tofu block in half horizontally to form two steaks. Place them side by side and wrap in a dish towel. Place a cast-iron skillet or something heavy on top to press out the excess water and set aside for 30 minutes. Cut the tofu into ¾ inch cubes.

*Secret salt and pepper spice mix*—Mix the ingredients in a small bowl.

*Toss tofu*—Place the tofu cubes in a bowl, sprinkle with ¾ teaspoon of the spice mix, then toss to coat. Sprinkle the cornstarch over, then toss to coat—this should be enough to lightly coat the tofu pieces so they feel dry. If required, add more cornstarch. Proceed to cooking immediately—don't leave them sitting around.

*Crispy tofu!*—Heat 2 tablespoons of oil in a 11 inch nonstick skillet over high heat. Using your hands, shake the excess cornstarch off the tofu, then place in the pan in a single layer. Start tossing the tofu cubes gently using a plastic spatula[3] and a wooden spoon—toss at least every 10 seconds for 3 minutes, using the spatula to scoop up and flip. If the tofu is browning too quickly, lower the heat. After 3 minutes, drizzle with another 1 tablespoon of oil, then toss for a further 3 minutes until light golden and crispy.

*Crispy aromatics*—Turn the heat down to medium–high. Add the garlic and the white part of the green onion to the skillet. Toss everything a few times, then add the chili pepper and toss for 1 minute until the garlic is golden and crispy. Lower the heat if the garlic is browning too quickly.

*Seasoning*—Push the tofu together, then sprinkle with 1¼ teaspoons of the spice mix. Toss a few times to coat the tofu.

*Serve*—Pile the tofu in a bowl, then scrape the tasty little bits of garlic and chili pepper from the pan and sprinkle these over the top. Taste a tofu cube (sorry to have to ask that of you!) and sprinkle with more spice mix, if desired. (You will have some spice mix left over.) Sprinkle with the reserved green part of the green onions and serve immediately, while hot and crispy! Add a side of Chinese Fried Rice (page 120) or steamed Asian greens with Asian Sesame Dressing (page 333) to complete your meal.

**NOTES**

1. Use firm or hard tofu—soft tofu will crumble when tossed. Pressing out the excess water helps make the tofu crispier.
2. Not to be confused with kosher salt,* which is the standard salt I use throughout this cookbook. Table salt is finer-grained, which is ideal for this dish to create the dust-like sprinkle used to season the tofu. Don't have table salt? Just grind up kosher salt in your mortar and pestle!
3. By spatula, I mean an egg flipper so you can scoop and flip plenty of tofu cubes in one go.

LEFTOVERS Fridge 3 days though best made fresh so the tofu is crispy!

# VIETNAMESE CARAMEL GROUND PORK

*A long-standing reader favorite!*

 **SERVES: 4 | PREP: 5 MINUTES | COOK: 10 MINUTES**

This ground pork dish isn't strictly authentic but the flavors are drawn straight from traditional Vietnamese dishes. I think my website readers love it because it's easy to put together (from mostly pantry staples), appeals to both little and big kids with its sweet, caramelly taste, and is a flavoring for meat that's a bit different! I find pork works best, but it's also excellent made with ground chicken, turkey, or beef. Try it with chunks of plain cucumber and tomato on the side—something you often see on dinner plates across South-East Asia!

---

1 1/2 tbsp canola oil

1/2 yellow onion, finely diced

2 tsp ginger,* finely minced

2 garlic cloves,* finely minced

1 bird's eye chili,* deseeded and finely minced (optional)

1 lb ground pork (or chicken, turkey, or beef)

5 lightly packed tbsp brown sugar

2 tbsp fish sauce[1]

**TO SERVE**

1 green onion,* finely sliced (optional)

Long red chili pepper,* deseeded (if desired) and finely sliced (optional)

Tomato wedges and cucumber* chunks (optional)

*Cook aromatics*—Heat the oil in a large skillet over high heat. Add the onion, ginger, garlic, and chili, then sauté for 2 minutes.

*Cook pork*—Add the pork and cook for 2 minutes, breaking it up as you go until it changes from pink to white.

*Caramelize it!*—Add the sugar and fish sauce, stir, then leave it to cook without touching until all the pork juices cook out and the meat starts to caramelize—about 2 minutes. Stir, then leave it again, without stirring, for around 30 seconds to get more caramelization. Repeat twice more until caramelized to your taste.

*Serve*—Serve over rice (pages 334–37) or vermicelli noodles, garnished with green onion and chili pepper, if desired. Add some chunks of tomato and cucumber on the side, if you like—no dressing necessary!

**NOTES**

1. Fish sauce is a key ingredient in this simple sauce to get good depth of flavor. It smells fishy when raw, but once cooked it just leaves behind a savory flavor without any trace of fishiness. You can substitute with soy sauce* but the sauce won't be quite the same.

LEFTOVERS Fridge 4 days, freezer 3 months.

# PAD THAI

*The dish by which every Thai restaurant is judged!*

 **SERVES: 2 I PREP: 15 MINUTES I COOK: 10 MINUTES**

Did you know pad Thai was actually invented by the Thai government in the 1930s? It was devised as a national dish to unite the Thai people, which was both delicious and easy to make. True story! It's also true that pad Thai is surprisingly simple to cook. With just a trip to your everyday grocery store, you can make a dead ringer for this Thai takeout staple! In fact, I find most takeout versions are often bland or too sweet. I really think once you've made it yourself, you'll never look at takeout versions the same way again!

---

4 oz pad Thai dried rice-stick noodles[1]

3 tbsp canola oil

½ yellow onion, cut into ¼ inch thick slices

5 oz boneless, skinless chicken breast or thighs, sliced into ¼ inch pieces

2 garlic cloves,* finely minced

2 eggs, lightly whisked

1½ cups bean sprouts

½ cup (3 oz) firm tofu batons (1 x ¼ inch)

¼ cup garlic chives,*[2] cut into 1½ inch lengths

¼ cup finely chopped roasted unsalted peanuts

**SAUCE**

1½ tbsp tamarind puree*[3]

3 tightly packed tbsp brown sugar

2 tbsp fish sauce

1½ tbsp oyster sauce

**TO SERVE**

Lime or lemon wedges (essential!)

Ground red chili* or cayenne pepper (optional)

Handful extra bean sprouts

*Sauce*—Mix the sauce ingredients in a small bowl and set aside.

*Noodles*—Prepare the noodles as per the package directions just before you start cooking. Don't leave them sitting around as they become more fragile.

*Cook chicken*—Heat 2 tablespoons of oil in a large nonstick skillet over high heat. Add the onion and cook for 30 seconds. Add the chicken and garlic, then cook for 1½ minutes until the chicken is mostly cooked through.

*Scramble egg*—Push the ingredients to one side of the pan, then pour the egg in on the other side. Scramble using a wooden spoon (add a touch of extra oil if the pan is too dry), then mix into the chicken.

*Add noodles*—Add 1 tablespoon of oil to the pan. Add the bean sprouts, tofu, and noodles, then pour the sauce over. Cook for 3–4 minutes, tossing gently every minute or so, until the sauce is absorbed by the noodles and the edges of the noodles start to caramelize.

Add the garlic chives and half the peanuts and toss through quickly. Remove from the heat.

*Serve*—Serve immediately, sprinkled with the remaining peanuts and lime wedges on the side. Add a sprinkle of ground red chili or cayenne pepper, if desired, and some extra bean sprouts on the side (this is the Thai way!). Squeeze over lime juice to taste before eating.

**NOTES**

1. Look for flat dried rice noodles that are ⅛–¼ inch wide.
2. Substitute with ordinary chives and use an extra garlic clove.
3. Tamarind puree is a soft paste sold in jars that is a key sour ingredient in pad Thai sauce. Labeled tamarind puree, concentrate, or paste, it is sold in the Asian section of most large grocery stores or in Asian stores. Use leftovers for the Devour—Maple Sweet Potato Salad with Maple Tamarind Dressing (page 192). Can't find tamarind? Use this sauce instead (works remarkably well!): Mix together 1 tablespoon ketchup, 2 tablespoons brown sugar, 2 tablespoons fish sauce, 2 teaspoons oyster sauce, 1 teaspoon dark soy sauce,* 2 tablespoons rice vinegar (or 1 tablespoon white vinegar).

LEFTOVERS Fridge 3 days though best made fresh. Not suitable for freezing.

# PEKING SHREDDED BEEF

*Crispy little strips of beef in a sticky sauce. So, so good!*

SERVES: 2 AS A MAIN WITH RICE | PREP: 15 MINUTES + 30 MINUTES (OR OVERNIGHT) MARINATING | COOK: 10 MINUTES

I first fell in love with this dish at an unremarkable little Chinese restaurant hidden behind an anonymous parking lot somewhere on Sydney's North Shore. The dish probably wasn't actually as good there as I fondly remember. But the memory of those crispy fingers of beef doused in a heavenly sweet and sticky sauce has always stayed with me. Here's my ode to that little restaurant from my food past, done right! The key to this dish is hitting the right balance of sweet and savory in the sauce, and ensuring your beef is super crispy on the outside yet tender on the inside.

**MARINATED BEEF**

10 oz boneless rib-eye steak,[1] cut into thin strips

1/4 tsp baking soda*[2]

2 tsp Shaoxing cooking wine*

1 tbsp finely grated yellow onion, juice and all (use a Microplane*)

2 tsp light soy sauce*[3]

1 tsp cornstarch

**PEKING SAUCE**

1/4 cup ketchup

1 1/2 tbsp light soy sauce*

1/4 tsp dark soy sauce*[4]

1/3 cup honey

2 tsp sesame oil*

1 tbsp Shaoxing cooking wine*

1 1/2 tbsp rice vinegar

1 tbsp water

1 tsp+ sriracha* (optional—for a hit of spiciness!)

**COATING**

2 1/2 tbsp cornstarch

1/3 cup rice flour[5]

**COOKING**

3 cups canola oil

2 tbsp finely shredded carrot, using a box grater (pieces 1 inch long)[6]

**TO SERVE**

1 oz dried vermicelli noodles (optional)[7]

1 tsp white sesame seeds (optional)

1 tbsp finely sliced green onion*

*Marinate beef*—Place the marinated beef ingredients in a bowl and toss with your fingers to coat. Marinate for at least 30 minutes, or even overnight, in the fridge.

*Peking sauce*—Place all the ingredients in a small saucepan and whisk until smooth. Simmer on medium-low for 5 minutes until it becomes a thick syrupy consistency like honey. Remove from the stove, cover, and keep warm while cooking the beef.

*Coat beef*—Add the cornstarch to the marinated beef bowl and toss with your fingers to mix together—it will make the beef sticky. Add the rice flour and toss to coat. Separate the beef strips with your fingers, shake off the excess rice flour, then spread the beef out on a plate.

*Fry 1*—In a large saucepan over medium-high heat, heat 1¼ inches of oil to 410°F.[8] Carefully scatter one-fourth of the beef into the oil and fry for 1½ minutes. Transfer to a paper towel-lined plate. Repeat with the remaining beef, working in batches, ensuring that the oil goes back up to 410°F before starting each new batch.

*Vermicelli noodles*—After the beef is fried, place the wad of vermicelli noodles into the oil—it will expand five times its volume in mere seconds! Use tongs to remove the noodles from the pan and drain on paper towels, then transfer what you need to a serving plate.

*Fry 2*[9]—Increase the oil temperature to 430°F. Line a bowl with paper towels. Place the carrot in bowl. Fry half the beef again for 30 seconds or until deep golden and crisp, then transfer to the bowl directly on top of the carrot so it wilts from the heat. Repeat with the remaining beef.

*Serve*—Remove the paper towels from the bowl, leaving the beef behind. Pour the warm Peking sauce over the beef, quickly toss to coat, then pile onto the vermicelli noodles. Sprinkle with sesame seeds (if using) and green onion (quickly, before the candied coating sets!). Serve with a side of Sesame Ginger Garlic Stir-fried Vegetables (page 108).

**NOTES**

1. A juicy tender cut of beef is best for this recipe, as the double-fry means the beef will be well done.
2. Baking soda tenderizes the beef to keep it as tender as possible during the double-cook process (the thin strips of beef cook through in a flash!).
3. Or all-purpose soy sauce. Do not substitute with dark soy sauce.
4. Can be substituted with light or all-purpose soy sauce, though the sauce color will not be quite as dark.
5. Makes the crispiest coating for the beef. Substitute with (in order of crispiest result) potato starch, cornstarch, tapioca flour, and (bringing up the rear) all-purpose flour.
6. Control the length of the carrot pieces by adjusting the angle of the carrot on the box grater.
7. This dish is commonly served on a bed of crispy white noodles, which are simply fried vermicelli noodles.
8. Best checked with an instant read thermometer.* If you don't have one, see Oil temperature testing in the Glossary (page 361)
9. Double-fry is the pro secret to extra crispy beef strips.

LEFTOVERS Fridge 4 days, but best made fresh. Not suitable for freezing.

# PAD SEE EW

*My favorite Thai noodles!*

**SERVES: 2 I PREP: 10 MINUTES I COOK: 10 MINUTES**

Whereas pad Thai is sweet, nutty, and a little tangy, pad see ew is straight-up savory with a more intensely flavored sauce. Most people plump for pad Thai but I say pad see ew is where it's at! I have a trick to recreate the restaurant-style caramelized edges on the noodles at home. If you cook the chicken and vegetables separately from the noodles, you can get some deliciously authentic charring by stir-frying the noodles alone—then just bring everything together at the end!

---

4 stems Chinese broccoli[1]

7 oz dried wide rice-stick noodles[2]

3 tbsp canola oil

2 garlic cloves,* finely minced

5 oz finely sliced boneless, skinless chicken thighs or breast

1 egg

**SAUCE**

2 tsp dark soy sauce*[3]

1 tbsp light soy sauce*[4]

1½ tbsp oyster sauce

2 tsp white vinegar

2 tsp sugar

*Prepare broccoli*—Trim the ends of the broccoli, then cut into 3 inch pieces and separate the leaves from the stems. Cut thick stems in half lengthwise if needed so they're no thicker than ¼ inch.

*Sauce*—Mix the ingredients in a small bowl until the sugar dissolves. Set aside.

Prepare the noodles according to the package directions, then drain. Time it so they're cooked just before using—do not leave cooked rice noodles lying around or they will break in the wok.

*Cook chicken*—Heat 1 tablespoon oil in a large nonstick skillet or wok over high heat. Add the garlic and stir for 10 seconds until light golden. Add the chicken and cook for 30 seconds until it mostly changes from pink to white, but is still raw inside.

*Add Chinese broccoli*—Add the Chinese broccoli stems and cook for 1 minute or until the chicken is just about cooked through.

Add the Chinese broccoli leaves, then stir for 20 seconds until just wilted.

*Scramble egg*—Push everything to one side, crack the egg in, and scramble it. This is the traditional Thai way! Transfer everything from the pan to a plate.

*Caramelize noodles*[5]—Return the pan to the stove, still over high heat. Heat 2 tablespoons of oil until it starts smoking (HOT is key!). Add the noodles and sauce and toss gently using two wooden spoons (not tongs or the noodles will break), as few times as possible just to coat the noodles with sauce and caramelize the edges—about 1–1½ minutes.

*Toss*—Quickly return the chicken, vegetables, and egg to the pan and toss to disperse.

*Serve*—Slide it all onto plates and serve immediately!

**NOTES**

1. Also known as *gai lan* or *kai lan*, sold at everyday grocery stores these days.
2. Traditionally made with Sen Yai fresh rice noodles, which are wide, flat rice noodles. These are hard to handle and quite difficult to find, even at Asian grocery stores. It's easiest to use wide, dried rice-stick noodles. I use pad Thai noodles—the widest you can find at everyday grocery stores. Otherwise, just use the widest flat rice noodles you can find.
3. Can be substituted with kecap manis.* If using, omit the sugar in the sauce. Light and all-purpose soy sauce won't provide the same level of flavor and color, but can be used if you have no other alternative.
4. Substitute with all-purpose soy sauce. Do not use more dark soy sauce—too intense!
5. The key to caramelizing the noodles without breaking them up too much is a very hot pan and tossing as few times as possible. But if the noodles do break, don't fret! They usually are quite broken up even at Thai restaurants, which is why this dish is traditionally served with a fork and spoon rather than chopsticks.

LEFTOVERS Fridge 3 days though best made fresh. Not suitable for freezing.

# CHINESE FRIED RICE

*The one I make "all the time."*

**SERVES: 3–4 AS A SIDE I PREP: 10 MINUTES I COOK: 5 MINUTES**

When I make fried rice properly (quote marks!), I use my grill's high-powered gas burner. I try to capture what the Chinese call *wok hei*, meaning "breath of the wok"—that delicious smoky flavor you get in wok dishes at good Chinese restaurants. I also make an egg omelet separately, which I diligently chop. I hunt down a specific type of ham, and peel small shrimp one by one (a mind-numbingly tedious business). That event happens about twice a year. This recipe? Much simpler and 90 percent as good, so it happens about once a week!

---

2 tbsp canola oil

½ yellow onion, finely chopped

2 garlic cloves,* finely minced

4 oz bacon, chopped into ½ inch squares (or ham)

1 cup frozen mixed diced vegetables (carrots, peas, and corn)[1]

2 tightly packed cups cooked day-old White Rice[2] (page 335)

3 eggs, whisked

2 green onions,* finely sliced

**SEASONING**

1 tbsp Shaoxing cooking wine*[3]

1 tbsp oyster sauce

1 tbsp light soy sauce*[4]

1 tsp sesame oil*

¼ tsp white pepper

*Cook aromatics*—Heat about 1½ tablespoons oil in a wok or large nonstick skillet over high heat until you see wisps of smoke. Add the onion, garlic, and bacon and cook until the bacon is light golden—about 1½ minutes.

*Cook vegetables*—Add the vegetables (still frozen is fine) and cook for 2 minutes so they defrost and the water evaporates.

*Rice*—Add the rice and seasoning ingredients and cook for 1½ minutes until the liquid evaporates.

*Scramble egg*—Shove the rice to the side of the wok/skillet. Add ½ tablespoon oil into the cleared space, then shift the wok so the heat is centered under the cleared space. Pour in the egg, then scramble—cook it through properly, don't "soft scramble."

*Serve*—Toss in the green onion, then stir the egg into the rice. Remove from the heat and serve immediately!

**NOTES**

1. I have always used a frozen vegetable mix for my fried rice and I'm pretty sure my local Chinese restaurant does too! Handy—and the right mix of vegetables.
2. Refrigerated or frozen and thawed (it's really handy having rice in the freezer!).
3. Or mirin* or dry sherry. If you can't consume alcohol, omit and add ¼ cup low-sodium chicken broth* and cook for 1 minute longer.
4. Dark soy sauce can also be used but your rice will be a darker color. All-purpose soy can be used as well.

LEFTOVERS Fridge 3 days, freezer 3 months.

# CHOW MEIN

*My most made noodles.*

**SERVES: 2 (GENEROUSLY) | PREP: 8 MINUTES + 10 MINUTES MARINATING | COOK: 7 MINUTES**

Chow mein are actually the noodles I make most frequently. Why? Sheer convenience, really. These noodles can make use of my Charlie Stir-Fry Sauce for one (I wasn't kidding when I said I often reach for that jar in my fridge!). It also contains a load of good vegetables, which makes it a pretty well-balanced meal. Not to mention, it's fast—15 minutes flat from start to finish, if you skip the marinating. These noodles are great for any meal, including breakfast! Yep, chow mein is actually a common way to start the day in China. I can totally get behind that!

---

7 oz boneless, skinless chicken breast or thighs, finely sliced[1]

7 oz chow mein noodles[2]

1½ tbsp canola oil

2 garlic cloves,* finely minced

4 lightly packed cups (8 oz) finely shredded green cabbage (or napa cabbage*)

1 carrot, julienned[3]

3 green onions,* cut into 2 inch lengths, white and green parts separated[4]

¼ cup water

1½ cups bean sprouts

**SAUCE OPTION 1**

⅓ cup Charlie Stir-Fry Sauce (page 94)

**SAUCE OPTION 2**

2 tsp cornstarch

1½ tbsp light soy sauce*[5]

1½ tbsp oyster sauce

1½ tbsp Shaoxing cooking wine*[6]

2 tsp sugar

½ tsp sesame oil*

Dash of white pepper

*Sauce*—If making the sauce from scratch (option 2), mix together the cornstarch and soy sauce in a small bowl until lump-free, then mix in the remaining ingredients. If using my Charlie Stir-Fry Sauce, just give the jar a shake and measure out ⅓ cup.

*Marinate chicken*—Pour 1 tablespoon of the sauce over the chicken, mix to coat, then set aside to marinate for 10 minutes (if time permits—I skip this more often than not).

*Noodles*—Prepare the noodles according to the package directions, then drain.

*Cook chicken*—Heat the oil in a wok or large nonstick skillet over high heat. Add the garlic and stir-fry for 10 seconds or until it starts to turn golden. Add the chicken and stir-fry until the surface gets a tinge of brown but the inside is still raw—about 1 minute.

*Cook vegetables*—Add the cabbage, carrot, and the white part of the green onion and stir-fry for 1½ minutes until the cabbage is mostly wilted.

*Noodles and sauce*—Add the noodles, sauce, and water and stir-fry for 1 minute, tossing constantly, until the sauce thickens and coats the noodles.

*Bean sprouts and green onion*—Add the bean sprouts and the green part of the green onion, toss for 30 seconds or until the bean sprouts just start to wilt.

*Serve*—Remove from the heat and serve immediately.

**NOTES**

1. Tenderizing option: Follow the directions in the Easy Everyday Chicken Stir-Fry on page 98 to tenderize the chicken using baking soda,* the Chinese-restaurant way. Chicken can also be substituted with pork or beef.
2. Helpfully labeled "chow mein noodles" on the package, these are a type of thin egg noodles sold in the fridge section of grocery stores and Asian stores, and are lightly dusted with flour (rather than the slippery oily type). Substitute with any other thin wheat noodles (not rice noodles).
3. I use a julienne shredding tool, but a box grater can also be used—or show off your chopping skills!
4. The white part takes longer to cook so we add that in first.
5. Or all-purpose soy sauce. Do not substitute with dark soy sauce.
6. Or dry sherry or mirin.* If using mirin, omit the sugar. For nonalcoholic, omit this and substitute the water with low-sodium chicken broth.*

LEFTOVERS Fridge 3 days though best made fresh. Not suitable for freezing.

# MALAYSIAN HOKKIEN MEE

*Pull this out when you want to impress.*

**SERVES: 2 | PREP: 15 MINUTES | COOK: 15 MINUTES**

With thick and satisfyingly chewy lo mein noodles stained with a deeply flavored dark sauce, this Malaysian hawker stall favorite is always a hit with my friends. I fry off the pork belly first until it's crispy, then use the fat to stir-fry the noodles. It gives everything an extra-tasty edge! Try not to skip the shrimp—they're a wonderful combination with the pork.

---

8 medium (4 oz) raw shrimp,* peeled and deveined

9 oz fresh[1] lo mein noodles

4 oz skinless, boneless pork belly, cut into ¼ inch batons

¼ tsp kosher salt*

1½ tbsp canola oil

½ yellow onion, halved, sliced ¼ inch thick

1 garlic clove,* finely minced

1½ tsp finely minced anchovies[2]

2 heaped cups chopped green cabbage

½ carrot, peeled, halved lengthwise and sliced ⅛ inch thick diagonally

**SAUCE**

2 tsp dark soy sauce*[3]

1½ tsp light soy sauce*[4]

1 tbsp oyster sauce

1½ tsp brown sugar

1 tsp cornstarch

1½ tbsp water

*Sauce*—Mix the ingredients in a jar, then set aside.

*Toss shrimp*—Toss the shrimp in a separate bowl with ½ tablespoon of sauce and set aside.

*Noodles*—Prepare the noodles as per the package directions. Rinse briefly under tap water, then leave in the colander to drain while you start to cook.

*Crispy pork belly*—Toss the pork belly with the salt. Heat the oil in a large nonstick skillet or wok over high heat. Cook the pork belly for 3 minutes until golden and crispy, then use tongs to transfer it to a bowl. Keep the fat in the skillet.

*Sear shrimp*—Still over high heat, spread the shrimp out in the skillet and cook each side for 1 minute, then transfer to a separate bowl.

*Cook vegetables*—You should have about 1 tablespoon of fat left in the pan. If not, add a bit of oil. Add the onion and cook for 1 minute, then add the garlic and anchovies and cook for 20 seconds. Add the cabbage and carrot and cook for 2½ minutes.

*Sauce and noodles*—Add the noodles and sauce, then toss using two wooden spoons for 4 minutes or until the noodles are stained a beautiful mahogany color and starting to caramelize. Add the shrimp and continue tossing for another 30 seconds.

*Serve*—Remove from the stove and divide the noodles between two serving bowls. Sprinkle with the crispy pork belly, then dig in!

**NOTES**

1. Lo mein noodles come in fresh, dried and vac-packed form. Fresh (from the fridge) is the best!
2. Secret ingredient that adds depth of flavor! Powdered anchovies are traditionally used in Malaysia. I use anchovies in oil, which are more readily accessible, for a similar hit of umami.
3. This stains the noodles and adds flavor to the dish. Though it can be substituted with light or all-purpose soy sauce, it won't be quite the same flavor or color. The best substitute would be kecap manis,* but omit the brown sugar in the sauce.
4. Or all-purpose soy sauce. Do not substitute with dark soy sauce.

LEFTOVERS Fridge 3 days though best made fresh. Not suitable for freezing.

# WHAT I DO WITH A PIECE OF . . .

. . . Chicken. Fish. Steak. Chops. And even big, fat mushrooms!

# Chicken breast

Poach it. Bake it. Or pan-fry it. Here's what I do with a piece of chicken breast!

# PAN-FRY IT

**SERVES: 2 LARGE SERVINGS OR 4 SMALL SERVINGS I PREP: 5 MINUTES I COOK: 5 MINUTES**

My default way to cook chicken breast—split it, dust it, sear it, sauce it.

---

2 x 8 oz boneless, skinless chicken breasts, each cut in half horizontally to form 2 thin steaks

1/2 tsp kosher salt*

1/4 tsp black pepper

2 tbsp all-purpose flour[1] (optional)

2 tbsp unsalted butter (or 1 1/2 tbsp extra-virgin olive oil)

**SAUCE OF CHOICE**

Any sauce from pages 324–31 (Honey Garlic Sauce on page 326, pictured, is my favorite quick and easy option)

*Prepare chicken*—Cover the chicken with a sheet of parchment paper or plastic wrap and, using the flat side of a meat tenderizer, rolling pin, or a small skillet, flatten to a ½ inch thickness (so each piece is roughly uniform in thickness[2]).

Sprinkle each side of the chicken with salt and pepper, then flour.

*Pan-fry chicken*—Melt the butter in a large nonstick skillet over medium–high heat. Cook the chicken for 2 minutes on each side until golden and crispy.

*Rest, then serve*—Transfer to a plate and rest for 3 minutes and serve with selected sauce.

**NOTES**

1. A dusting of flour creates a light golden crust on the chicken, which adds texture and flavor as well as giving the sauce something to cling to (without it, the sauce just slides off). Substitute with cornstarch for a gluten-free alternative.
2. Pounding is a key tip for even cooking as well as tender chicken.

# POACH IT

**MAKES: 1–2 CHICKEN BREASTS | PREP: 1 MINUTE | COOK: 20 MINUTES**

Gently poaching chicken breast is both healthy and locks in all the moisture. This recipe will give you the juiciest poached chicken of your life, every time! Read on for a bunch of great ideas for using the meat.

---

1–2 skinless, boneless chicken breasts, up to 8 oz each, fridge-cold

**OPTIONAL FLAVORINGS (I RARELY USE THEM)**

1 lemon, quartered

1 bay leaf,* dried or fresh

2 garlic cloves,* smashed

*Poach chicken*—In a large saucepan, bring 10 cups of water to a boil over high heat.

Place the chicken and flavorings (if using) in the water. Bring back up to a boil, then immediately turn the heat off and cover the pan with a lid. Leave the pan on the turned-off stove for 20 minutes (up to 50 minutes is fine).

*Serve*—Remove the chicken from the pan. Slice or shred and marvel at the incredible juiciness! Use for any recipe that calls for cooked chicken. See the suggestions below.

**NOTE**

This recipe works consistently, every time, because chicken breast meat cooks at 150°F, so while the boiled water is at, or above, this temperature, the chicken is cooking. Once it falls below this temperature (as the water cools), the chicken stops cooking and thus prevents the breast from overcooking. This yields a guaranteed perfectly cooked juicy chicken breast every single time!

**USE FOR:**

- The Bangkok—Satay Chicken Noodle Salad (page 183)
- The Kyoto—Chicken Soba Salad with Creamy Sesame Dressing (page 191)
- Ms. Saigon—Vietnamese Chicken Salad (page 195)

**ADD IT AS A PROTEIN TO:**

- Sun-Dried Tomato Pesto Pasta Salad (page 36)
- Crispy Korean Pancakes (page 40)
- Vietnamese Rice Paper Rolls (page 234)
- Chinese Noodle Soup (page 242)
- Cheesy Baked Broccoli Fritters (page 26)

**MAKE A MEAL OUT OF IT:**

- Make it dinner with any sauce from pages 324–31 + a starch from pages 338–339 + a side salad with a dressing (pages 332–33)
- Serve over cooked pasta with Creamy Mushroom Sauce (page 325) or My Favorite Blue Cheese Sauce (page 330) tossed with baby spinach and a handful of cherry tomatoes
- Sandwiches, omelets, frittatas

# BAKE IT

 **MAKES: 4 CHICKEN BREASTS | PREP: 3 MINUTES | COOK: 20 MINUTES**

Here's a simple and great way to cook chicken breast in the oven. High heat is the trick here to avoiding dry meat. A touch of brown sugar in the seasoning also helps create a sauce!

4 skinless, boneless chicken breasts (8 oz each)

4 tsp extra-virgin olive oil

**SEASONING**

1 1/2 tbsp brown sugar

1 tsp paprika

1 tsp dried oregano (or thyme)

1/4 tsp garlic powder

3/4 tsp kosher salt*

1/2 tsp black pepper

Preheat the oven to 425°F.

*Seasoning*—Mix the seasoning ingredients in a small bowl.

*Prepare chicken*—Place the chicken, smooth-side down, on a work surface. Cover with a sheet of parchment paper or plastic wrap and, using the flat side of a meat tenderizer, rolling pin, or a small skillet, flatten until 3/4 inch thick at the thickest part.[1]

Place the chicken on a baking tray. Rub the chicken on both sides with the olive oil, then use your fingers to sprinkle evenly with the seasoning.

*Cook chicken*—Bake the chicken for 15 minutes or until the internal temperature is 155°F (it will rise to 160°F once rested).

*Serve*—Remove the tray from the oven and immediately transfer the chicken to serving plates. Scrape the tray juices over the chicken. Rest for 3 minutes before serving!

**NOTE**

1. Pounding is a key tip for even cooking as well as tender chicken.

# Chicken thighs

Whether boneless or bone-in, chicken thighs are my most used cut of chicken! They have it all—flavor, juiciness, and some richness in the meat. Some people avoid thighs on health grounds, but did you know that, when trimmed of excess fat, thighs have virtually the same calories as chicken breast?

# CRISPY GARLIC CHICKEN THIGHS

 **SERVES: 4 | PREP: 3–5 MINUTES | COOK: 10 MINUTES**

Here's my favorite no-prep way to cook skinless, boneless chicken thighs. However, if I have time, I like to marinate the thighs for more flavor. You can use these in Greek Chicken Gyros on page 24 (my pick!) or Chicken Shawarma (page 46).

---

1½ lb boneless, skinless chicken thighs (5–6 pieces)

1 tsp garlic powder

¾ tsp kosher salt*

¼ tsp black pepper

1 tbsp extra-virgin olive oil

**WHITE WINE PAN SAUCE**

2 large garlic cloves,* finely minced

1½ tbsp unsalted butter

½ cup chardonnay or other dry white wine*[1]

*Prepare chicken*—Sprinkle each side of the chicken with the garlic powder, salt, and pepper.

*Fry chicken*—Heat the oil in a large nonstick skillet over medium heat. Place the thighs in the skillet, smooth-side down, and press down lightly on them with a spatula. Cook for 5 minutes until deep golden and crispy.

Flip the chicken and again press lightly with a spatula. Cook for 2 minutes.

*Sauce*—Add the garlic and butter, cook for 1 minute until the garlic is light golden and smells amazing.

Add the wine, then turn up the heat so the wine is simmering. Stir around the chicken to dissolve the golden bits stuck on the bottom of the skillet into the wine. Simmer rapidly for 1½ minutes or until the alcohol smell evaporates.

*Serve*—Remove from the heat and transfer the chicken to serving plates. Rest for 3 minutes, drizzle with the pan sauce, and serve!

**NOTE**

1. Substitute with nonalcoholic white wine, which is widely available these days. Or use low-sodium chicken broth.*

# CRAZY CRISPY NO-OIL CHICKEN

**SERVES: 4 | PREP: 3 MINUTES + 6–24 HOURS FRIDGE-DRYING (IF TIME PERMITS) | COOK: 30 MINUTES**

Bone-in, skin-on chicken thighs are my favorite cut of chicken! Here's my current favorite way to cook them, with shatteringly crispy skin all done on the stove. No messing with deep-frying! Devour fresh off the stove, dipped in the pan juices.

---

4 x 8 oz skin-on, bone-in chicken thighs

3/4 tsp kosher salt*

1/2 tsp black pepper

NO OIL!

Salt flakes for sprinkling (optional)

*Prepare chicken*—Dry the chicken flesh and skin with paper towels.

Slash the flesh side of the chicken along the bone. Do two more slashes on either side of the bone (in the same direction) halfway down into the flesh (goal: even meat thickness).

Sprinkle the salt and pepper evenly on each side of the chicken.

*Optional fridge-dry*—Place the chicken on a plate, skin-side up, and leave uncovered in the fridge for a minimum of 6 hours and up to 24 hours.[1] If you can't wait 6 hours, skip this step and immediately proceed to cooking. (Do not leave salted chicken lying around.)

*Cook chicken*—Place the chicken, skin-side down, in a cold, large, nonstick skillet[2] (preferably one with a lid). Place the pan over medium heat. Cover with a lid[3] and let the chicken cook for 10 minutes. The chicken juices and fat will leach out into the pan.

Uncover, then turn the heat down to medium–low and cook for another 20 minutes.[4] The liquid will evaporate, leaving only chicken fat in which the skin fries, making it super golden and crispy. Regulate the heat as needed. At the end of cooking time, the flesh side should be virtually cooked through (you will be able to tell just by looking at it).

Flip the chicken and cook the flesh side for 2 minutes, or until cooked through.

*Rest*—Transfer the chicken to a plate and rest for 3 minutes.

*Serve*—Chicken cooked this way is incredibly flavorful so I usually just eat it plain, sometimes sprinkled with salt flakes. The chicken fat left in the pan can be used as the sauce, if desired, for extra indulgence. Though, if you really want to take it over the top, make Gravy (page 326) for dunking.

**NOTES**

1. If you refrigerate the salted chicken, you need to leave it in there for at least 6 hours. This is because the salt makes the chicken skin sweat, and it needs time to dry out again if the skin is to become ultra crispy. You can't pat it dry because then you lose the salt. So if you don't have 6 hours, skip this step. The chicken will still be very, very crispy. It's just even crispier if you do the fridge-dry!
2. Nonstick is best but it does also work in a well-seasoned cast-iron pan. However, you will need to regulate the heat more carefully as cast-iron tends to retain heat much better and get quite hot.
3. If your pan doesn't have a lid, either cover with aluminum foil or a baking tray.
4. 20 minutes is the optimum time for the skin to become really crispy after removing the lid. Check at 10 minutes—if the pan is still looking watery, increase the heat. If the chicken is browning too fast, turn the heat down.

# Steak

If I'm going all in, the best way to serve a great piece of steak, for me, is with a great sauce. I adore all the steakhouse classics: béarnaise, chimichurri, blue cheese, red wine sauce—yum! (And you'll find all these on pages 327–31.) But, as with all things, simple is often just as good. Here's my way to make steak without the fuss.

# BUTTER-BASTED STEAK

**SERVES: 1–2 | PREP: 3 MINUTES | COOK: 10 MINUTES**

Choosing a steak around 1 inch thick means you don't need to mess around finishing it in the oven. This is perfect for fast midweek meals—who's got time for that sort of fluff on a Monday night!? The basting method isn't just about showing off (but, well, that too!), it's also about getting more flavor on the steak as well as being a good cooking technique. The butter has a tempering effect and moderates heat. This means more evenly cooked steak, and less smoking/burning of fats and meat in the pan.

---

1–2 x 10 oz boneless rib-eye steaks,[1] 1 inch thick, removed from the fridge 30 minutes prior to cooking, patted dry with paper towels

½ tsp kosher salt* per steak

2 pinches black pepper per steak

1½ tbsp canola oil

3½ tbsp unsalted butter,[2] cut into ½ inch cubes

5 garlic cloves,* smashed

6 thyme sprigs (or 3 rosemary sprigs)

*Season*—Sprinkle each side of the steak with salt and pepper.

Turn your exhaust fan on high and open the windows! Set a rack over a tray for resting the steak[3] (optional, but recommended).

Heat the oil in a cast-iron skillet over high heat just until you see the first wisps of smoke.

*Cook steak*—Use tongs to hold the steak upright (if cooking two steaks, grip both together at once) and sear the fat side of the steak—around 1½ minutes in total. (Skip this step if the steak does not have fat on the sides.) Once the side is nicely colored, lay the steak down in the pan, which should be smoking hot by now!

Cook for 2½ minutes until you get a great crust, then turn the steak. Leave the steak for 1 minute, then toss in the butter, garlic, and thyme (the thyme will splutter!). Turn the heat down to medium–high.

*Baste*—As soon as the butter melts (10 seconds), tilt the pan slightly so the butter pools on one side. Using a large spoon, continuously spoon the butter over the steak until it's cooked to your liking—1½ minutes in total for medium-rare (internal temperature 125°F, see page 351 for other doneness temperatures).

*Rest*—Transfer the steak to the rack[3] and rest for 5–10 minutes. Never skip this step with steak!

*Serve*—Transfer to serving plates and serve the steak with a bit of the butter from the pan (which is now brown butter!).

**NOTES**

1. In my personal opinion boneless rib-eye steak is the best cut of beef to cook as a pan-seared steak, followed by New York strip, then T-bone, porterhouse. Strip will take 45 seconds less to cook than a boneless rib-eye, and a T-bone steak will take the same time as a boneless rib-eye. Beef tenderloin, although very tender, has less beefy flavor. Also note this method of cooking is not suitable for flank, skirt, or bavette. It is also not suitable for slow-cooking cuts of beef (like chuck, beef ribs, or brisket) or lean thin steaks (such as "minute" or "sizzle steak" and beef schnitzels).
2. You need this amount of butter whether cooking one or two steaks in order to have enough to baste. You won't use all the butter for serving. Frankly, it's so flavorful, though, it's worth saving. Freeze it for up to 6 months, then melt and serve over the next steak you throw on the grill where you can't use this basting method.
3. Resting steak on racks is best practice (good restaurants always do it) but I ordinarily don't bother unless it really adds to the steak dish. For good steak, though, it's worth it! The rack prevents the underside of the steak from sweating, which compromises the crust.

# Fish

When I have a beautiful piece of fish, more often than not I'll do as little to it as possible.

# PAN-FRIED FISH FILLETS

**SERVES: 2 | PREP: 2 MINUTES | COOK: 4 MINUTES**

For easy cooking, I opt for thin, flat fish fillets like the John Dory pictured (a favorite Australian fish). While I've written the recipe for two fillets, you can cook more in the same pan as long as you have a bit of space around each piece, or they will stew instead of fry!

---

2 x 5 oz skinless white fish fillets,[1] ½ inch even thickness, such as dory, snapper, or tilapia

½ tsp kosher salt*

2 pinches black pepper

¼ cup all-purpose flour[2]

1 tsp paprika[3] (optional)

2–3 tbsp canola oil[4]—enough to cover the base of the pan

Lemon wedges, to serve

Finely chopped parsley, to serve (optional)

**OPTIONAL SAUCE—CHOOSE**

Lemon Butter Sauce—my most used sauce (see Brown Butter & Lemon Butter Sauce on page 328)

White Wine Sauce (page 328)

Chimichurri (page 330)

*Prepare fish*—Pat the fish dry with paper towels (extra well if using thawed frozen fish).

Sprinkle salt and pepper on both sides of the fish. Mix the flour and paprika on a plate, then coat the fish, pressing firmly so it adheres. Shake off the excess very well.

Heat a large nonstick skillet[5] over medium–high heat until you see the first wisps of smoke. Add the oil and swirl to coat the pan (it heats in seconds!).

*Cook fish*—Place the fish in the pan, presentation-side down. It should sizzle straight away. Shake the pan lightly to move the fish. Cook for 2½ minutes until golden and crisp, pressing down gently once or twice with a spatula, then flip. If it's browning too quickly, just remove the pan from the stove briefly. Cook the other side for 45 seconds until crisp, then remove the fish from the pan.

*Rest*—Transfer the fish to a plate and let it rest for 2 minutes.

*Serve*—Sprinkle with parsley (if using), then either serve the fish just with lemon wedges (my default option!), or with a sauce of your choice.

**NOTES**

1. See the Glossary (page 359) for a list of white fish fillets suitable for pan-frying. Note that while I emphasize the need for thin fillets, this method of cooking can actually be used for fillets of any thickness! See Crispy Skin Fish on page 67 for directions on how to cook thicker fish fillets. If your fish has skin, that's fine. Put the fish, skin-side down, first and press down lightly with a spatula so the skin seals flat rather than curling up. Then flip and cook the underside.
2. Use cornstarch to make this recipe gluten-free, though note that the crust won't become as golden.
3. I like to add this for an extra touch of warm color on the crust and a bit of extra flavor.
4. If you skimp on oil, the fish will just burn instead of becoming golden. So—don't skimp on oil!
5. You don't actually need a nonstick skillet but it does make life a bit easier. With a pan that is not nonstick, the fish will initially stick to the pan but, once cooked, it naturally releases. In fact, that is the indicator of when it is ready to flip!

# Salmon

I love salmon baked and even poached, but pan-seared is a fast and easy way to bring out the best in this fish. Being such a flavorful and rich fish, salmon doesn't really need anything more than a squeeze of fresh lemon. If you're a sauce person though, I've included a list of my favorite sauces for salmon.

# PAN-SEARED SALMON

**SERVES: 4 I PREP: 2 MINUTES I COOK: 7 MINUTES**

This recipe is intended for skinless salmon, but feel free to keep the skin on. I cook my salmon so it's just-set, for the ideal juiciness and melting texture.

---

4 x 6 oz boneless, skinless salmon fillets,[1] removed from the fridge 30 minutes prior to cooking

1/2 tsp kosher salt*

1/4 tsp black pepper

1 1/2 tbsp extra-virgin olive oil

Lemon wedges, to serve

**SAUCE OPTIONS**

Honey Garlic Sauce—my most used sauce (page 331)

Béarnaise Sauce—restaurant classic (page 331)

Brown Butter & Lemon Butter Sauce—luxuriously rich (page 328)

White Wine Sauce—elegant and easy (page 328)

Chimichurri—fresh and vibrant (page 330)

*Season salmon*—Sprinkle the salmon all over with salt and pepper.

*Cook salmon*—Heat the oil in a large nonstick skillet over medium–high heat (or medium, on strong burners). Add the salmon, presentation-side down,[2] and cook for 3 minutes until golden in color.

Flip, then cook the other side for 3 minutes. The best internal temperature for cooked salmon is 125°F[3] (the flesh should flake easily).

*Serve*—Transfer the salmon to a plate. Rest for 3 minutes, then serve. Being such an oily fish, well-cooked salmon doesn't need anything more than a squeeze of lemon juice. However, take it to the top with your choice of sauce.

**NOTES**

1. Though this recipe calls for skinless salmon fillets, it doesn't matter if there is skin. Just add 2 minutes to the cooking time on the skin side, and eat the flesh off the skin!
2. The presentation side is the nice side you want facing up on the plate.
3. 125°F is the optimum internal temperature for salmon when you take it off the stove.The salmon is at its juiciest but fully cooked—this is the temperature that restaurants target (it will rise to 130°F when resting). But because salmon is a very oily fish, there is a good margin for error—up to 140°F and it will still be juicy! See the Internal Cooked Temperatures chart on page 351 for more information.

# Big mushrooms

Give me big, meaty mushrooms and I think “meat-free steak.” That’s how to treat them, and here’s how I cook them! Serve on toast for a quick, hearty meal.

# GARLIC ROASTED MUSHROOMS

**SERVES: 2 | PREP: 5 MINUTES | COOK: 35 MINUTES**

This is my go-to way to cook big mushrooms—with butter and garlic, roasted until browned. Serve as a "meaty" main or as a side dish with steak!

---

2 tbsp unsalted butter[1]

2 garlic cloves,* finely minced

½ tsp each kosher salt* and black pepper

4 BIG mushrooms! Use portabella or large mushrooms, 4 inches+ wide, stalks trimmed

½ tbsp extra-virgin olive oil[1]

2 tsp finely chopped chives or parsley, to serve (optional)

Preheat the oven to 425°F.

*Melt butter*—Place the butter, garlic, salt, and pepper in a heatproof jar. Microwave on High for 45 seconds or until the butter is melted, then stir.

*Prepare mushrooms*—Brush the mushroom caps (smooth side) with garlic butter, then place on a tray, gills side up (i.e., stalk facing up). Brush the remaining butter onto the rims and gills, being sure to scrape up all the garlic in the jar. Drizzle with olive oil.

*Cook mushrooms*—Roast for 25 minutes, then flip the mushrooms. Brush the mushrooms with the tray juices, then roast for a further 10 minutes or until the center of the mushrooms is tender.

*Serve*—Transfer to plates, sprinkle with chives or parsley, if desired, and drizzle with the tray juices.

PS: I have been known to top the mushrooms with a slice of Swiss cheese and return to the oven for a few minutes.

**NOTE**

1. Using both butter and olive oil is key here. While I love the flavor of butter, it burns at high temperatures and the mushrooms won't brown very well. This is easily rectified by adding a bit of oil so you get the best of both worlds!

# Pork chops

Pork chops are lean, quick to cook, and affordable. Avoid overcooking them and you'll be rewarded with succulent, flavorful meat!

# SMOKY PORK CHOPS

 **SERVES: 4 | PREP: 5 MINUTES | COOK: 10 MINUTES**

My first instinct with pork chops? Sprinkle with a smoky savory rub. Sear, then add a knob of butter toward the end for a flavor-soaked instant sauce. YUM.

---

4 x 5 oz boneless pork chops,[1] 3/4 inch thick

1 1/2 tbsp olive oil

3 1/2 tbsp unsalted butter

**SMOKY PORK RUB**[2]

1 tbsp smoked paprika

2 1/4 tsp kosher salt*

1 1/2 tsp garlic powder

1 1/2 tsp onion powder

1 tsp dried oregano

3/4 tsp mustard powder

3/4 tsp black pepper

1/2 tsp ground cumin

1/2 tsp ground sage

*Smoky pork rub*—Mix the rub ingredients in a small bowl.

*Prepare pork*—Pat the pork chops dry with a paper towel. Sprinkle both sides evenly with the rub—use it all!

Place a rack over a tray (for resting).[3]

*Cook pork*—Heat the oil in a large nonstick skillet over medium–high heat. Cook the chops for 3 minutes on each side until deep golden. Don't crowd the pan or the pork will stew instead of sear!

*Rest*—Let the pork rest on the rack for 3 minutes.

*Make sauce*—Melt the butter in the same skillet, stirring to dissolve the rub that's left in the pan into the butter.

*Serve*—Transfer the pork to serving plates, pour over the melted butter and serve. These are great with Creamy Mashed Potato (page 338).

**NOTES**

1. As with steak, for effortless midweek cooking I opt for pork chops up to 3/4 inch thick so they can be cooked entirely on the stove rather than finished in the oven (which is best for pork chops thicker than 3/4 inch). If yours are thinner, just cook for a shorter length of time.
2. Rub spice substitutes:
   - Smoked paprika: use normal or sweet
   - Onion and garlic powder: double up on either if you are missing one
   - Oregano: use 1 teaspoon mixed herbs or thyme
   - Mustard powder: use 1/4 teaspoon extra onion or garlic powder
   - Cumin: use ground coriander
   - Sage: use ground coriander or extra mustard powder
3. Resting cooked meat on racks is best practice but I ordinarily don't bother unless it's really necessary. In this recipe, it is! It keeps the underside of the chops from sweating, which makes the rub come off.

# Lamb rib chops

Lamb rib chops are the Rolls-Royce of lamb cuts. With meat this prime I like to keep it simple and stick to classic flavor partners—garlic and rosemary do the trick very nicely!

# ROSEMARY GARLIC LAMB CHOPS

**SERVES: 2 (4 CHOPS PER PERSON) | PREP: 5 MINUTES + 1 HOUR (OR OVERNIGHT) MARINATING | COOK: 4 MINUTES**

Lamb rib chops are ideal for pan-searing. You have precise control so you can cook them perfectly medium-rare (or how you want), and they cook so quickly that dinner is done in the blink of an eye!

---

8 x 3 oz lamb rib chops,[1] trimmed, ½ inch thick

1½ tbsp extra-virgin olive oil

**MARINADE**

1 tbsp finely minced rosemary leaves

¾ tsp finely minced garlic* (1 clove)

½ tsp kosher salt*

¼ tsp black pepper

3 tbsp extra-virgin olive oil

Set a rack over a tray (for resting the meat).

*Marinade*—Combine the ingredients in a small bowl.

*Prepare lamb*—Lay the lamb chops on a plate and smear both sides with the marinade, using it all up. Leave on the counter to marinate for 1 hour (or even overnight in the fridge!).

Brush the excess rosemary and garlic off the lamb, or they will burn (little bits remaining is okay).

*Cook lamb*—Heat the olive oil in a large nonstick skillet over high heat until you see the first wisps of smoke. Place the lamb in the pan and cook each side for 2–2½ minutes or until the internal temperature is 145°F for medium-rare.[2]

*Rest*—Transfer the lamb to the rack and rest for 3 minutes.

*Serve*—Serve immediately! You won't need a sauce as the lamb is so tender and juicy, and infused with flavor from the marinade.

**NOTES**

1. Lamb rib chops are often sold trimmed of excess fat with the bone scraped clean for a neater presentation. These are also referred to as "frenched" lamb rib chops. The cooking times in this recipe assume 8 lamb chops that fill the pan. If you are using less, they will cook faster so you will need to reduce the cooking time.
2. Lamb is best served medium-rare so the flesh is pink and at its juiciest. This is the default doneness that restaurants will serve lamb at, but see the Internal Cooked Temperatures chart on page 351 for more information.

# PASTA & COZY FOOD

Heads up—there's a lot of cheese here. I make no apologies!

# SAUCY BAKED PORK MEATBALLS

*Just when you thought meatballs couldn't get any better . . .*

**SERVES: 4–5 I PREP: 20 MINUTES I COOK: 70 MINUTES**

When you bake plump, juicy meatballs in tomato sauce, then top them with stretchy, bubbling mozzarella, very good things happen. The meatballs absorb the sauce and become juicier, while also releasing their flavor into the sauce. It's an all-round win!

**SAUCY TOMATO SAUCE**

2 tbsp extra-virgin olive oil

½ yellow onion, finely chopped

2 garlic cloves,* minced

1 bay leaf*

¼ tsp each dried thyme and oregano

3 tbsp tomato paste

⅓ cup chardonnay wine*[1]

14 oz can crushed tomatoes

2 cups low-sodium vegetable broth*

¾ tsp sugar

½ tsp kosher salt*

¼ tsp black pepper

**MEATBALLS**

Olive oil spray

1 lb ground pork[2]

1 cup panko bread crumbs*

1 egg

2 green onions,* finely chopped

¼ tsp dried thyme

1 tsp each ground sage and onion powder

½ tsp black pepper

¾ tsp kosher salt*

**TO FINISH**

½ cup (2 oz) finely grated parmesan*

1 cup (4 oz) shredded* mozzarella

2 tsp chopped chives or parsley (optional)

14 oz spaghetti, cooked as per package directions

*Sauce*—Heat the oil in a large saucepan over medium heat. Add the onion, garlic, bay leaf, thyme, and oregano. Cook for 3–4 minutes until the onion is translucent. Add the tomato paste and stir for 1 minute. Stir in the wine, then increase the heat to high and simmer rapidly until mostly evaporated (about 2 minutes). Add the tomatoes, broth, sugar, salt, and pepper. Stir and reduce the heat to medium–low. Simmer for 20 minutes.

*Blitz*—Remove the bay leaf and blitz the sauce until smooth using an immersion blender. Simmer for 1 minute, then remove from the stove. Cover with a lid to keep warm.

Preheat the oven to 475°F. Cover a baking tray with aluminum foil, place a wire rack on top and spray the rack with oil.

*Meatballs*—Place all the meatball ingredients in a bowl and mix well with your hands. Roll 2 tablespoons of mixture into 1½ inch balls, then place on the rack. Spray the meatballs generously with oil. Bake for 15 minutes until lightly browned on the outside (they will still be raw inside).

*Bake in sauce*—Remove the meatballs from the oven, then lower the heat to 350°F. Pour the sauce into an 7 x 12 inch baking dish[3] and place the meatballs in the sauce. Sprinkle with parmesan, then mozzarella. Bake for 25 minutes.

*Serve*—Serve the meatballs and sauce over spaghetti, sprinkled with chives (if using). Add a side salad of arugula leaves tossed with Balsamic Dressing (page 333) and shavings of parmesan.

**NOTES**

1. Or any dry white wine, or nonalcoholic white wine.
2. Ground pork is best as it's juiciest, however ground beef or chicken can be used.
3. Don't use a dish too large otherwise the sauce may reduce too much in the oven.

LEFTOVERS Fridge 4 days. Not suitable for freezing. Baked meatballs in the sauce (unbaked)—fridge 3 days, freezer 3 months.

# FRENCH SAUSAGE & BEAN CASSEROLE

*Unexpectedly so, so good.*

**SERVES: 4 | PREP: 15 MINUTES + 15 MINUTES RESTING | COOK: 1 HOUR**

This is a simplified take on cassoulet, the famous French bean casserole studded with sausages and hearty meats. I skip the confit duck and affectionately dub it "Poor Man's Cassoulet." One bite though and you'll know there's nothing poor about this dish! Serve this as a complete meal. It's got it all—protein, starch, and vegetables!

---

2 tbsp extra-virgin olive oil

7 oz speck block,[1] cut into 1½ x ¼ inch batons

8 x 4 oz short, thick pork sausages

2 yellow onions, finely chopped

3 garlic cloves,* minced

2 carrots, peeled, quartered lengthwise and sliced into ½ inch thick pieces

1 tbsp tomato paste

2 thyme sprigs

2 rosemary sprigs

2 bay leaves*

¼ cup chardonnay wine*[2]

3 x 15 oz cans cannellini beans, drained[3]

2 cups low-sodium chicken broth*

¼ tsp kosher salt*

½ tsp black pepper

12 cherry tomatoes

**TOPPING**

½ cup panko bread crumbs*

2 tbsp chopped parsley

2 tbsp extra-virgin olive oil

¼ tsp kosher salt*

Preheat the oven to 400°F.

*Topping*—Mix the topping ingredients in a bowl.

*Brown speck*—Heat the oil in a shallow 12 inch ovenproof casserole dish (or large pot) over medium–high heat. Cook the speck for 2½ minutes until golden, then transfer to a large bowl, leaving behind the speck fat.

*Brown sausages*—Brown the sausages in the same pot (I brown three sides, 1½ minutes on each side), then add to the bowl with the speck.

*Sauté aromatics*—Add the onion, garlic, and carrot to the pot and cook, stirring, for 3 minutes until the onion is softened. Add the tomato paste, thyme, rosemary, and bay leaves and stir for 1 minute.

*Deglaze*—Add the wine and simmer for 1 minute, scraping the base of the pot, until reduced by half.

*Combine ingredients in pot*—Add the beans, broth, salt, and pepper. Stir, then put the sausages and speck back in. Scatter over the cherry tomatoes and sprinkle with the topping, avoiding the sausages and tomatoes (so they can brown).

*Bake and grill*—Bring to a simmer, then place in the oven, uncovered, for 30 minutes. Flick the oven broiler to high and leave for 3 minutes to allow the surface to brown. Move the shelf up if necessary.

*Rest and serve*—Remove from the oven and rest for 15 minutes. The starch from the beans thickens the sauce slightly as it rests. Spoon into bowls and serve!

**NOTES**

1. Block is best so you can cut batons, because biting into chunks of salty, golden meat is part of the greatness of this dish! Substitute with block bacon or thick bacon slices.
2. Or any dry white wine, or nonalcoholic white wine.
3. Can be substituted with other beans of choice.

LEFTOVERS Fridge 4 days, though, regrettably, you won't be able to resurrect that crunchy topping! Not suitable for freezing.

# BAKED RATATOUILLE WITH BEANS

*My most made vegetarian dish in recent years.*

**SERVES: 5–6 AS A MAIN, 8–10 AS A SIDE | PREP: 15 MINUTES | COOK: 1 HOUR**

Despite being a devout meat-loving gal, I'm totally mad for ratatouille. I just adore the sunny flavors of this Provençal vegetable stew and it's become one of my favorite ways to cook up a big basket of vegetables! Traditionally in a ratatouille you would cook each vegetable separately, but this baked version is much more hands-off. I also add beans to turn it into a hearty meal. Serve with crusty bread, always!

---

1 eggplant (14 oz, 7 inches long)

½ tsp kosher salt*

2 tbsp extra-virgin olive oil

**VEGETABLE BEAN MEDLEY**

2 zucchini, halved lengthwise, sliced into ½ inch thick half-moons

1 each red and yellow bell pepper, cut into ¾ inch squares

2 yellow onions, cut into ½ inch dice

2 x 15 oz cans cannellini beans,[1] drained

1 tsp finely chopped thyme leaves

1 garlic clove,* minced

1 tsp kosher salt*

¼ tsp black pepper

2 tbsp extra-virgin olive oil

**TOMATO AND OLIVE SAUCE**

28 oz can crushed tomatoes

1 cup pitted kalamata olives,[2] drained

1 garlic clove,* minced

1 tsp minced thyme leaves

¼ tsp kosher salt*

¼ tsp black pepper

1 tbsp extra-virgin olive oil

**TO SERVE**

½ cup finely sliced basil, plus extra for serving

Extra-virgin olive oil, for drizzling

Preheat the oven to 475°F.

*Sweat eggplant*—Cut the eggplant into 1 inch cubes, then place in a large bowl. Sprinkle with salt and toss to coat. Transfer to a colander set over the sink and leave for 30 minutes to sweat. Tip the eggplant into a bowl, drizzle with olive oil, and toss to coat.

*Vegetable bean medley*—Place the ingredients in a bowl and mix.

*Sauce*—Place the sauce ingredients in a 13 x 9 inch roasting pan.[3] Mix to combine, then spread out in the pan.

*Top with vegetables*—Spread the vegetable bean medley evenly across the surface of the sauce, then top with the eggplant.

*Bake*—Bake for 30 minutes to brown the eggplant, then remove from the oven. Turn the oven down to 400°F. Give everything a good mix and return to the oven for a further 30 minutes.

*Serve*—Remove from the oven. Give everything a quick mix, then stir in the basil leaves. Transfer to a serving bowl if you are more civilized than me. Serve at room temperature in summer, warm in winter! Just before serving, drizzle everything with olive oil and sprinkle with the extra basil. Serve with Easy Crusty Artisan Bread (page 341) or No-Yeast Rolls (page 344).

**NOTES**

1. Any beans will work here. Chickpeas are also great!
2. Try to use good-quality kalamata olives as they are key for flavoring the tomato sauce. Whole, unpitted in oil are best for flavor, but pitted are more convenient.
3. This dish works best in a heavy-based metal or cast-iron roasting pan as it conducts heat better than ceramic or glass baking dishes.

LEFTOVERS Fridge 3 days. Not suitable for freezing.

# CHILLI CON CARNE

*A big pot of beefy Texan deliciousness.*

 **SERVES: 5–6 I PREP: 15 MINUTES I COOK: 45 MINUTES**

Chilli con carne is a bit like America's bolognese—there are a zillion ways to make it and every household has its own recipe they're fiercely proud of. I love mine full-flavored with my secret homemade spice blend and seasoned with beef bouillon cubes, which bring more flavor than just plain old salt. Serve over rice for a belly-rubbing midweek meal, or with tortilla chips for dunking on a lazy Friday TV night. Whatever you do, don't skip the toppings!

---

1 tbsp extra-virgin olive oil

3 garlic cloves,* minced

1 yellow onion, finely chopped

1 red bell pepper, deseeded and diced into ½ inch squares

1 lb ground beef

3 tbsp tomato paste

28 oz can crushed tomatoes

15 oz can red kidney beans, drained and rinsed (or other beans)

2 beef bouillon cubes,* crumbled

1½ tsp brown sugar

½ cup water

**SPICE MIX**

5 tsp ground cumin

4 tsp paprika

2 tsp each garlic powder, onion powder, and dried oregano

1½ tsp cayenne pepper[1] (adjust to taste)

1½ tsp kosher salt*

**TO SERVE**[2]

Sour cream

Shredded* cheese (colby, monterey jack or cheddar)

Avocado, diced

Cilantro

White Rice (page 335) or other rice of choice (pages 334–37), tortilla chips or warmed tortillas* (page 225)

*Spice mix*—Combine the ingredients in a small bowl.

*Sauté aromatics*—Heat the oil in a large heavy-based pot over high heat. Add the garlic and onion, cook for 1 minute, then add the bell pepper and cook for 2 minutes until the onion is translucent.

*Cook chili*—Add the beef and cook, breaking it up as you go, until the meat changes color, around 2 minutes. Add the spice mix and cook for a further 2 minutes. Add the remaining chili ingredients, then stir. Bring to a simmer, then reduce the heat to medium–low or low so it's bubbling gently.

Simmer for 30 minutes, uncovered, stirring every now and then, until the sauce reduces and thickens.

*Slow-cook option*—For even better flavor and more tender beef, add an extra 1 cup of water and simmer on the lowest heat for 1½–2 hours, covered.

*Serve*—Serve over rice, or ladle into bowls and serve with tortilla chips or warm tortillas on the side. Add your toppings of choice.

**NOTES**

1. Chilli con carne is supposed to be spicy—1½ teaspoons cayenne pepper gives this a nice spicy hit but it's not ragingly hot! If you're concerned, start with less and just add more, if desired, toward the end of cooking time.
2. Serve in a bowl topped with sour cream, guacamole or diced avocado, shredded cheese,* and fresh cilantro with tortilla chips or warm tortillas on the side for dunking and scooping. All these combine for an exceptionally delicious eating experience!

LEFTOVERS Fridge 4 days, freezer 3 months.

# CREAMY TUSCAN CHICKEN PASTA BAKE

*My fully loaded creamy pasta bake.*

**SERVES: 6 I PREP: 20 MINUTES I COOK: 45 MINUTES**

This is everything you want in a creamy pasta bake. Loads of cheesy sauce, juicy chunks of chicken, and tangy pops of sun-dried tomato (plus some spinach for your veggie quota!). Is it really Tuscan? Not at all! The flavors are vaguely reminiscent of what I think of as Tuscan-like. But the truth is, I just think "Tuscan" has a nice ring to it. Taste is all that matters in the end, after all!

---

2 tsp kosher salt*

12 oz penne or ziti[1]

5 oz bacon slices

2 tightly packed cups baby spinach

½ cup sun-dried tomato strips in oil, drained, roughly chopped

2 tsp chopped parsley, to serve (optional)

**CHICKEN**

1 lb boneless, skinless chicken thighs[2]

¾ tsp each kosher salt* and black pepper

2 tbsp unsalted butter

**TUSCAN SAUCE**

2 tbsp unsalted butter

2 garlic cloves,* minced

¼ cup chardonnay wine*[3]

⅓ cup all-purpose flour

2 cups whole milk, hot

1 cup heavy cream*

1½ cups low-sodium chicken broth*

½ tsp each onion powder and garlic powder

1 tsp kosher salt*

¾ tsp black pepper

1 cup (4 oz) finely grated parmesan*[4]

2½ cups (9 oz) shredded* mozzarella[4]

Preheat the oven to 350°F.

*Pasta*—Bring 12 cups of water to a boil with the salt. Cook the pasta as per the package directions, then drain and let cool.

*Bacon*—Lay the bacon in an unheated, large pot (no oil) over medium-high heat. Cook for 3 minutes until golden, then turn and cook the other side for 2 minutes or until golden. Cool on a paper towel-lined plate then chop into ½ inch pieces. Discard the bacon fat in the pot.

*Cook chicken*—Sprinkle the chicken with salt and pepper. Using the same pot over medium-high, melt the butter. Cook the chicken for 4 minutes on each side, then transfer to a plate. Rest for 5 minutes and cut into ½ inch thick slices.

*Tuscan sauce*—Melt the butter in the same pot, still on medium-high heat. Add the garlic and cook for 20 seconds. Add the wine, stir, then simmer rapidly for 2 minutes or until mostly evaporated. Lower the heat to medium, add the flour and stir for 1 minute. Switch to a whisk. While whisking, slowly pour in the milk—the mixture will thicken. Once the flour and milk are combined, add the cream and chicken broth. Whisk until lump-free. Bring to a simmer and stir regularly with a wooden spoon for 4–5 minutes until the sauce is thick enough to coat the back of the wooden spoon.

Stir in the onion and garlic powder, salt, pepper, and two-thirds of both the parmesan and mozzarella. Once the cheese melts, the sauce should be thick and creamy.

*Assemble and bake*—Stir in the spinach, chicken, sun-dried tomato, most of the bacon (reserve some for topping), and pasta. Pour into a 13 x 9 inch baking dish, sprinkle with the remaining parmesan, followed by the mozzarella and bacon. Bake for 25 minutes or until the cheese is melted and golden.

*Serve*—Stand for 5 minutes before serving. Garnish with parsley, if desired.

**NOTES**

1. Or other short pasta of choice, such as macaroni.
2. Thighs work best as they stay juicy. For chicken breast, cut in half horizontally to form two thin steaks, then cook for 2 minutes on each side.
3. Can be substituted with more chicken broth.
4. A knockout combination for cheesy ooze and flavor. But can substitute with other cheese, such as cheddar or colby.
5. Make ahead: Assemble the pasta bake but do not cook. Cool, uncovered, then top with the remaining cheese and bacon. Cover with plastic wrap, refrigerate for up to 5 days, or freeze for up to 3 months. Thaw, then bake for 20 minutes at 350°F covered with aluminum foil, then uncovered for 20 minutes.

LEFTOVERS Fridge 3 days.

# ZUPPA TOSCANA

*Ridiculously good for something with so few ingredients!*

**SERVES: 4–5 | PREP: 15 MINUTES | COOK: 75 MINUTES**

This hearty soup is a copycat of a popular dish at an Italian–American chain restaurant called Olive Garden. A reader gave me the recipe many years ago, and I find myself making it regularly because it's so quick to make yet tastes so good! Sausage is the key here. It adds so much flavor!

---

4 oz bacon,[1] chopped into ½ inch pieces

1 large yellow onion, diced

4 garlic cloves,* minced

1 lb good-quality Italian pork sausages,[2] meat removed from casings[3]

2 tbsp all-purpose flour

4 cups low-sodium chicken broth*

1 lb russet potatoes,[4] peeled and cut into ½ inch cubes

¼ tsp kosher salt*

½ tsp black pepper

1 cup heavy cream*

2 lightly packed cups kale leaves,* chopped into ¾ inch pieces

*Cook bacon*–Scatter the bacon across the base of an unheated, heavy-based pot, then place the pot over medium–high heat. As the pot starts heating up, the bacon fat will melt–yes, we are cooking bacon in its own fat! Stir for 3 minutes until golden, then use a slotted spoon to transfer the bacon to a paper towel–lined plate. Leave the bacon fat in the pot.

*Cook aromatics and sausage*–Add the onion and garlic to the pot and cook for 2 minutes. Turn the heat up to high and add the sausage meat. Cook for 4 minutes, breaking it up as you go, until the sausage meat is cooked and there are some golden bits.

*Simmer*–Add the flour and stir for 1 minute. Add the broth, potato, most of the bacon (reserve some for garnish), salt, and pepper, then bring to a simmer. Cover with a lid, reduce the heat to low, and simmer gently for 1 hour. Stir in the cream, add the kale, and simmer for a further 2 minutes until just wilted.

*Serve*–Ladle into bowls and garnish with the reserved bacon.

**NOTES**

1. If you cheat yourself into using lean bacon, you will need about 1½ teaspoons of olive oil to cook the bacon.
2. The sausage here is key for flavor, so skip the really economical sausages. Look for good-quality ones made with more meat and less fillers. (Tip: Read the ingredients label or ask your friendly butcher, aim for 90%+ meat.) I like to use Italian fennel sausages, to be on theme. But honestly I think any sausage flavor will work great here, made of any meat–pork, beef, lamb, or chicken!
3. To remove the meat from the sausage casings, just think of squeezing toothpaste out of a tube! Hold one end of the sausage firmly, then squeeze and push the meat out the other end of the casing.
4. While russet potatoes are ideal, this recipe is enjoyable with any type of potato, whether it's all-purpose, waxy or starchy. Don't use sweet potato, it will get too soft.

LEFTOVERS Fridge 4 days, freezer 3 months.

# PUMPKIN SOUP

*Classic and perfect.*

 **SERVES: 4–6 I PREP: 10 MINUTES I COOK: 15 MINUTES**

If I am ever reminded that the original is always the best, it's when I make pumpkin soup. Sometimes I'll trick it up, sauté aromatics, blend in other vegetables, add fancy garnishes and so on. But I always come back to the classic. Bursting with pumpkin flavor, smooth and beautifully creamy, this is the definition of cozy food. You don't need the extra bells and whistles!

---

2½ lb pumpkin or butternut squash, any type (unpeeled weight)

1 yellow onion, cut into ½ inch thick slices

2 garlic cloves, kept whole, peeled

3 cups low-sodium vegetable broth*

1 cup water[1]

¾ tsp kosher salt*

¼ tsp black pepper

½ cup heavy cream,* plus extra for drizzling (optional)

2 tsp finely chopped Italian parsley, to serve (optional)

*Prepare pumpkin*—Cut the pumpkin into 1¼ inch thick slices. Cut the skin off and scrape the seeds out with a spoon, then cut into 1½ inch pieces.

*Cook soup*—Place the pumpkin and all the other ingredients, except the cream, in a pot—the liquid should just about cover the pumpkin. Bring to a boil, uncovered, then reduce the heat to medium or medium-high so it is simmering rapidly. Cook for 10 minutes or until the pumpkin is very tender—check with a knife.

*Blitz*—Remove from the heat and use an immersion blender to blitz until completely smooth. Stir through the cream, then put it back on the stove for a minute or two to reheat, but do not let it boil as the cream may split.

*Serve*—Ladle the soup into bowls and drizzle with extra cream and a sprinkling of parsley, if desired. Serve with Easy Crusty Artisan Bread (page 341) or No-yeast Rolls (page 344) for dunking!

**NOTE**

1. I like to use a bit of water for the liquid rather than just all broth because it lets the flavor of the pumpkin shine through more.

LEFTOVERS Fridge 4 days, freezer 3 months.

# MORROCAN HARIRA SOUP WITH LAMB

*This soup is downright delicious.*

**SERVES: 4–5 I PREP: 15 MINUTES + 12–24 HOURS CHICKPEA SOAKING I COOK: 1 HOUR**

Meat-free versions of harira, a delicately spiced Moroccan soup, are quite common and delicious. But the tender lamb bits add such great flavor to the broth that I just can't pass it up! This soup is traditionally eaten to break the fast during Ramadan, though it's served year-round. I've opted for a slightly streamlined version here, using tomato passata as a shortcut instead of whole tomatoes, which is not only easier but gives it a better flavor, I think. Win-win!

¾ cup dried chickpeas[1]

2 tbsp extra-virgin olive oil

10 oz lamb leg steaks or shoulder,[2] cut into ½ inch cubes

2 tbsp unsalted butter

1 yellow onion, finely chopped

2 garlic cloves,* minced

2 celery stalks, finely chopped

⅓ cup dried green or brown lentils[1]

1 cinnamon stick (or ¼ tsp ground cinnamon)

1½ tsp ground turmeric

½ tsp ground cumin

1½ tsp ground ginger

½ tsp black pepper

4 cups low-sodium chicken broth*

4 cups water

1¼ cups tomato passata*

¾ cup short-cut angel hair pasta[3]

1¼ tsp kosher salt*

1½ tbsp fresh lemon juice

¼ cup chopped fresh cilantro

**THICKENER**

2 tbsp all-purpose flour

½ cup water

*Soak chickpeas*—Soak the chickpeas in 4 cups of water for 12–24 hours, then drain.

*Brown lamb*—Heat the olive oil in a large heavy-based pot over high heat. Add half the lamb and cook for 3 minutes until browned on the outside (it will still be raw inside), then transfer to a plate. Repeat with the remaining lamb.

*Sauté aromatics*—Turn the heat down to medium, then add the butter to the pot. Once melted, cook the onion, garlic, and celery for 4 minutes until the onion is softened. Add the browned lamb, soaked chickpeas, lentils, cinnamon, turmeric, ginger, cumin, pepper, broth, water, and passata. Stir, then let it come to a boil. Lower the heat so it's simmering and cook for 45 minutes, uncovered, or until the chickpeas are cooked through but still firm, not mushy.[4]

*Cook pasta and thicken soup*—Increase the heat to medium to bring the soup up to a rapid simmer. Add the pasta and salt and cook for 2 minutes. Mix the thickener ingredients in a small bowl until lump-free. Add the thickener to the soup, stir to dissolve, then cook for 1 minute until the broth thickens so it lightly coats the back of the wooden spoon.

*Serve*—Stir in the lemon juice just before serving and ladle into bowls. Sprinkle with a generous amount of cilantro and serve with Easy Flatbreads (page 342) for slopping!

**NOTES**

1. Dried chickpeas and lentils can be substituted with 1½ x 15 oz cans chickpeas plus a 15 oz can lentils (drained). Leave out the water in the recipe, simmer the soup broth for 15 minutes before adding, then simmer for a further 30 minutes as per the recipe.
2. Suitable for virtually any cut of lamb because small pieces are slow-cooked until tender. Shoulder, leg, neck, shanks, and lamb labeled "'stewing meat" will all work. Skip expensive lamb cuts, such as tenderloin or rib chops.
3. Also called "broken angel hair," this is thin spaghetti broken into 1 inch lengths. Fairly easy to find these days in the pasta aisle. Can't find it? Get normal angel hair pasta or egg vermicelli pasta and break it yourself (it's fun!). Use any left over to make the Fried Cabbage with Noodles & Bacon on page 57 (it's crazy delicious—and fast!).
4. Exact cooking time for the chickpeas will depend on the age of the dried chickpeas (older = longer to cook).
5. Make this gluten-free by swapping the flour for 1 tablespoon cornstarch and adding 1½ cups cooked rice at the end (instead of using pasta).

LEFTOVERS Fridge 4 days, freezer 3 months. After cooling it thickens and becomes stew-like, which I love! Or just add a little slosh of water to loosen it up a bit when reheating.

# SPINACH & RICOTTA CANNELLONI

*This will really hit the spot!*

**SERVES: 5–6 I PREP: 25 MINUTES I COOK: 50 MINUTES**

This is one of my go-to recipes when I need a cozy vegetarian meal to shake off the winter weather. It's also perfect for making ahead to give to grateful friends and family! Here in Australia I make this with cannelloni, which are just a slightly smaller version of manicotti tubes. Despite what the package says, there is no need to pre-boil the tubes if you bake them with a sufficient amount of sauce. Also, trying to stuff a wet floppy manicotti tube is insanity!

---

2 x quantities of Saucy Tomato Sauce (see Saucy Baked Pork Meatballs, page 150)

2/3 cup basil leaves,[1] roughly torn, plus extra leaves to serve (optional)

20 dried cannelloni tubes or 14 manicotti tubes (8.8 oz package)*[2]

1/2 cup (2 oz) finely shredded parmesan,* plus extra to serve (optional)

1 1/4 cups (4 oz) shredded* mozzarella

**FILLING**

10 oz frozen chopped spinach, thawed

1 lb ricotta

1/3 cup (1 oz) finely shredded parmesan*

1 cup (3 1/2 oz) shredded* mozzarella

1 egg

1 large garlic clove,* minced

1/8 tsp ground nutmeg

3/4 tsp kosher salt*

1/2 tsp black pepper

*Sauce*—Make a double batch of the Saucy Tomato Sauce from the baked meatballs recipe, except use a small pot (rather than a small saucepan) and simmer for 35 minutes. Stir in the basil leaves. Keep warm until required.

*Filling*—Grab handfuls of the thawed spinach and squeeze out most of the water, then place the spinach in a bowl. Add the remaining filling ingredients and mix well with a wooden spoon.

Preheat the oven to 400°F.

*Make cannelloni*—Spread 1½ cups of the tomato sauce across the base of a 13 x 9 inch baking dish.

Transfer the filling to a piping bag, or use a strong zip-top bag* and snip the corner so it fits into the cannelloni tubes. Pipe the filling into each tube until full. Place the cannelloni in the baking dish, lined up so they are touching each other.

*Bake*—Pour over the remaining sauce, covering all the cannelloni tubes. Cover with aluminum foil, then bake for 30 minutes. Remove the aluminum foil, sprinkle with the parmesan, then the mozzarella. Return to the oven for 15 minutes until the cheese is melted.

*Serve*—Garnish with extra basil and parmesan, if desired, and serve with a side of arugula tossed with Balsamic Dressing (page 333).

**NOTES**

1. Fresh basil can be omitted if you don't have it. It's not a make-or-break in this dish!
2. Cannelloni are dried pasta tubes that are popular in Australia. While they can be found online and in speciality stores, there is no need to hunt them down as they can be directly substituted with manicotti tubes. They are basically the same except manicotti are ridged and slightly larger. As I mentioned in the introduction, do not pre-cook the tubes no matter what the package says! They will cook in the sauce in the oven.
3. Make ahead: Add an extra ½ cup water to the cooled sauce. Assemble the cannelloni, including sprinkling the top with cheese, but do not bake. Cover tightly with plastic wrap, then refrigerate for 3 days or freeze for up to 3 months. To bake, thaw first, then bake, covered with aluminum foil for 35 minutes, then uncovered for 10 minutes. Use a knife to check that the inside is piping hot!

LEFTOVERS Fridge 3–4 days, freezer 3 months.

# MY FOREVER SPAGHETTI BOLOGNESE

*I will never stray from this recipe.*

**SERVES: 5 I PREP: 15 MINUTES I COOK: 30 MINUTES (OR 3 HOURS—WORTH IT!)**

Everyone seems to have an opinion on bolognese sauce and secret tips they say make theirs special. I've experimented with many over the years, but this is the one I always come back to. Rich and tomatoey with a deep meaty flavor, it's my idea of the perfect bolognese. My tricks? There are a few. But the two things that people stop me in the streets for, to declare changed their bolognese game forever, are a touch of sugar and beef bouillon cubes. Trust me, you'll also become a convert!

---

1½ tbsp extra-virgin olive oil

1 yellow onion, finely chopped

2 garlic cloves,* minced

1 lb ground beef

½ cup pinot noir wine*[1]

2 beef bouillon cubes,* crumbled

28 oz can crushed tomatoes[2]

2 tbsp tomato paste

2 tsp Worcestershire sauce

2 bay leaves*

2 thyme sprigs (or ½ tsp dried thyme)

½ tsp black pepper

¾ tsp kosher salt*

1 tsp sugar[2] (optional)

**TO SERVE**

14 oz dried spaghetti, or other pasta[3]

Parmesan,* freshly grated

Finely chopped parsley (optional)

*Cook beef*—Heat the oil in a large heavy-based pot over medium–high heat. Cook the onion and garlic for 3 minutes until softened. Turn the heat up to high and add the beef. Cook, breaking it up as you go, until browned. Add the wine, bring to a simmer and cook for 1 minute, scraping the bottom of the pot, until the alcohol smell is gone.

*Simmer*—Add the remaining ingredients. Stir, bring to a simmer, then turn the heat down to medium so it bubbles gently. Cook for 20–30 minutes, uncovered, adding water if the sauce gets too thick for your preference. Stir occasionally.

*Check seasoning*—At the end of the cook time, taste the bolognese sauce and add more salt or sugar if needed.

*Toss sauce with pasta[4]*—Cook the pasta in a large pot of salted water as per the package directions minus 1 minute. Just before draining, scoop out a mug of pasta cooking water, then drain the pasta. Add the pasta to the pot of hot bolognese sauce. Add ½ cup of the pasta cooking water. Toss the pasta over medium heat, continuously, using two wooden spoons for 1½ minutes until the spaghetti turns red and the bolognese sauce is clinging to the pasta rather than pooled at the bottom of the pot. If the pasta sauce gets too thick, add a splash of the reserved pasta cooking water to loosen it up.

*Serve*—Divide the spaghetti among bowls. Garnish with the parmesan, and parsley, if desired. Serve immediately with a salad of leafy greens tossed with Italian Dressing (page 333).

*Slow-cook option (premium!)—Add ¾ cup water, cover with a lid and simmer on the lowest heat for 2 hours, stirring every 30 minutes or so. Uncover and simmer for another 20 minutes to thicken the sauce.[5]*

**NOTES**

1. Any red wine that's not too sweet can be used or nonalcoholic red wine or water.
2. Many economical canned tomato brands can have a sour edge, so be sure to use the sugar in your bolognese. Start with 1 teaspoon, simmer, taste, then add more if needed.
3. Despite what you may have been doing for years, 1 lb ground meat doesn't make enough sauce for 1 lb pasta, only 14 oz! This quantity serves five people (2¾ oz pasta is a standard serving size per person in general).
4. You can just put bolognese sauce over cooked spaghetti, but it is better tossed with the pasta. It would be unacceptable in Italy to skip this step!
5. Slow-cooker: After the beef is browned, transfer everything into a slow-cooker and cook for 6 hours on Low.

LEFTOVERS Bolognese sauce keeps 4 days in the fridge or 3 months in the freezer.

# CREAMY CHICKEN & MUSHROOM FETTUCCINE

*When you've just gotta have a creamy pasta for dinner . . . fast!*

**SERVES: 2 I PREP: 10 MINUTES I COOK: 15 MINUTES**

The Italian trick to making a silky-smooth, emulsified sauce that coats every strand of pasta, is tossing through a splash of pasta cooking water at the last minute. What seemed like black magic before was a total lightbulb moment when I learned how Italians did it! In this creamy fettuccine, the pasta water gently thickens the creamy sauce so it becomes luscious and gorgeous, clinging to the fettuccine rather than pooling in your bowl. Translation: Pasta perfection with every bite!

---

**SEASONED CHICKEN**

7 oz boneless, skinless chicken breasts or thighs, sliced into 1 x ¼ inch pieces

¼ tsp each garlic powder, onion powder, kosher salt,* and black pepper

**PASTA**

1 tbsp kosher salt*

6 oz fettuccine, or other long pasta of choice

**SAUCE**

2 tbsp unsalted butter, cut into ¾ inch cubes

1¾ cups (4 oz) button mushrooms, sliced ¼ inch thick

¼ tsp each kosher salt* and black pepper

1 garlic clove,* minced

¼ cup chardonnay wine*[1]

¾ cup heavy cream*[2]

½ cup (2 oz) finely grated[3] parmesan*

**TO SERVE**

Freshly grated parmesan*

Pinch of finely chopped chives or Italian parsley

*Season chicken*—Toss the chicken with the seasoning.

*Cook pasta*—Bring 8 cups of water to a boil with the salt. Add the pasta and cook per the package directions minus 1 minute. Just before draining, scoop out 1 cup of the pasta cooking water (reserve for the sauce). (Meanwhile, start the sauce while the pasta is cooking.)

*Cook chicken*—Melt half the butter in a large deep nonstick skillet (or pot) over high heat. Add the mushrooms with half the salt and pepper and cook for 1½ minutes. Add the remaining butter and, once melted, add the chicken and garlic. Stir for 3 minutes until the chicken is cooked, then transfer everything to a plate.

*Sauce*—Pour the wine into the now-empty pan. Bring to a simmer while stirring, then let it simmer rapidly for 1½ minutes or until mostly evaporated. Turn the heat down to medium, then add the cream. Once it comes to a simmer, stir in the parmesan and remaining salt and pepper. Stir to melt, then simmer for 2 minutes until the sauce thickens.

*Toss pasta*—Add the chicken and mushroom to the sauce, then add the pasta with ⅓ cup of the pasta cooking water. Still over high heat, using two wooden spoons, toss the pasta for 1–1½ minutes until the sauce thickens and is coating the pasta rather than pooling in the pan. Use the remaining pasta cooking water to adjust the looseness of the pasta, as needed.

*Serve*—Serve immediately, garnished with extra parmesan and a pinch of fresh chives or parsley. Add a side of leafy greens tossed with my Everyday Salad Dressing (page 333).

**NOTES**

1. Or any dry white wine, or nonalcoholic white wine.
2. This recipe will work with low-fat cream but the sauce will not have the same luxurious mouthfeel. I don't recommend evaporated milk.
3. When measuring grated parmesan using cups, be sure to pack it in tightly—push it right in—otherwise you will be seriously short, and parmesan is essential here for flavor! For a silky smooth sauce, it's essential to grate your own parmesan rather than using store-bought pre-shredded, which doesn't melt properly in sauces. I use a Microplane.*

LEFTOVERS Fridge 3 days, though pastas are always best freshly made! Not suitable for freezing.

# RESTAURANT-WORTHY EASY SHRIMP LINGUINE

*Use the shrimp shells to make a quick homemade broth!*

**SERVES: 2 I PREP: 15 MINUTES I COOK: 35 MINUTES**

One of the key things that distinguishes really excellent restaurant pastas from home cooking is a great homemade broth. This is especially the case with seafood pastas. Store-bought fish broth is garbage! But who has time to make broth on a Monday night? You do! Based around a super quick and easy broth using the shells and heads of the shrimp, this is a pasta that's dinner party–worthy, date-worthy, Valentine's-worthy, and absolutely restaurant-worthy.

---

12 oz whole shrimp* (10 pieces), peeled and deveined,[1] shells and heads reserved

6 oz linguine (or other long pasta)

1/8 tsp each kosher salt* and black pepper

2 tbsp extra-virgin olive oil

1 large garlic clove,* minced

1/4 tsp dried red pepper flakes

8 cherry tomatoes, halved

1 tbsp roughly chopped parsley

**EASY SHRIMP BROTH**

1 tbsp extra-virgin olive oil

1 garlic clove, roughly chopped

1 shallot* or 1/2 yellow onion, roughly chopped

2 anchovies[2]

1 bay leaf*

Reserved shrimp heads and shells (see above)

1/2 cup chardonnay wine*[3]

1 1/2 cups low-sodium chicken broth*

1/2 tsp kosher salt*

*Shrimp broth*—Heat the olive oil in a medium saucepan over medium–high heat. Cook the garlic, shallot, anchovies, and bay leaf for 3 minutes, mashing up the anchovies with a wooden spoon. Add the shrimp heads and shells, then cook, stirring, for 4 minutes.

*Reduce broth*—Add the wine, turn the heat up to high, then simmer for 2 minutes until mostly evaporated. Add the broth and salt, bring to a boil, then turn the heat down and simmer gently on low for 25 minutes. Crush the shrimp heads twice with a potato masher to extract their flavor as the broth cooks. Strain the broth through a fine-mesh strainer into a bowl, pressing all the juice out of the shrimp shells. Discard the solids. You should have around 1 1/4 cups of broth. Don't worry if you have a bit more or less, it will self-correct later!

*Cook linguine*[4]—Bring 10 cups of water to a boil in a large saucepan and cook the linguine according to the package directions minus 1 minute. (Start cooking the shrimp once the pasta is in the water.) Stir the pasta regularly to ensure it doesn't stick together. Just before draining, scoop out a mugful of pasta cooking water (reserve), then drain the pasta.

*Cook shrimp*—Toss the shrimp with salt and pepper. Heat 1 tablespoon of oil in a large nonstick skillet over medium heat. Cook the shrimp for 1 1/2 minutes on each side until just cooked, then transfer to a plate.

*Pasta sauce*—Heat the remaining 1 tablespoon of oil in the same pan. Cook the garlic and red pepper flakes for 15 seconds until the garlic is golden. Add the shrimp broth, then turn the heat up to high[5]. Simmer rapidly for 2–3 minutes, stirring to scrape the base of the pan, until the liquid reduces down to about 1/2 cup. (You can pause at this point if the pasta is not yet cooked.)

*Toss with pasta*—Add 1/3 cup of the pasta cooking water, the cooked pasta and cherry tomatoes. Still over high heat, toss for 1–2 minutes using two wooden spoons until the sauce thickens and coats the pasta rather than pooling at the bottom of the pan[6].

*Serve*—Working quickly, toss the shrimp and parsley through the pasta. Divide between bowls and serve, stat! I like to serve with butter lettuce drizzled with Mediterranean Dressing (page 333).

*See Notes on page 174.*

## NOTES

1. Sadly, pre-peeled shrimp can't be used because the sauce flavor comes from the shrimp broth made using the shells.
2. Anchovies are a secret ingredient for a boost of seafood flavor in the sauce!
3. Or any dry white wine, or nonalcoholic white wine.
4. This recipe specifically calls for the pasta to be cooked in as little water as possible for a higher concentration of starch in the cooking water, which is necessary to thicken the sauce.
5. It will look like a lot of liquid in the pan at first. Have faith! Once you start tossing the pasta, the sauce magically reduces and thickens!
6. If the pasta gets too thick and gluggy instead of being smooth and slick with sauce, just add a slosh of the reserved pasta cooking water and keep tossing!
7. If you double the recipe, reduce the double batch of shrimp broth down to 1¾ cups.

LEFTOVERS Fridge 3 days, though pastas are always best freshly made! Not suitable for freezing.

# MAC & CHEESE

*When you want the best, this is the one you make.*

**SERVES: 4–5 AS A MAIN, 6–8 AS A SIDE I PREP: 15 MINUTES I COOK: 40 MINUTES**

If, like me, you love your mac and cheese oozing irresistibly with stringy cheese and creamy sauce, you're looking at the right page. This has been one of the most popular recipes on my website for years. I've even had restaurants asking permission to use the recipe! I hope you try it at least once. If you can, use gruyere. It's the best cheese for the job, both for flavor and melting qualities (take it from this self-confessed cheese addict!).

---

1 tbsp kosher salt*

8 oz macaroni (elbow pasta)

1 tbsp unsalted butter (or 2 tsp extra-virgin olive oil)

Pinch of finely chopped parsley (optional)

**TOPPING**

2/3 cup panko bread crumbs*

2 tbsp unsalted butter, melted

1/4 tsp kosher salt*

**SEASONINGS**

1 tsp garlic powder

1/2 tsp onion powder

1/2 tsp mustard powder

3/4 tsp kosher salt*

**CHEESE SAUCE**

4 tbsp unsalted butter

1/3 cup all-purpose flour

3 cups whole milk, hot (I microwave it)

2 cups (7 oz) shredded* gruyere[1]

1 cup (4 oz) shredded* mozzarella[1]

*Cook pasta*—Bring 12 cups of water to a boil in a pot with the salt. Add the macaroni and cook as per the package directions minus 1 minute. Drain, return the pasta to the pot, add the butter and toss until melted. Set aside to cool while making the topping and cheese sauce.

*Topping*—Mix the topping ingredients together in a small bowl, then set aside.

Preheat the oven to 400°F.

*Seasonings*—Mix the seasoning ingredients together in a small bowl.

*Cheese sauce*—Melt the butter in a 10 inch ovenproof cast-iron pan[2] over medium heat. Add the flour and stir for 1 minute—it will become a paste. Switch to a whisk. While whisking, slowly pour in about 1 cup of the milk and whisk to dissolve the paste into the milk. Add the remaining milk and whisk until lump-free. Whisk in the seasonings.

Keep cooking the sauce, stirring regularly with a wooden spoon, for 5–8 minutes until thickened to a cream consistency. You should be able to draw a path with your finger when the sauce coats the back of the wooden spoon.

Add both cheeses and stir until melted. The sauce will become thicker. Adjust the salt to taste (if you use the recommended cheeses, you won't need more).

*Assemble*—Pour the sauce into the pot with the cooled macaroni. Stir quickly, then pour back into the pan used for the sauce (I do this) or a 2½ quart baking dish. Sprinkle with the topping. Bake for 25 minutes or until the top is light golden.

*Serve*—If you want to be posh, sprinkle with a little parsley and serve with leafy greens tossed in Italian Dressing (page 333).

**NOTES**

1. Your mac and cheese is only as good as the cheese you use! The combination of gruyere plus mozzarella yields the most superior, luscious, creamy, cheesy sauce (in my humble cheese-loving opinion). I would not recommend substituting the mozzarella as its melting qualities are excellent in creamy sauces. However, the gruyere can be substituted with cheddar, Swiss, colby, monterey jack, or other flavorful cheese that melts well.
2. If you don't have an ovenproof pan, just use a regular pot to cook the sauce and transfer the macaroni mixture to a baking dish before putting it in the oven.
3. Make ahead: Assemble the dish (including the topping) in a glass or ceramic dish, then let it cool completely. Cover tightly with plastic wrap, then refrigerate for up to 4 days, or freeze for up to 3 months. Thaw, then bake, covered with aluminum foil, for 15 minutes at 400°F, then uncovered for 25 minutes.

LEFTOVERS Fridge 4 days, freezer 3 months, though best made fresh for optimum molten cheesy goodness!

# CHICKEN FRICASSEE

*Chicken stew, the French way. The gravy is CREAMY!*

**SERVES: 4 I PREP: 15 MINUTES I COOK: 50 MINUTES**

If I could bottle the sauce in this country-style French stew, I would! This is a dish taught to me by the super talented Chef Jean-Baptiste Alexandre. He was born, raised, and trained in France, and now resides right here in my hometown of Sydney. So it goes without saying this recipe is *par excellence*! Creamy, silky, and rich with the flavors of chicken, herbs, and wine, you'll be mopping your plate clean with bread. While this is terrific made with store-bought broth, if you can manage homemade, I highly recommend it as it will catapult this dish into wow territory!

---

4 x 8 oz skin-on, bone-in chicken thighs[1]

4 x 5 oz chicken drumsticks[1]

1 tsp kosher salt*

½ tsp black pepper

4 tbsp unsalted butter

**CREAMY MUSHROOM SAUCE**

10 oz small-ish white button mushrooms, halved

2 yellow onions, halved, then sliced ¼ inch thick

1 fresh bay leaf* (or 1 dried bay leaf)

3 thyme sprigs (or ½ tsp dried thyme)

2 garlic cloves,* finely minced

3 tbsp all-purpose flour

½ cup chardonnay wine*[2]

3 cups low-sodium chicken broth*

¼ tsp kosher salt*

¼ tsp black pepper

⅔ cup heavy cream*

2 tbsp roughly chopped parsley (optional)

*Brown chicken*—Pat the chicken dry with paper towels and sprinkle all over with salt and pepper. Melt the butter over medium–high heat in a very large, deep skillet[3] (or similar) with a lid. Add the chicken thighs, skin-side down, and cook for 4–5 minutes until the skin is golden brown. Turn and cook the other side for 1 minute. Transfer to a plate. Add the drumsticks to the pan and brown them as best you can. I do three sides, about 2 minutes each. Transfer from the skillet to the plate with the thighs.

*Creamy mushroom sauce*—Add the mushrooms, onion, bay leaf, and thyme to the pan. Cook for 5 minutes until the mushrooms are lightly golden. Add the garlic and stir for 30 seconds. Add the flour and cook for 1 minute. Add the wine, chicken broth, salt, and pepper and stir, scraping the base of the pot to dissolve the brown residue stuck to the pan (the "fond") into the sauce.

*Simmer covered*—Return the chicken, skin-side up, to the pan with the sauce. Once the sauce comes to a simmer, adjust the heat so it's bubbling gently (not rapidly) but constantly. This is medium–low on my stove. Cover with a lid and simmer for 10 minutes.

*Simmer uncovered*—Remove the lid and let the fricassee simmer for a further 20 minutes. The chicken will be cooked when the meat's internal temperature is 165°F or slightly higher.

*Finish sauce*—Transfer the chicken to a plate, leaving the sauce in the pan. Add the cream to the sauce and stir. Once the sauce comes back up to a simmer, taste it and add more salt if desired.

*Serve*—Return the chicken to the sauce, then remove the pan from the stove. Sprinkle with parsley (if using) and serve! Traditionally, fricassee is served over Creamy Mashed Potato (page 338) or White Rice (page 335). It's also ideal with short pasta like penne, ziti, or macaroni. For a side dish, steamed vegetables, or leafy greens drizzled with French Dressing (page 333) would be a lovely accompaniment.

**NOTES**

1. The chicken needs to be skin-on, bone-in thigh and leg pieces so they don't overcook and dry out. If you are dead set on making this with boneless breast, brown it as per the recipe, then simmer the sauce with the lid off for 15 minutes (to reduce), then add the breast and simmer with the lid on for 6 minutes or until the internal temperature reaches 155°F. For boneless thigh, do the same except the internal temperature should be 160°F.
2. Any dry white wine will work here, though chardonnay is my preference because it adds good flavor. For a nonalcoholic substitute, replace with more chicken broth.
3. A large pot also works. The shallow casserole pot I use is 12 inches wide and 2½ inches deep (3½ quarts). No lid? Just use aluminum foil.

LEFTOVERS Fridge 4 days, freezer 3 months.

# MEAL-WORTHY SALADS

All Asian. Because they're the best!

# THE BANGKOK—SATAY CHICKEN NOODLE SALAD

*The satay dressing is everything!*

**SERVES: 2 AS A MAIN | PREP: 20 MINUTES | COOK: 10 MINUTES**

This salad is heavily inspired by a dish from a popular Asian salad bar in my neighborhood. They shall remain nameless but everybody in my area knows exactly the place I'm talking about! The pineapple and bean sprouts are two killer additions that keep things interesting, and the satay dressing is impossibly good. However, I cut down on the sugar in my dressing and dial up the satay flavor—both good things in my opinion. Another benefit of making this at home? It's about 75 percent cheaper than to buy!

---

**SATAY DRESSING**

1 tbsp canola oil

1 small garlic clove,* finely grated

1 tbsp red curry paste*

1/4 cup natural unsweetened peanut butter,* smooth

1/2 cup full-fat coconut milk*

1/2 cup low-sodium chicken broth*

1 tbsp apple cider vinegar

4 tsp sugar

1 tsp fish sauce

1/4 tsp dark soy sauce*[1] (optional)

1/4 tsp kosher salt*

1/4 cup water

**SALAD**

3 heaped cups baby spinach leaves

1 cup fresh pineapple pieces, 1/2 inch x 1 1/4 inches

1/2 cup bean sprouts

1 green onion,* finely sliced diagonally

3 baby cucumbers,*[2] finely sliced diagonally

1 x 6 oz poached chicken breast (page 130), sliced 1/4 inch thick diagonally

1/3 cup roasted salted peanuts, finely chopped

Lime wedges, to serve

**NOODLES**

5 oz white fresh wheat noodles[3] (about 1/8 inch wide)

1/2 tsp sesame oil*

1/2 tsp light soy sauce*

*Satay dressing*—Heat the oil in a small saucepan over low heat. Cook the garlic and curry paste for 2 minutes until fragrant. Whisk in the remaining ingredients, then simmer very gently for 10 minutes on low until it reduces to a maple syrup consistency (thinner than honey, thicker than water).[4]

Pour the dressing into a measuring jar—you should have around 1 cup. Cover with plastic wrap and allow to cool to lukewarm. It will thicken into a honey consistency.[4]

*Noodles*—Cook the noodles following the package directions. Drain, rinse under cold water and shake well to remove excess water. Leave to drain for a few minutes, then drizzle with sesame oil and soy sauce and toss. Set aside for at least 20 minutes to cool to room temperature.

*Salad*—Put the baby spinach, pineapple, bean sprouts, green onion, and cucumber in a large bowl and toss to mix them up. Divide the salad between two bowls. Place the noodles on one side, then top with the sliced chicken. Spoon 1/3 cup of the dressing over the salad and sprinkle 1 tablespoon of peanuts over each bowl.

*Serve*—To eat, jumble it all up yourself so the dressing gets mixed in with everything, serve with the lime wedges, and devour! I like to serve the leftover dressing on the side, for spooning extra on the chicken pieces.

**NOTES**

1. Optional as it's mainly to slightly darken the sauce color.
2. Small cucumbers around 4 inches long. Substitute with 1 cucumber.*
3. Or other noodles of choice—fresh, dried, yellow, white, thick, thin, flat, round! Vermicelli and soba noodles would also work well.
4. If the dressing is too thick, add a dash of water and simmer to bring together until your desired thickness is achieved. If too thin, keep simmering.
5. Make ahead: All the separate components can be prepared the day before.

LEFTOVERS Leftover satay dressing can be frozen for 3 months. Excellent over rice (pages 334–37) and steamed vegetables!

# ISLAND BLISS—SHRIMP SALAD WITH COCONUT LIME DRESSING

*As unique as it is addictive. Summer food perfection!*

 **SERVES: 4 AS A STARTER, 2 AS A MAIN | PREP: 20 MINUTES + 1 HOUR REFRIGERATION | COOK: NONE**

This is a stellar combination of super fresh flavors and great textures combined with the silky richness of the lime coconut dressing. The combination of plump shrimp with sweet apple, crunchy cabbage, and vibrant herbs is unbeatable! I've also got a great tip for thickening the tangy lime coconut dressing so it clings to every vegetable (spoiler: chill in fridge!). Make this one for hot summer days or as a fantastic starter for Asian-themed menus.

---

1 green apple

¼ tsp lime juice

2½ tightly packed cups finely shredded baby napa cabbage*[1]

2 green onions,* finely sliced on the diagonal

5 oz (about 12) peeled and cooked shrimp,*[2] halved horizontally

¼ cup finely sliced mint

¼ cup roughly chopped cilantro, plus extra to serve

**COCONUT LIME DRESSING**[3]

7½ tbsp full-fat coconut cream*

1¼ tsp lime zest

1½ tbsp lime juice

3½ tsp fish sauce

2¼ tsp superfine sugar

¾ tsp finely grated ginger*

½ tsp finely grated garlic*

*Dressing*—Measure out the coconut cream into a jar and refrigerate for 1 hour to thicken.[4] Do not leave for hours as it will get too thick!

Add the remaining dressing ingredients and whisk to combine. Set aside for 10 minutes to let the flavors meld.

*Slice apple*—Slice the apple into thin batons—you need ½ cup in total. (Cut the apple just before serving and toss with the lime juice.)

*Make salad*—Place the cabbage, apple, and green onion in a bowl. Drizzle with three-fourths of the dressing and toss gently. Add the shrimp, mint, and cilantro and toss gently again.

*Serve*—Pile the salad high into serving bowls and drizzle with the remaining dressing. Sprinkle with extra cilantro and serve immediately!

**NOTES**

1. Baby napa is the small, young version of standard napa cabbage. The leaves are slightly more tender, which works well in this salad. If you can't find it, ordinary napa cabbage is fine.
2. I use store-bought whole cooked shrimp. These are naturally seasoned, so you don't need to salt them. See page 361 for how to peel shrimp. You can also cook your own raw shrimp: Toss the shrimp in 2 teaspoons of oil and ⅛ teaspoon of salt. Cook in a nonstick skillet over medium–high heat for 1–1½ minutes on each side (depending on their size). Remove, cool, then use as per the recipe.
3. The dressing is best made fresh to preserve the lime flavor. Salad components can be prepared ahead (except the apple, which is always best cut fresh) but keep them separate.
4. Refrigerating the coconut cream thickens it so the dressing is nice and creamy, rather than runny.

LEFTOVERS Once dressed, serve immediately. Leftover salad does not keep well.

# THE RAINBOW—QUINOA SALAD WITH GINGER DRESSING

*Still my very best quinoa salad.*

**SERVES: 4–5 AS A MAIN, 8–10 AS A SIDE | PREP: 20 MINUTES | COOK: 35 MINUTES**

I'm not going to lie: I never got into quinoa. Maybe I just like rice so much better (the Japanese blood in my Aussie veins). Maybe it's because it gets stuck in my teeth. Or maybe I just don't care for nutrition fads. Quinoa in *this* salad, though, I can definitely get into. The nutty grains are just perfect in this riot of fresh and crunchy vegetable textures! Don't skip the wasabi peas. They're the cherry—err, peas—on top!

1 x 6 inch cucumber,* cut into 1/4 inch cubes

1 carrot, peeled and finely julienned[1]

3 lightly packed cups finely shredded red cabbage[2]

2 green onions,* finely sliced

1/2 lb cherry tomatoes, small ones quartered, large ones cut into 6

1 cup frozen shelled edamame,[3] cooked as per package directions, then cooled

1 red bell pepper, deseeded and chopped into 1/4 inch cubes

1/2 lightly packed cup finely chopped cilantro

**QUINOA**

1 cup tricolor or white quinoa

2 cups water

**DRESSING**

5 tbsp light soy sauce*[4]

2 tbsp mirin*

2 tbsp rice wine vinegar[5]

2 tbsp sesame oil*

2 1/2 tbsp grapeseed oil

2 1/2 tbsp Kewpie mayonnaise*[6]

2 1/2 tsp sugar

2 tsp finely grated ginger*

1/2 tsp finely grated garlic*

**TO SERVE**

1/3 cup wasabi peas[7]

1 tbsp toasted white sesame seeds*

*Toast quinoa (gives it extra flavor!)*—Preheat the oven to 400°F. Spread the quinoa on a large baking tray and bake for 15 minutes, stirring halfway through cooking, until it's lightly browned and smells nutty. Rinse under running water for 10 seconds using a fine-mesh strainer and shake off the excess water well.

*Cook quinoa*—Place the quinoa in a medium saucepan, add the water, and cover with a lid. Bring to a simmer over medium heat, then reduce the heat to low and simmer for 15 minutes (or until all the water is absorbed). Remove from the stove (lid still on) and rest for 10 minutes. Fluff the quinoa with a fork and allow to fully cool before using.

*Dressing*—Place all the dressing ingredients in a jar and shake well to combine.

*Crush wasabi peas (it's fun!)*—Bundle the wasabi peas up in a clean dish towel and bash using a meat tenderizer or rolling pin to crush them into irregular sizes—some larger pieces, some will end up like dust. (Mortar and pestle also works well.)

*Assemble*—Place the cooled quinoa in a large bowl. Add the remaining salad ingredients, then pour the dressing over and toss very well.

*Serve*—Transfer the salad to a large serving platter or individual bowls. Sprinkle generously with the crushed wasabi peas and sesame seeds. Eat!

**NOTES**

1. I use a julienne shredder. A standard box grater will work fine as an alternative—otherwise, sharpen your knives and get chopping!
2. About one-fourth of a small, or one-eighth of a large, cabbage. Green cabbage is fine too.
3. Fresh young soybeans, easily found these days in the freezer section of grocery stores alongside peas!
4. Can be substituted with all-purpose soy sauce, but not dark or sweet soy sauce.
5. Substitute with apple cider vinegar, sherry vinegar, or champagne vinegar.
6. Substitute with whole egg mayonnaise.* For a no-mayo version, use more oil (same quantity).
7. Crispy/sweet/salty/spicy! Common these days in the Asian snack section of grocery stores.

LEFTOVERS Keeps pretty well until the next day! Toss well and serve at room temperature. If intentionally making ahead, keep the dressing separate.

# THAI BEEF SALAD

*The perfect way to serve beef as a healthy meal without being boring!*

 **SERVES: 2 AS A MAIN | PREP: 20 MINUTES | COOK: 5 MINUTES**

I've always been madly in love with Thai beef salad, a fixture at Thai restaurants all over Australia. With rosy-pink slices of beef, pops of sweet cherry tomato, and a zesty, fiery dressing, this salad epitomizes all that is great about Asian salads–big, bold flavors yet light and fresh. The trick is getting the perfect balance in the dressing. I've played with it a lot over the years and think I've nailed it. An extra tip is to chop all those peanuts really well, so you get a bit of peanut "dust." Trust me, this really cranks it up a notch!

---

9 oz sirloin beef[1] (3/4 inch thick)

1/4 tsp kosher salt*

1/4 tsp black pepper

1 tbsp canola oil

**DRESSING**

1/2 tsp red bird's eye chili,*[2] deseeded and finely minced

1/4 tsp finely minced garlic*

1 tbsp finely chopped cilantro stems

Small pinch of kosher salt*

1 tbsp grapeseed oil

2 1/4 tsp sugar

3 tbsp lime juice

2 tbsp fish sauce

**SALAD**

2 heaped cups mixed baby leafy greens[3]

10 cherry tomatoes, halved

1/4 small red onion, very finely sliced

1/2 x 6 inch cucumber,* sliced into 1/4 inch thick half moons

1/4 cup lightly packed cilantro

1/4 cup lightly packed mint leaves

**GARNISHES**

1/4 cup finely chopped roasted, unsalted peanuts[4]

Extra cilantro and mint leaves (optional)

*Cook beef*–Remove the beef from the fridge 30 minutes before cooking. Just before cooking, pat it dry with paper towels and sprinkle both sides with the salt and pepper. Heat the oil in a cast-iron skillet over high heat until screaming hot. It should be smoking! Cook the beef, done to your liking. For a 3/4 inch thick steak, it will take 2 minutes on the first side, then 1 1/2 minutes on the second side for medium-rare (target internal temperature 125°F, see page 351 for the Internal Cooked Temperatures chart).

*Rest*–Transfer the beef to a rack set over a tray. Cool (uncovered) for 20 minutes to room temperature.

*Dressing*–Put the chili, garlic, cilantro stems, and salt into a mortar and pestle[5] then grind until it becomes a smooth paste. Mix in remaining dressing ingredients. Taste, then adjust with extra sugar, lime juice, or fish sauce as desired.

*Slice beef*–Cut the beef by finely slicing it against the grain[6] and place in a bowl. Drizzle over 1 tablespoon of the dressing and gently toss to coat.

*Make salad*–Place all the salad ingredients in a separate large bowl. Add one-fourth of the peanuts and toss with 2 tablespoons of dressing.

*Serve*–Divide the salad between two plates and top with the sliced beef. Sprinkle generously with most of the remaining peanuts, then drizzle each plate with 1 tablespoon of dressing. Sprinkle over the remaining peanuts, garnish with extra cilantro and mint leaves (if using), and serve immediately!

**NOTES**

1. Use any beef suitable for serving as a steak. Boneless rib-eye, porterhouse, flank, or flat iron.
2. This amount of chili makes it a bit spicy, but not blow-your-head-off. Adjust to your taste.
3. See Note 2 on page 191. Substitute with baby spinach, or a 50/50 mix of baby spinach and arugula.
4. Peanuts are traditional but can be substituted with cashews.
5. No mortar and pestle? Make the paste by finely chopping the ingredients, then smearing them against the chopping board with the side of a knife. Scrape into a jar and shake with the remaining ingredients.
6. See Cutting beef against the grain in the Glossary (page 358).

LEFTOVERS You dress it, you eat it! This salad really needs to be served straight away as the dressing wilts the salad leaves.

# THE KYOTO—CHICKEN SOBA SALAD WITH CREAMY SESAME DRESSING

*That creamy sweet soy sesame dressing is everything!!!*

**SERVES: 4 AS A MAIN | PREP: 20 MINUTES | COOK: 20 MINUTES**

Another copycat of a salad from the popular neighborhood salad bar I mentioned on page 183 (shh! No names, I'll get in trouble!). This Japanese-inspired salad has crisp vegetables that provide crunch while cool soba noodles and juicy poached chicken bring the bulk.

The insanely addictive, creamy sesame and soy dressing is based on a style of dressing popular in Japan. Though you can buy similar in bottles, freshly made is far superior with real sesame flavor unlike any you've had before!

---

4 oz soba noodles,[1] green tea if you can find them (optional)

2 x 7 oz poached chicken breasts (see page 130), cooled to room temperature

4 heaped lightly packed cups mixed leafy baby greens[2]

2½ lightly packed cups finely sliced napa cabbage*

¼ red onion, very finely sliced

1 x 6 inch cucumber,* halved lengthwise and finely sliced diagonally

1 large avocado, halved and cut into ½ x 1 inch chunks

½ lb cherry tomatoes, halved

¾ lightly packed cup mint leaves

¾ lightly packed cup cilantro

1 tsp black sesame seeds (or more white)

**DRESSING**

¼ cup toasted white sesame seeds*

¼ cup Kewpie mayonnaise*

¼ cup grapeseed oil

2 tbsp light soy sauce*

1½ tbsp rice vinegar

2¾ tsp mirin*

4 tsp honey

¾ tsp sesame oil*

⅛ tsp white pepper

*Dressing*—Place the toasted sesame seeds in a mortar and pestle.[3] Grind into a fine powder, then tip into a jar. Add the remaining dressing ingredients and shake well to form a creamy dressing.

*Noodles*—Cook the soba noodles by following the package directions. Drain, rinse briefly with tap water, then leave to dry and cool to room temperature. Transfer to a bowl.

Slice the chicken on an angle into ¼ inch thick slices, then place in a separate bowl.

*Make salad*—Place all the salad ingredients in a third (large!) bowl with ½ teaspoon of the black sesame seeds. Drizzle with half the dressing, then toss. Drizzle the remaining dressing over the chicken and soba noodles and toss to coat.

*Serve*—Divide the salad among four serving bowls. Place a pile of soba noodles to one side. Top with chicken, then sprinkle with remaining black sesame seeds. Enjoy!

**NOTES**

1. Use green tea–infused soba noodles rather than the standard beige ones, if you can find them. They don't taste any different but look nice!
2. Mixed baby greens or a store-bought mix of small leafy greens. Substitute with baby spinach, a 50/50 mix of baby spinach and arugula, finely sliced romaine, or iceberg lettuce. More napa cabbage would also work, or substitute with more leafy greens.
3. Alternatively, just blitz together until smooth using a Nutribullet or immersion blender.
4. Make ahead: Cut/prepare all the components (other than the avocado) the day before, then assemble when desired.

LEFTOVERS Best eaten fresh once dressed!

# DEVOUR—MAPLE SWEET POTATO SALAD WITH TAMARIND DRESSING

*Put this in your Show-Off Salads folder!*

 **SERVES: 2 AS A MAIN | PREP: 20 MINUTES | COOK: 35 MINUTES**

This salad takes a bit more effort than ripping open a bag of leaves, but it's absolutely worth it! Tamarind puree and maple syrup in the dressing seem like an unlikely team but work incredibly well, giving the salad an unusual sweet and bright flavor. I love to cook the sweet potatoes so they develop lovely caramelized edges. Marinating the kale is my other trick, which tenderizes and seasons these robust leaves. The crowning glory is a hefty shower of toasted pumpkin seeds and crunchy wild rice (yes, I need you to do a 10-second mini deep-fry). It's a celebration of flavors and textures dialed up to 11!

---

2 tightly packed cups kale leaves,* cut into 1¼ inch pieces

12 cherry tomatoes, halved

¼ red onion, very finely sliced

2 tbsp pumpkin seeds, toasted[1]

**MAPLE-ROASTED SWEET POTATO**

14 oz sweet potato, skin on, cut into 1 inch cubes

1 tbsp extra-virgin olive oil

¼ tsp kosher salt*

⅛ tsp black pepper

2 tsp maple syrup

**TAMARIND DRESSING**

1½ tbsp tamarind puree*

2 tbsp grapeseed oil

3 tbsp maple syrup

2 tsp light soy sauce*

¼ tsp finely grated garlic*

¼ tsp kosher salt*

⅛ tsp white pepper (or use black)

1½ tbsp Kewpie mayonnaise*[2]

**CRISPY WILD RICE**

1 cup canola oil

2 tbsp wild rice[3]

Pinch of kosher salt*

*Maple-roasted sweet potato*—Preheat the oven to 425°F. Toss the sweet potato with olive oil, salt, and pepper. Spread on a baking tray lined with parchment paper and roast for 20 minutes. Remove from the oven, push the potato together on the tray, drizzle with maple syrup, then briefly toss. Spread out again on the tray and roast for 10 minutes. Flip the sweet potatoes, then roast for a final 5 minutes until golden. Remove from the oven and allow to cool to room temperature on the tray (20 minutes).

*Tamarind dressing*—Place all the dressing ingredients in a jar and shake well until combined.

*Marinate kale*—Tenderize the leaves and season the kale by placing it in a large bowl with 1 tablespoon of the dressing. Scrunch firmly with your hands for 20 seconds (don't hold back here!), then set aside for 20 minutes. This will soften and flavor the kale.

*Crispy wild rice*—Heat the canola oil to 410°F[4] in a small saucepan. Add the rice and cook for 10 seconds—it will pop, puff, and the white insides will be exposed. Scoop out and place onto a paper towel–lined plate and immediately sprinkle with salt. You will end up with about ⅔ cup crispy rice—it expands a lot!

*Make salad*—Place the kale, roasted sweet potato, cherry tomato, and red onion in a bowl. Toss with about three-fourths of the dressing.

*Serve*—Transfer the salad to a large serving bowl or plate. Drizzle over the remaining dressing and sprinkle with the crispy rice and pumpkin seeds. Serve!

**NOTES**

1. Or almond flakes or sunflower seeds. Toast the pumpkin seeds in a small skillet over medium heat for 2 minutes until lightly golden on each side.
2. Just a bit of mayonnaise really improves this dressing by adding a luxurious mouthfeel. However, to omit, add 1 tablespoon extra grapeseed oil plus ¼ teaspoon sugar.
3. Wild rice has a beautiful nutty flavor. Find it at independent grocery stores and some large grocery stores (rice or health-food aisle). The recipe won't work with other rice (I tried). Substitute with store-bought plain puffed rice (sprinkle with a pinch of salt) or ¼ cup store-bought crispy fried shallots.*
4. See Oil temperature testing in the Glossary (page 361) for directions.

LEFTOVERS Fridge 2 days, though it's best made fresh.

# MS. SAIGON—VIETNAMESE CHICKEN SALAD

*You will make this over and over (and over) again.*

 **SERVES: 3–4 AS A MAIN | PREP: 20 MINUTES | COOK: NONE**

Another hit from my website, think of this a bit like a loaded Vietnamese-style slaw. It's big, fresh, and colorful with a zesty lime dressing based on nuoc cham, the sauce that's used for "everything"' in Vietnam. I like using napa rather than regular cabbage as it gives the slaw a juicy crunch. I also cut the chicken into thin batons because I find this shape jumbles nicely with the other ingredients. Use plenty of herbs (you can't have too much!) and dial the chili right up to where you like it. You will love this salad, I promise!

---

2 x 7 oz poached chicken breasts (see page 130), cooled to room temperature

6 lightly packed cups finely shredded napa cabbage*

½ red onion, very finely sliced (so it's floppy)

1 red bell pepper, deseeded and finely sliced into thin batons

2 x 6 inch cucumbers,* halved lengthwise, seeds scraped out, then finely sliced into half moons

1 large carrot, peeled, then julienned[1]

1 long red chili pepper,* deseeded, then julienned (optional)[2]

1 tightly packed cup mint leaves[3]

1 tightly packed cup cilantro

⅓ cup finely chopped roasted unsalted peanuts[4]

**DRESSING**

2 tbsp lime juice

2 tbsp rice vinegar

¼ cup fish sauce[5]

¼ cup grapeseed oil

1 tbsp sugar

¾ tsp finely grated garlic* (about 1 clove)

2 tsp deseeded and very finely minced red bird's eye chili*[6]

*Dressing*—Put the ingredients in a jar, shake, then set aside for 10 minutes to let the flavors meld.

*Cut chicken*—Slice the chicken diagonally into ¼ inch thick slices, then cut into ¼ inch thick batons.

*Make salad*—Place the remaining salad ingredients, except the peanuts, in a large bowl. Pour over half the dressing and toss well to coat. Set aside for 5 minutes so the vegetables soften slightly, making it more "slaw-like."

*Toss*—Just before serving, add most of the remaining dressing, then toss the salad again. Taste and add more dressing if you want.

*Serve*—Sprinkle with ALL the peanuts! It's part of what makes this salad so great.

**NOTES**

1. I use a julienne shredder. A standard box grater will work fine as an alternative. Otherwise, sharpen your knives and get to work!
2. Long chili peppers are not very spicy but can be omitted if you are concerned.
3. Tear large/giant mint leaves (as they sometimes are!) by hand into smaller pieces.
4. Finely chop the peanuts so you get some "dust." It makes them extra good! Peanut alternative—cashews are best, though sunflower seeds or pumpkin seeds would be lovely too.
5. It won't be quite the same but can be substituted with light soy sauce,* if you must! Or "vegetarian fish sauce," if you can find it.
6. This amount of chili gives this salad a warm tickle—it's not that spicy. It gets dispersed among a lot of other "stuff"! If you're concerned, reduce or leave it out.
7. Make ahead: Prepare the ingredients and assemble when required.

LEFTOVERS Best served fresh because the cabbage continues to wilt and leach water, which dilutes the flavor.

# MEXICAN FOOD

Simple. Unpretentious. Big flavors. That's why I love it!

# CHICKEN TINGA TACOS

*Quick, easy, for any night of the week.*

 **SERVES: 5–6 (MAKES 20 TACOS) I PREP: 15 MINUTES I COOK: 1 HOUR 15 MINUTES**

Chicken tinga is a classic homestyle dish from Puebla of shredded chicken in a flavorsome tomato and chipotle sauce. It's found all across Mexico, its popularity no doubt partly because it's simple to prepare yet tastes surprisingly complex and full-flavored—my kind of food! It's a classic taco filling, but is great in, or on, just about anything, from burritos to enchiladas to tortas (sandwiches).

---

2 tbsp extra-virgin olive oil

3 garlic cloves,* finely minced

1 yellow onion, finely chopped

2½ tsp dried oregano

1 cup low-sodium chicken broth*

⅓ cup chipotle in adobo,*[1]
1 tbsp sauce + whole chipotle chilies from the jar, finely chopped

28 oz can crushed tomatoes

1 tsp ground cumin

1½ tsp kosher salt*

1½ lb boneless, skinless chicken thighs[2]

**TO SERVE**

20 x 6 inch small tortillas,* warmed (page 225)

½ cup cilantro, roughly chopped

Guacamole (page 220)

Plain sour cream, or Lime Crema (page 219) (optional)

*Cook aromatics*—Heat the oil in a large pot over high heat. Add the garlic, onion, and oregano, then cook for 3 minutes until the onion is tinged with gold on the edges.

*Slow-cook chicken*—Add all the remaining ingredients, except the chicken. Stir to combine. Add the chicken (in a single layer), pushing down to submerge it in the sauce. Bring to a boil, then reduce the heat to low so it's simmering very gently. Cook for 1 hour, uncovered. Stir every now and then toward the end of cooking time so the base doesn't catch, until the chicken is tender and easy to shred.

*Shred and toss*—Transfer the chicken from the sauce to a large rectangular pan. Shred the chicken quite finely using two forks. Meanwhile, keep the sauce simmering on low for a further 10 minutes until it becomes quite thick. Return the shredded chicken to the sauce and toss to coat well.

*Serve*—Transfer the tinga to a serving bowl. Stuff into warmed tortillas to make tacos! In Mexico, chicken tinga tacos are typically served with just basic toppings such as a sprinkling of cilantro. But I can't resist adding a dollop of guacamole and drizzle of sour cream or Lime Crema. See the Essential Sauces & Sides section on pages 218–25 for more topping options. Mix 'n' match as you please!

**NOTES**

1. For gluten-free, ensure the chipotle in adobo is gluten-free (not all brands are). I'd ordinarily offer a substitution for the chipotle in adobo but it's the main flavor for the sauce in this dish so I can't!
2. Most chicken tinga recipes use a shortcut with store-bought roast chicken or poach the chicken separately. I prefer to cook the chicken in the sauce to capture the meat juices for extra flavor. Chicken thighs work best because they stay juicier and are more tender. To use breast, cook for 10 minutes in the sauce, flip, then cook for a further 5 minutes. Remove the chicken, then cook the sauce for a further 20 minutes to thicken. Shred the chicken and toss in the sauce.

LEFTOVERS Fridge 4 days, freezer 3 months.

# CHIPOTLE SALMON TACOS

*I saved this one especially for the cookbook!*

**SERVES: 4 (MAKES 12 TACOS) I PREP: 25 MINUTES + 20 MINUTES (OR UP TO 2 HOURS) MARINATING I COOK: 5 MINUTES**

No, this isn't authentic but everything in these salmon tacos just works so well that it still rates as one of the best tacos I've invented in recent years! The salmon marinade is a little bit spicy, a little bit smoky, and so good with the oily salmon. Having both lime slaw and Mango Avocado Salsa for the toppings requires a bit of added effort, but the refreshing effect they bring is unbeatable. I promise they're worth the work! However if you're pressed for time, suggestions for simpler alternatives are in the notes.

---

1¼ lb skinless salmon fillets, cut lengthwise into ½ inch thick slices[1]

1 tbsp extra-virgin olive oil

**CHIPOTLE MARINADE**

½ tsp each paprika, ground coriander, and onion powder

1 tsp ground cumin

1½ tsp chipotle powder*

1½ tsp kosher salt*

1 tbsp lime juice

1 tbsp extra-virgin olive oil

**TO SERVE**

12 x 6 inch small tortillas,* warmed (page 225)

1 quantity Taco Slaw (page 222)

1 quantity Mango Avocado Salsa (page 222)

3 limes, cut into wedges

*Marinate salmon*—Mix the chipotle marinade ingredients in a zip-top bag.*[2] Add the salmon, seal the bag, and massage to coat the salmon in the marinade. Leave on the counter for 20 minutes.[3]

*Cook salmon*—Heat the oil in a large nonstick skillet over medium–high heat. Cook the salmon for 1 minute on each side, then transfer to a plate.

Rest the salmon for 3 minutes, then roughly break into chunks (or leave whole for DIY option).

*Serve*—Stuff the warmed tortillas with the taco slaw and top with salmon chunks. Spoon over some Mango Avocado Salsa,[4] add a squeeze of lime juice, and enjoy!

**NOTES**

1. The idea here is to cut thinner strips of salmon to increase the surface-area-to-flesh ratio for extra flavor and speedy marinating. No need to get too hung up about perfect slices—it gets flaked anyway! If you can only get skin-on salmon, it's not a big deal—just flake the salmon flesh off the skin once cooked.
2. The used zip-top bag can be washed in warm soapy water for reuse. Otherwise use a bowl, but increase the marinade by 50%.
3. Only marinate up to 2 hours at most. Don't marinate overnight as the fish is too delicate and may become overly soft.
4. For a faster option, skip the slaw and mango salsa. Instead, use finely sliced iceberg lettuce, avocado, sliced tomato, finely chopped red onion, cilantro, a dollop of sour cream, and a squeeze of lime juice. YUM.

LEFTOVERS Fridge 3 days (cooked salmon). Not suitable for freezing.

# STEAK FAJITAS

*With ALL the trimmings!*

 **SERVES: 4 (MAKES 12 FAJITAS) I PREP: 15 MINUTES + 2–24 HOURS MARINATING + 30 MINUTES RESTING I COOK: 15 MINUTES**

Steak fajitas are a staple of Tex-Mex restaurants. Yet I've seen far too many bad examples in my time, with tough, bland beef being the common stumble. There are two essential things for a great steak fajita. One: Good-quality steak, cooked to a perfect medium-rare and not a hair more. Two: A great fajita steak marinade is a must, to infuse the beef with flavor and tenderize it. Get these two things right and your fajitas will be *exquisito* every time!

---

1½ lb skirt steak (or flank),[1] ¾ inch thick

2½ tbsp canola oil

1 large yellow onion, halved and sliced ¼ inch thick

3 bell peppers—yellow, red, and green—deseeded and sliced ¼ inch thick

¼ tsp kosher salt*

¼ tsp black pepper

**FAJITA MARINADE**

¼ cup orange juice[2]

2 tbsp lime juice

2 garlic cloves,* finely minced

½ tsp each ground coriander, cumin, and onion powder

1 tsp chipotle powder*

1½ tsp kosher salt*

**FAJITA FIXINGS**

¼ cup roughly chopped cilantro

12 x 6 inch small tortillas,* warmed (page 225)

2 large avocados, halved, peeled, and sliced

Pico de Gallo (page 224) (optional)

2 limes, cut into wedges

¾ cup sour cream or Lime Crema (page 219)

*Marinate beef*—Mix the marinade ingredients in a zip-top bag.*[3] Add the beef, seal, then massage the bag to coat the beef with the marinade. Refrigerate for 24 hours (2 hours absolute minimum!).

*Prepare beef*—Remove the beef from the fridge and pat dry with a paper towel. Discard the marinade. Leave the beef to rest on the counter for 30 minutes.

*Cook beef*—Heat a cast-iron skillet on high heat until it is screaming hot. We want it smoking! Drizzle ½ tablespoon of oil on each side of the beef. Cook the beef for about 2 minutes on each side (aim to get a nice sear) or until the internal temperature is 125°F for medium-rare. (See the Internal Cooked Temperatures chart on page 351.) Transfer the beef to a rack set over a tray. Rest the beef while you cook the vegetables.

*Char vegetables*—Return the skillet to the stove, still on high heat. Heat the remaining 1½ tablespoons of oil. Add the onion and bell pepper and sprinkle with the salt and pepper. Cook, stirring regularly, until soft and charred, about 5 minutes. Transfer to a serving platter.

*Serve*—Cut the beef into ¼ inch thick slices against the grain[4] for the most tender bite. Pile onto the platter and pour any beef juices on the cutting board over the beef. Sprinkle with cilantro. Serve with the fajita fixings! To make a fajita, put some bell pepper and onion in a tortilla, followed by avocado, steak, pico de gallo (if using), a squeeze of lime, then a dollop of sour cream.

**NOTES**

1. Or other steak of choice, such as boneless rib-eye or strip.
2. Orange juice is a secret marinade ingredient in Mexican cooking. You can't taste orange in the end result, but it adds sweetness and unique flavor. Any bottled fresh (real) orange juice is fine, though if you want to go all the way you can use freshly squeezed (I rarely do). Skip the reconstituted fake orange-flavored stuff, though!
3. If you prefer not to use a zip-top bag, use a container that the beef fits in quite snugly so the marinade coats it well. Turn the beef once or twice during the marinating time.
4. See Cutting beef against the grain in the Glossary (page 358) for directions.

LEFTOVERS Fridge 3 days. Not suitable for freezing.

# NACHOS OF YOUR DREAMS

*Promise me you won't skip the cheese sauce. It totally makes it!*

 **SERVES: 6–8 | PREP: 45 MINUTES | COOK: 40 MINUTES**

Here's my pro tip that will supercharge your nachos game for good: Don't rely only on shredded cheese. What you also want is cheese *sauce* drizzled edge-to-edge over the nachos to ensure complete molten cheese coverage. Do this and sad cheese-less bites of tortilla chips will be a thing of the past! There's a fair few components needed for truly great nachos. The good news is that most of them can be prepared the day before, so you can just build your nachos in a flash when you're ready!

Nachos Cheese Sauce (page 219), warm

10 oz lightly salted tortilla chips[1]

3 cups (10 oz) shredded* monterey jack cheese[2]

1/3 cup pickled jalapeños, chopped

**NACHOS SEASONING**

1/4 tsp cayenne pepper (optional)

1 tsp each dried oregano, garlic powder, and onion powder

2 tsp each ground cumin and paprika

1 tsp kosher salt*

1/4 tsp black pepper

**BEEF TOPPING**

1 tbsp canola oil

2 garlic cloves,* finely minced

1 yellow onion, finely chopped

1 lb ground beef

15 oz can black beans, drained

1 cup canned refried beans*

2 tbsp tomato paste

3/4 cup water

**TO SERVE**

Guacamole (page 220)

3/4 cup sour cream

Pico de Gallo (page 224)

1/4 cup fresh cilantro

1 fresh jalapeño, sliced (optional)

*Beef topping*—Heat the oil in a large nonstick skillet over high heat. Cook the garlic and onion for 4 minutes until tinged with gold. Add the beef and cook for 2 minutes, breaking it up as you go, until it changes to light brown. Add the nachos seasoning ingredients and cook for 1 minute. Add the black beans, refried beans, and tomato paste, stir until combined, then stir in the water. Cook for 5 minutes or until the water is evaporated and you're left with a juicy but not watery mixture. Keep warm.

Preheat the oven to 350°F. Make sure the cheese sauce and beef topping are warm.

*Cheese protection layer*—Spread two-thirds of the tortilla chips evenly across a baking tray. Sprinkle with one-fourth of the shredded cheese, then bake for 5 minutes (tortilla chip crispiness insurance policy).

*Build nachos*—Leaving a 1 inch border on the outer ring of tortilla chips (for chip-gripping purposes), dollop, then spread half the beef topping across the tortilla chips. Scatter with half the pickled jalapeños, then pour two-thirds of the cheese sauce over. Top with the remaining tortilla chips, one-third of the remaining cheese, and all the remaining beef topping, jalapeños, and cheese sauce. Sprinkle the whole thing with the remaining shredded cheese, then bake for 15 minutes until the cheese is melted.

*Serve*—Remove the nachos from the oven. Top with a big dollop of guacamole and sour cream, then spoon over some pico de gallo. Sprinkle with cilantro and fresh jalapeño, if desired. Serve any leftover toppings on the side in little dishes. Eat immediately—prepare to get messy!

**NOTES**

1. Opt for good-quality, sturdy tortilla chips. Cheap ones tend to go soggy easily.
2. Monterey jack has excellent melting qualities that are perfect for nachos—it's not oily, doesn't go crusty, and stretches nicely. Cheddar and colby cheese are all great substitutes.

LEFTOVERS Unlikely! And best made fresh!

# BEEF ENCHILADAS

*Juicy and generously stuffed (just as they should be!).*

**SERVES: 4 I PREP: 20 MINUTES I COOK: 1 HOUR**

This is the way I've been making beef enchiladas for as long as I can remember, and they're as devilishly good as ever. The secret? Refried beans in the filling. They make the enchilada meat stuffing juicy so it holds together, as well as adding flavor. Heads up, these enchiladas are plump! As they should be. Because there's nothing sadder in my world than wimpy, skinny enchiladas.

---

8 x 8 inch flour tortillas* warmed, (page 225)

1½ tightly packed cups (6 oz) shredded* monterey jack cheese or cheddar

1 tbsp roughly chopped cilantro, to serve (optional)

**ENCHILADA SPICE MIX**

½–1 tsp ground cayenne pepper (optional)

1 tsp each onion powder and garlic powder

1 tbsp each ground cumin, paprika, and dried oregano

**ENCHILADA SAUCE**

2 tbsp extra-virgin olive oil

3 tbsp all-purpose flour

2 cups low-sodium chicken broth*

1½ cups tomato passata*

¼ tsp kosher salt*

¼ tsp black pepper

**BEEF FILLING**

1 tbsp extra-virgin olive oil

2 garlic cloves,* finely minced

1 yellow onion, finely chopped

1 lb ground beef

15 oz can refried beans*[1]

15 oz can black beans, drained

½ tsp kosher salt*

¼ tsp black pepper

*Enchilada spice mix*—Combine the spices in a small bowl.

*Enchilada sauce*—Heat the oil in a large saucepan over medium heat. Add the flour and mix to form a paste. Cook for 1 minute, stirring constantly. While whisking, pour in about ½ cup of the chicken broth. The mixture will turn into a thick smooth paste quite quickly. Add the remaining chicken broth, passata, salt, pepper, and 2 tablespoons of the spice mix. Whisk until incorporated, then increase the heat to medium–high. Cook for 3–5 minutes, whisking regularly, until the sauce has the consistency of thick syrup. Remove from the stove and keep warm.

Preheat the oven to 350°F.

*Beef filling*—Heat the oil in a large skillet over high heat. Cook the garlic and onion for 2 minutes. Add the beef and cook for 2 minutes, breaking it up as you go. Add the remaining spice mix and cook for a further 2 minutes. Add the refried beans, black beans, about ¼ cup of the enchilada sauce, salt, and pepper and mix. Cook for 2 minutes, stirring regularly, then remove from the stove. The filling should be juicy but not watery.

*Assemble*—Smear a bit of enchilada sauce on the bottom of a 13 x 9 inch baking dish (this stops the enchiladas from sliding). Spoon one-eighth of the beef filling on the lower third of a tortilla. Roll up, then place in the baking dish, seam-side down. Repeat with the remaining beef filling and tortillas, arranging them snugly side by side in the baking dish. Pour the remaining sauce all over the enchiladas.

*Bake*—Loosely cover with aluminum foil, then bake for 10 minutes. Remove the foil, sprinkle with cheese, and bake for a further 15 minutes.

*Serve*—Sprinkle with cilantro (if using) and serve! Great served as is! However, if I'm making enchiladas for guests, I put toppings, such as sour cream and Pico de Gallo (page 224), on the side for people to help themselves.

**NOTES**

1. The secret ingredient that bulks out the filling and makes it nice and juicy!
2. Make ahead: Wrap the rolled enchiladas in plastic wrap (bundle them together) or place in an airtight container. Store the sauce separately. Keep in the fridge for 5 days or freezer for 3 months. Thaw, assemble, then bake as per the recipe.

LEFTOVERS Fridge 4 days.

# MEXICAN SHREDDED BEEF

*Quick prep, big flavors, highly versatile!*

 **MAKES: 12 BURRITOS, 25–30 TACOS | PREP: 15 MINUTES | COOK: 3½ HOURS**

This shredded beef is inspired by barbacoa. In Mexico, barbacoa is a catch-all term for hunks of seasoned meat often buried underground and slow-cooked for hours until it's so tender it falls apart. This is a simpler version done in a kitchen! I like a good bit of spice for flavor with the beef, and the natural sweetness from orange juice really adds a delicious special touch. This makes a big batch, which is perfect because it freezes well. It's especially good in burritos or tacos, and is also excellent piled over rice or stuffed into soft rolls.

---

3 lb beef chuck steak, cut into 4 equal pieces

2 tbsp extra-virgin olive oil

5 garlic cloves,* finely minced

1 yellow onion, finely chopped

¾ cup orange juice[1]

2 tbsp lime juice

14 oz can crushed tomatoes

2 cups low-sodium beef broth* (for homemade, see page 348)

½ cup water

**SPICE MIX**

1 tsp each allspice, ground coriander, kosher salt,* and black pepper

2 tsp onion powder

1 tbsp each paprika and dried oregano

1½ tbsp chipotle powder*[2]

*Spice mix*—Combine the ingredients in a bowl. Sprinkle 4 teaspoons over the beef pieces and pat well so it sticks.

*Brown beef*—Heat the olive oil in a large heavy-based pot over high heat. Sear the beef pieces so they are browned all over, around 4 minutes. Transfer to a plate.

*Braising liquid*—Turn the stove down to medium, add the garlic and onion, and cook for 3 minutes until translucent. Add the orange juice, lime, tomatoes, beef broth, water, and the remaining spice mix. Stir, then add the beef—the liquid should just about cover the meat.

*Slow-cook*—Once the liquid starts bubbling, reduce the heat to low so it is simmering very, very gently. Place the lid on and cook for 3 hours or until the beef shreds easily. (See Note 3 for other cooking methods.)

*Shred*—Remove the beef from the sauce and transfer to a casserole dish. Shred with two forks.

*Reduce sauce*—Meanwhile, keep the sauce simmering rapidly on high heat for 15 minutes or until reduced to 2 cups. Pour the sauce over the shredded beef and toss. Taste and add more salt if desired.

*Serve*—Use the shredded beef for all things Mexican—tacos, Burritos (page 210), enchiladas, taquitos, chimichangas, or make Mexican dinner plates by adding a side of Mexican Red Rice (page 223) and Quick Pickled Cabbage (page 224).

**NOTES**

1. See Note 2 of Steak Fajitas on page 202 for information about this secret ingredient!
2. This dish is not overly spicy but the chipotle powder does add a hum of warmth! If you are concerned, reduce slightly but don't reduce it too much or you won't have enough flavor in the sauce, which would be a terribly sad situation to find yourself in.
3. Oven: Place the heavy-based pot in the oven, covered with aluminum foil or a lid, for 3–3½ hours at 350°F, then reduce the sauce on the stove as per the recipe as needed. Slow-cooker: 10 hours on Low, 6 hours on High. Pressure cooker: 50 minutes on High. After you remove the beef, reduce the sauce to 2 cups by simmering rapidly in a large skillet for about 25 minutes.

LEFTOVERS Fridge 4 days, freezer 3 months.

# BURRITOS

*Excellent freezer food and for feeding a crowd (no plates!).*

**MAKES: 12 I PREP: 30 MINUTES I COOK: 15 MINUTES (OPTIONAL)**

I have strong opinions about burritos. They involve burritos being plump and generous, for one—we're not making spring rolls here! Juicy fillings are also a must, because biting into a dry burrito is a distressing experience. I also believe you should ALWAYS make a double batch of burritos. Why? Because they're a bit time-consuming to make if you have a good variety of fillings (as I always insist on), but freeze exceptionally well. I always sleep better knowing I have a stash of frozen burritos on hand! These burritos are a perfect vehicle for my Mexican Shredded Beef (page 208), but you can use any filling you like such as Chicken Tinga (page 198), Beef Topping (see Nachos of Your Dreams on page 204), or Pork Carnitas (page 214).

## WHAT YOU NEED

| INGREDIENTS | FOR 12 BURRITOS | PER BURRITO |
|---|---|---|
| 10 inch (jumbo) flour tortillas,* warmed if needed (see page 225) | 12 | 1 |
| Mexican Red Rice (page 223) | 2 batches | ½ cup |
| Mexican Shredded Beef (page 208) or other filling of choice (see page 210) | 1 batch | ½ cup (4 oz) |
| Shredded* cheese (monterey jack, colby, cheddar) | 3¾ cups (13 oz) | ⅓ cup (1 oz) |
| Canned black beans, drained | 2 x 15 oz cans | 2 tbsp |
| Canned corn kernels, drained | 2 x 15 oz cans | 2 tbsp |
| Tomatoes,* deseeded and cut into ¼ inch dice | 5 tomatoes | 1½ tbsp |
| Red onion, finely chopped | 1 onion | 1 tsp |
| Jalapeños, deseeded and finely chopped | 2 jalapeños | ½ tsp |
| Finely chopped cilantro | ¼ cup | 1 tsp |
| **FOR DUNKING** | | |
| Guacamole (page 220) or Avocado Crema (page 220) | 1 batch | 3 tbsp |
| Sour cream or Lime Crema (page 219) | 1 batch | 2 tbsp |
| Sriracha* or other hot sauce, as desired | | As much as you dare |

## METHOD

When measuring the rice and beef, be sure to use tightly packed cups or the burrito will be short on stuffing.

*Warm tortilla if needed*[2]—See page 225. Warm the beef, rice, corn, and black beans using your method of choice.*

*Burrito wrapping*—If you're making ahead (fridge or freezer), line a sheet of aluminum foil with parchment paper. If serving now, just use foil.

*Fillings*—Place the tortilla on a piece of foil. On the lower third of the tortilla, using the quantities listed above, spread the rice in a 5 x 2 inch rectangle, then top with beef, cheese, beans, corn, and tomato. Sprinkle with onion, jalapeño (if using), then cilantro.

*Roll up*—Start rolling the burrito up from the bottom, folding in the sides when you're halfway, then finish rolling up. Wrap tightly in foil to hold it in place.

*Serve*—Serve as is with dunking options of choice (my favorite is guacamole and sour cream). Or warm through in the oven if desired.

*Warming (optional)*—Bake, wrapped in aluminum foil, for 20 minutes at 400°F. Optional crisping: Remove the foil, then return the burritos to the oven for 10 minutes to crisp the exterior slightly.

**NOTES**

1. Usually jumbo tortillas are intentionally made soft and pliable so they don't necessarily need to be warmed before rolling.
2. These are best warmed beforehand as they take quite a long time to become warm in the oven once rolled up in the burrito. I usually just use the microwave. You won't quite use all the rice, corn, or black beans. Leftovers will keep in the fridge for 4 days. Toss the corn and beans into soup, an omelet, or Chinese Fried Rice (page 120)!
3. Make ahead: Wrap each aluminum foil-wrapped burrito in plastic wrap, then place in an airtight container or zip-top bag.* Fridge 5 days, freezer up to 3 months. Thaw, then remove the plastic wrap and reheat in a 325°F oven for 45 minutes (or bake for 1 hour from frozen). To crisp the exterior slightly, remove the wrapping and bake for a further 15 minutes.

# BAJA FISH TACOS

*Crispy battered spiced fish stuffed inside tacos? Off-the-charts good!*

**SERVES: 4 (MAKES 12 TACOS) I PREP: 25 MINUTES I COOK: 15 MINUTES**

Scoffing brand-spanking-fresh fried fish tacos from little beachside shacks was a highlight of my last trip to Mexico, and I couldn't wait to replicate it back home! This recipe hails from Baja California. I don't know if they use beer in the batter, but I find it helps the fried fish batter stay crispy and light. Top tip: Keep the toppings simple. When you have a great piece of fresh fish, less is more! The gently tangy cabbage and creamy-but-not-cloying Avocado Crema I've suggested are ideal accompaniments, and are typical in Mexico.

1 lb skinless, boneless cod or other firm white fish fillets, 3/4 inch thick[1]

1/4 tsp ground cumin

1/4 tsp garlic powder

1 1/2 tsp chipotle powder*

1/4 tsp kosher salt*

1/4 cup rice flour,[2] for dusting

**CRISPY BATTER**

3/4 cup all-purpose flour

1/4 cup rice flour[2]

1 1/4 tsp baking powder*

1/4 tsp kosher salt*

1 cup Corona or other pale beer,[3] ice-cold

4 cups canola oil

**TO SERVE**

12 x 6 inch corn tortillas,* warmed (page 225)

Quick Pickled Cabbage (page 224)

Avocado Crema (page 220)

1/3 cup fresh cilantro, roughly chopped

Fresh jalapeños, finely chopped (optional)

*Marinate fish*—Cut the fish into twelve 3 x 1/2 inch batons. Place in a bowl and toss with the cumin, garlic, and chipotle powder. Set aside for 20 minutes to marinate.

*Start batter*—Whisk the flours, baking powder, and salt in a bowl. Place in the fridge until required.

*Heat oil*—Fill a pot or large saucepan with 2 inches of oil and heat it over medium-high heat to 375°F.[4]

*Dust fish*—Meanwhile, sprinkle the fish in the bowl with the salt. Still in the bowl, coat the fish in rice flour, shake off the excess, then transfer to a plate. Set aside while you finish the batter.

*Finish batter*—Remove the flour bowl from the fridge and whisk in the beer just until it is incorporated. Some lumps are okay—better than overwhisking![5] The batter should be fairly thin but thick enough to coat the back of a spoon (don't worry, it puffs up a lot).

*Fry*—Dip a piece of fish into the batter, then carefully lower it into the oil. Repeat with 2–3 more pieces, depending on your saucepan size—don't crowd the pan! Fry for 1 minute and 20 seconds, turning once, until golden and crisp. Transfer to a paper towel-lined tray. Repeat with the remaining fish. The fish will stay hot for 10 minutes so there's no need to keep it warm in the oven while you fry the batches, though you can if you want.

*Serve*—Pile the crispy fish in a bowl alongside the stack of tortillas, Avocado Crema, Quick Pickled Cabbage, cilantro, and jalapeño (if using). To make a taco, stuff a tortilla with some cabbage, then top with battered fish. Drizzle over avocado crema and sprinkle with cilantro and jalapeño. Take a huge bite and be happy!

**NOTES**

1. See Fish in the Glossary (page 359) for a list of other suitable fish. Fillets around 3/4 inch thick are ideal. If yours are much thicker, slice them in half horizontally.
2. Substitute cornstarch (though rice flour is crispier!).
3. Use any pale or amber lagers or ales. Corona is on theme!
4. See Oil temperature testing in the Glossary (page 361) for directions.
5. Cold batter and minimal batter whisking are key to a light, remarkably ungreasy coating that stays crispy for long after the fish has gone cold! This is why we use ice-cold beer and refrigerate the dry ingredients until required. On hot days, or if you're doubling the recipe, keep the batter cold by setting it over another bowl filled with ice, or keep the batter in the fridge as you cook.

LEFTOVERS Best served hot and fresh! However, leftover fish can be kept in the fridge for 3 days. Blast in the oven at 475°F for 5 minutes to partially resurrect the crispy coating.

# PORK CARNITAS

*The king of all taco stuffings!*

**SERVES: 8–10 (MAKES 30–35 TACOS) | PREP: 10 MINUTES | COOK: 10 HOURS**

Of all the wonderful things you can tuck into a taco, pork carnitas is among the greatest! Traditionally slow-cooked in gallons of lard, my recipe is a (much!) more practical homemade version. It's richly porky, with juicy meat that has that bewitching crispy-yet-soft texture. This has been a Top 5 recipe on my website since 2016 and is loved by readers all over the world. Now it's your turn to experience the Mexican magic that is carnitas!

**PORK RUB**

1 tsp black pepper

2 tsp ground cumin

2½ tsp kosher salt*

1 tbsp dried oregano

1 tbsp extra-virgin olive oil

**PORK**

4 lb skinless, boneless pork shoulder[1] (5 lb bone-in)

1 yellow onion, finely chopped

1 jalapeño, deseeded and finely minced (optional)

4 garlic cloves,* finely minced

¾ cup orange juice[2]

4 tbsp canola oil

**CARNITAS TACOS**

30–35 x 6 inch small corn tortillas,* warmed (page 225)

Pico de Gallo (page 224) or Taco Sauce (page 221)

White onion, finely diced

Cilantro

Lime wedges, to serve

*Pork rub*—Combine the pork rub ingredients in a small bowl. Pat the pork dry with paper towels, then cover the pork all over with the rub, massaging it in.

*Prepare pork*—Place the pork in a slow-cooker, fat-cap up. Spread the onion, jalapeño, and garlic on the surface of the pork, then pour the orange juice over gently.

Slow-cook the pork on Low for 10 hours or High for 7 hours. (For other cooking methods, see Note 3.) The pork should be tender enough to easily shred. Transfer the pork to a large dish (leave juices in slow-cooker), then shred using two forks.

*Reduce juices*—Skim and discard the excess fat from the surface of the juices remaining in the slow-cooker. Pour the juices into a large saucepan and simmer rapidly on medium–high until it reduces to 2 cups, around 10 minutes (depends how much juice you have).

*Crisping (important step!)*[4]—Heat 1 tablespoon of oil in a large nonstick skillet over high heat. Spread one-fourth of the shredded pork in the pan and drizzle over ¼ cup of the juice. Leave untouched until the juice evaporates and the underside of the pork is golden brown, around 1½–2 minutes. Flip the pork and sear the other side for just 30 seconds, then transfer to a serving platter. Repeat with the remaining oil and pork.

*Serve*[5]—Just before serving, drizzle ¾ cup of the reduced juices all over the pile of carnitas. Serve hot, stuffed into warm corn tortillas, topped with Pico de Gallo or Taco Sauce. Finish with a sprinkle of white onion and cilantro, and a squeeze of lime juice.

**NOTES**

1. There's really no other cut of pork that will easily yield the same results as pork shoulder for this recipe! Don't trim off all the fat from the surface of the shoulder—leave some because it keeps the pork juicy. It can be removed later once cooked, if you want.
2. See Note 2 of the Steak Fajitas recipe (page 202).
3. I like the slow-cooker for ease and retention of meat juiciness. However, other cooking methods also work well. Electric pressure cooker: Same recipe, 1½ hours on High, depressurize naturally. Stove pressure cooker: Use a rack or scrunched-up balls of aluminum foil to elevate the pork off the base of the cooker and add ¾ cup of water. Cook for 1½ hours on High. Oven: Add 2 cups of water around the meat in a roasting pan. Roast at 350°F, tightly covered in a double layer of aluminum foil, for 3½ hours or until the meat can be shredded easily. Shred, then pan-fry as per the recipe.
4. The idea with the crisping is to make one side of the pork golden and crispy but leave the other side soft and juicy, so you get the best of both worlds!
5. Carnitas tacos are typically served quite simply, with just a fresh salsa, onion, cilantro, and lime juice. However, feel free to use any of the sauces and toppings on pages 218–24.

LEFTOVERS Fridge 4 days, freezer 3 months, with meat and juices stored separately. Thaw, then pan-fry and drizzle with the juices, as per the recipe, just before serving.

# MUSHROOM QUESADILLAS

*My team's pick of the chapter!*

**SERVES: 2 | PREP: 5 MINUTES | COOK: 10 MINUTES**

Quesadillas are like the pizza of Mexico. You can pretty much make them with anything and they'll be delicious, so long as they're hot, crispy, and oozing with cheese. These meatless quesadillas are quick to make and fabulously tasty. It's amazing what just a sprinkle of chipotle powder brings to the party! If a serious food emergency is leaving you short on time, skip the guacamole and just dunk in sour cream with a splash of hot sauce.

3 tbsp extra-virgin olive oil

7 oz portabella mushrooms,[1] sliced ¼ inch thick (or other mushrooms of choice)

½ tsp chipotle powder*

¼ tsp kosher salt*

¼ tsp black pepper

¾ cup (3 oz) shredded* colby cheese[2]

2 x 8 inch flour tortillas*

**TO SERVE**

Sour cream

Pico de Gallo (page 224)

Guacamole (page 220) or Avocado Crema (page 220)

Lime wedges

*Cook mushrooms*—Heat 2 tablespoons of oil in a nonstick skillet over medium-high heat. Add the mushrooms and cook for 1 minute, using a spatula to toss them regularly. Add the remaining 1 tablespoon oil, toss to coat the mushrooms, then add the chipotle powder, salt, and pepper. Cook for a further 1½ minutes until the surface of the mushrooms is golden. Transfer the mushrooms to a bowl and wipe any loose bits out of the pan with a paper towel.

*Assemble quesadilla*—Sprinkle half the cheese on one half of a tortilla, top with half the mushrooms, then fold the other half over. Repeat with the other tortilla.

*Cook quesadillas*—Return the skillet to the stove on medium heat (no extra oil is needed). Transfer the tortillas to the skillet and cook for 1½ minutes until crisp and golden. Flip and cook for a further 1 minute until crisp.

*Serve*—Cut each quesadilla in half and serve with sour cream and Pico de Gallo, Guacamole, or Avocado Crema for dunking. Finish with a squeeze of lime.

**NOTES**

1. I like using portabella mushrooms because they are big and meaty, but smaller mushrooms will work just fine too.
2. Colby cheese can be substituted with other good melting cheeses such as cheddar, gruyere, or Swiss. Mozzarella works fine but doesn't have as much flavor.

LEFTOVERS Best made fresh, because nobody likes a soggy quesadilla!

# Essential sauces & sides

Many Mexican dishes are as much about the toppings, sauces, and salsas as they are the meat for stuffing into tacos! Here is my selection of essentials to stuff in burritos, spoon over tacos, scoop with tortilla chips, and serve on the side of big dinner plates piled high with your favorite Mexican mains. All are very versatile, quick, and easy to make.

# NACHOS CHEESE SAUCE

**MAKES: 2½ CUPS | PREP: 5 MINUTES | COOK: 10 MINUTES**

I have a dirty secret: Processed cheese is non-negotiable for making the best version of this warm, silky, gooey cheese sauce. You can use all-natural cheese, but it won't be the same. Trust me, I went through a lot of cheese to figure this out! Use this as a dunking sauce for burritos, taquitos, or tortilla chips. My ultimate use, though? On nachos. The cheese oozing over every tortilla chip is a nachos-lover's dream come true! (See page 204 to experience this greatness.)

---

7 oz American cheese, cut into ½ x ¼ inch batons

½ tightly packed cup (2 oz) shredded*[2] mozzarella

1 tbsp cornstarch

12 fl oz can evaporated milk

½ tsp each garlic powder and onion powder

¼ tsp kosher salt*

1 tbsp sriracha* (optional)

1 tbsp finely chopped pickled jalapeño (optional for extra spiciness!)

½ cup heavy cream*

In a medium saucepan, toss the cheeses with the cornstarch. Add the remaining ingredients, except the cream. Stir, then place over low heat. As the mixture starts to heat up, stir regularly so the base doesn't burn. Once the cheese is fully melted and the mixture is completely smooth, stir in the cream. Stir for another 1 minute, then remove from the stove. Serve warm!

**NOTES**

1. I love a good gruyere as much as the next person, but for a silky nachos cheese sauce you want a very specific "meltability" that only comes from processed cheese! If you substitute with all-natural cheese (like cheddar) the sauce will have a very mild grainy texture, which doesn't bother most people, but I notice!
2. Shred the cheese yourself using a box grater. Store-bought shredded cheese contains anti-caking agents that will make your sauce unpleasantly grainy.
3. This cheese sauce is molten and pourable when warm, soft, and creamy at room temperature (still great for chip dipping), and will be like soft butter when it is refrigerated. Reheat in the microwave to make it pourable again.

LEFTOVERS Fridge 7 days, freezer 3 months. Thaw, reheat gently, then mix well. Loosen as needed with milk.

# LIME CREMA

**MAKES: ½ CUP, ENOUGH FOR 12 TACOS | PREP: 5 MINUTES | COOK: NONE**

I love the fresh and sharp bite of this creamy dressing. The zest really lifts the sauce and pushes through the lime flavor. This one is especially good with tacos.

---

¼ tsp finely grated garlic*

½ cup sour cream (substitute with plain yogurt)

1 tbsp mayonnaise*

1 tsp lime zest

2 tsp lime juice

¼ tsp kosher salt*

Place the ingredients in a small bowl and mix well to combine. Refrigerate until required.

LEFTOVERS Fridge 3 days.

# AVOCADO CREMA

 **MAKES: JUST OVER 1 CUP, ENOUGH FOR 24 TACOS | PREP: 5 MINUTES | COOK: NONE**

The complete package—tangy, creamy, yet fresh. And it stays green for days!

---

1/2 cup (4 oz) avocado flesh[1]

1/4 cup sour cream

1/4 cup mayonnaise*

2 1/2 tbsp lime juice

1/2 lightly packed cup cilantro

1/4 tsp finely grated garlic*

1/4 tsp kosher salt*

1/4 tsp black pepper

Place everything in a jar just wide enough to fit the head of an immersion blender. Blitz until smooth. Cover and refrigerate until required.

**NOTE**

1. 1 small or 1/2 large avocado. Cut in half, scoop out the flesh, and smoosh into a 1/2 cup measure.

LEFTOVERS Fridge 5 days. It will not go brown—yay!

# GUACAMOLE

 **MAKES: 1 1/2 CUPS, ENOUGH FOR 12 TACOS | PREP: 10 MINUTES | COOK: NONE**

The secret to great guac? Making an onion paste. It's the traditional Mexican way. Try it. It will change your guac game forever.

---

2 tbsp finely chopped white onion (or shallot* or red onion)

1 tbsp deseeded and finely minced jalapeños (adjust to taste)

1/2 tsp kosher salt,* plus extra to taste

1/4 cup roughly chopped cilantro

2 medium avocados (or 1 very large one)

2 tsp lime juice, plus extra to taste

1 tomato,* peeled, deseeded, and chopped (optional)[1]

Place the onion, jalapeño, salt, and half the cilantro in a mortar and pestle and grind to a paste. Alternatively, do this on a cutting board and use a fork or smear with the side of a knife to mash until juicy.

Scrape into a bowl, add the avocado flesh, lime juice, and remaining cilantro. Mash to your desired consistency with a spoon or fork. Do a taste test, adjusting the salt and lime juice as desired. If using tomato, stir it through.

Best made fresh, but to make ahead, prepare the paste, then mix in the avocado just before serving.

**NOTE**

1. Not strictly authentic to include, but that's okay!

LEFTOVERS To keep leftover guacamole green and fresh, place in an airtight container and smooth the surface as best you can. Then cover with a thin film of extra-virgin olive oil (prevents oxidization that makes avocados go brown). Fridge 3 days. To use, pour off the oil and mix well.

# INSTANT SPICY PINK SAUCE

**MAKES: ½ CUP, ENOUGH FOR 12 TACOS | PREP: 2 MINUTES | COOK: NONE**

Not really a Mexican sauce, but great with so many Mexican foods all the same! Don't let the simplicity of this sauce fool you. It's my go-to sauce for tacos, in part because it's instant! I also use this as a dipping sauce for things like Crunchy Baked Chicken Tenders (page 29) and Cheesy Baked Broccoli Fritters (page 26).

---

½ cup sour cream[1]

4 tsp sriracha*[2]

Mix the ingredients together in a small bowl until smooth. Ready for use!

**NOTES**

1. Swap sour cream for mayo for a richer version, or yogurt for a lighter version.
2. To make a non-spicy version, omit the sriracha and use 3 tablespoons ketchup with ¼ teaspoon finely minced garlic,* ¼ teaspoon kosher salt,* plus ½ teaspoon lemon juice.

LEFTOVERS Fridge 7+ days, depending on the shelf life of the ingredients.

# TACO SAUCE

**MAKES: 1 CUP, ENOUGH FOR 12 TACOS | PREP: 10 MINUTES | COOK: 35 MINUTES**

This homemade version of store-bought taco sauce is infinitely better. Real flavor, no preservatives–woo! Serve as a sauce for drizzling on your favorite tacos, or as a salsa dip for tortilla chips!

---

3 x 4 oz tomatoes, cut in half and core cut out

1 jalapeño, cut in half lengthwise and deseeded

3 garlic cloves, kept whole, peeled

¼ yellow onion, kept whole, peeled

1 tbsp extra-virgin olive oil

⅛ tsp chipotle powder*

⅛ tsp ground cumin

¼ tsp dried oregano

¼ tsp sugar

½ tsp kosher salt*

2 tsp lime juice

3 tbsp water

¼ cup lightly packed cilantro

Preheat the oven to 425°F. Line a baking tray with parchment paper.

Toss the tomato, jalapeño, garlic, and onion with the olive oil in a bowl.

Place the onion and tomato on the prepared tray, cut side up, then roast for 20 minutes. Add the jalapeño and garlic to the tray and roast for another 15 minutes so you get some nice browning on the edges of the vegetables–borderline charring!

Remove the tray from the oven and let the vegetables cool. Transfer everything to a jar or tall container. Add the remaining ingredients, except the cilantro. Blitz until pretty smooth using an immersion blender[1]–it will only take 5 seconds or so.

Add the cilantro and blitz just until the leaves get chopped into little bits. The taco sauce is ready for use!

**NOTE**

1. You can also blitz in a small food processor like a Nutribullet or similar.

LEFTOVERS Fridge 5 days. Freezes fine but you do lose some of the fresh flavor.

# MANGO AVOCADO SALSA

 **MAKES: 3 CUPS, ENOUGH FOR 12 TACOS | PREP: 10 MINUTES | COOK: NONE**

This fresh and summery salsa is so juicy you won't need a separate sauce with your tacos. It's particularly great with Chipotle Salmon Tacos (page 201), but also excellent with Chicken Tinga Tacos (page 198) and Baja Fish Tacos (page 212).

---

1 1/2 cups (9 oz) cubed mango (1/4 inch pieces)

1 1/2 cups (8 oz) cubed avocado (1/4 inch pieces)

1/4 cup finely chopped red onion

3 tbsp finely chopped cilantro

1 1/2 tbsp deseeded and finely minced jalapeño (adjust to taste)

3 tbsp lime juice

1 1/2 tbsp extra-virgin olive oil

1/2 tsp kosher salt*

Place everything in a bowl and toss. Serve immediately.

LEFTOVERS Best made fresh. To prepare ahead, don't add the lime, oil, and salt until just before serving.

# TACO SLAW

 **MAKES 5 1/2 CUPS, ENOUGH FOR 12 TACOS | PREP: 10 MINUTES | COOK: NONE**

Here's a slightly more involved cabbage salad that's more substantial and a bit richer than the Quick Pickled Cabbage on page 224. It's great stuffed into burritos and tacos, but a heap on a plate also makes a great side salad to cut through rich, spicy meats—this slaw goes with everything! Six cups of shredded cabbage sounds like a lot for 12 tacos, but it collapses to almost half the volume once it wilts.

---

6 tightly packed cups finely shredded green cabbage

1 cup finely sliced green onion* (sliced diagonally)

1/2 cup finely chopped cilantro

**DRESSING**

1/2 tsp finely minced garlic*

1/2 cup sour cream (or use plain yogurt)

2 tbsp mayonnaise* (or 4 tsp olive oil)

2 tsp lime zest[1]

4 tsp lime juice[1]

1/2 tsp kosher salt*

Mix the dressing ingredients in a large bowl. Add the cabbage and toss to coat. Set aside for 20 minutes until the cabbage wilts. Nobody wants spiky bits of cabbage in their tacos!

Add the green onion and cilantro and toss well again. Ready for use!

**NOTE**

1. No limes? Use lemon instead, but skip the zest. Otherwise, apple cider vinegar makes a good substitute.

LEFTOVERS Fridge 3 days. Toss before use.

# MEXICAN RED RICE

 **MAKES 3 CUPS, SERVES: 3–4 AS A SIDE | PREP: 5 MINUTES | COOK: 20 MINUTES**

A rice so tasty you'll eat it straight from the pot! With a gentle tomato flavor and attractive orange tint, it's perfumed with garlic, cilantro, and jalapeño. Red rice is excellent in a burrito, taco, or as a side dish with all things Mexican.

---

1½ tbsp extra-virgin olive oil

2 garlic cloves,* finely minced

½ small yellow onion, finely chopped

1 cup long-grain white rice[1]

1¾ cups low-sodium chicken broth*

¼ tsp kosher salt*

2½ tbsp tomato paste

1 jalapeño, whole (optional)

1 cilantro sprig

**OPTIONAL GARNISHES**

Cilantro

Sliced jalapeño

Heat the oil in a small (roughly 6 inch) saucepan over medium–high heat. Add the garlic, stir briefly, then add the onion. Cook for 3 minutes until the onion is translucent but not golden.

Add the rice, broth, salt, and tomato paste and stir until the tomato paste is dissolved. Drop in the jalapeño (if using) and cilantro. Bring to a boil, then cover with a lid and reduce the heat to low so the water is simmering gently. Cook for 15 minutes (no peeking, no stirring!) or until the liquid is absorbed.

Remove from the stove, then rest for 10 minutes with the lid on. Fluff with a fork and serve, garnished with cilantro, if desired.

**NOTE**

1. The type of rice you use significantly alters the outcome! Jasmine and basmati rice give a similar result but have a slightly different fragrance. Medium-grain rice will also work okay. Short-grain, sushi rice, risotto, and paella rice are not suitable.

LEFTOVERS Fridge 3 days, freezer 3 months.

# PICO DE GALLO

 **MAKES: 1¾ CUPS, ENOUGH FOR 12 TACOS | PREP: 10 MINUTES | COOK: NONE**

Pico de gallo is a condiment you'll find on every table across Mexico. It's bright, fresh, juicy, and spicy—the perfect topping or side for tacos, enchiladas, quesadillas etc.

---

3 large tomatoes,* deseeded and cut into ¼ inch cubes

⅓ cup roughly chopped cilantro

¼ cup finely chopped white onion (or red onion)

1½ tbsp finely chopped jalapeño (adjust to taste)

1–2 tbsp lime juice

½ tsp kosher salt*

Gently mix all the ingredients in a bowl and set aside for 5–20 minutes so the juices are drawn out of the tomato. Toss again and serve as a topping or side for things like tacos, burritos, enchiladas, quesadillas, and any Mexican dish!

**NOTE**

1. Best made fresh as the tomato goes soggy the next day. To get ahead, prepare the ingredients but only add the salt and lime juice just before serving.

# QUICK PICKLED CABBAGE

 **MAKES 2½ CUPS, ENOUGH FOR 12 TACOS | PREP: 5 MINUTES | COOK: NONE**

Another super simple but incredibly versatile accompaniment for just about anything. I especially love making it with red cabbage. The cabbage turns a brilliant crimson that looks so striking as a topping!

---

4½ packed cups (14 oz) finely shredded green or red cabbage

4 green onions,* finely sliced diagonally

2½ tbsp red wine vinegar[1]

½ tsp kosher salt*

Toss all the ingredients in a bowl and set aside for 40 minutes until wilted.

**NOTE**

1. You can also use white wine vinegar or apple cider vinegar.

LEFTOVERS Fridge 5 days.

# WARMING TORTILLAS

Warming tortillas makes them pliable as well as bringing out the flavor. The same methods can be used for both flour and corn tortillas. My default method is the oven, for convenience, because you can heat a lot of tortillas in one go. My ideal method is toasting the tortillas over an open flame. Charred bits = extra flavor!

---

## WHAT YOU NEED

### OVEN

Separate the tortillas (sometimes they are stuck together), then stack (up to eight tortillas) and wrap with aluminum foil. Make more foil packages as needed, for more tortillas. Place in a preheated 400°F oven for 15 minutes. Keep the tortillas warm in the foil packages until serving.

### NAKED FLAME

Place the tortilla directly onto the flame of a gas stove on medium heat. Leave for 15–20 seconds until you get some charred spots, but before it goes crispy. Flip with tongs and repeat on the other side. I will typically have multiple burners going at the same time!

### STOVE

Heat a nonstick skillet over medium–high heat. Place the tortilla in the pan (no oil) and leave for 20 seconds. Flip and heat the other side for 25 seconds or until you get a few little brown spots, but don't let it go crispy or it will break when folded/rolled. Remove and repeat. Speed things up: Get a few pans going at the same time.

### MICROWAVE

Separate the tortillas, then stack six to eight on a paper towel–lined plate and cover with another paper towel. Microwave on High for 40 seconds. Method not recommended for tacos as they get a bit too steamy and soft.

## METHOD

*Remove tortillas from package*—Separate one by one, because sometimes they are stuck together, then proceed with one of the methods.

*Keeping tortillas warm*—Stack warmed tortillas in a clean dish towel and keep wrapped so they stay warm. If warming ahead of time, they can be kept wrapped in aluminum foil in a 125°F oven.

### NOTES

1. Most flour tortillas are pliable enough straight out of the package, so I only warm them up for tacos because they taste better.
2. Corn tortillas are much more brittle than flour tortillas. They MUST be warmed thoroughly to make them soft and pliable before use or they will break!
3. Once corn tortillas become even a bit stale, they are much more prone to breaking. Resuscitate them by dunking briefly in water, then reheat using the stove or naked flame method. Or spritz lightly with water and reheat using the oven method.

# ASIAN BITES & SOUPS

If you can nibble it or slurp it, it's got my name on it.

# THAI CHICKEN SATAY SKEWERS

*This one's all about the peanut sauce!*

**MAKES: 15 SKEWERS, SERVES 5–6 AS A STARTER | PREP: 20 MINUTES + 20 MINUTES (OR 24 HOURS) MARINATING | COOK: 15 MINUTES**

This is the litmus test of Thai restaurants everywhere! For me, the peanut sauce makes or breaks a satay skewer. The secret to a great sauce? A touch of Thai red curry paste for extra savory oomph. Also, using natural peanut butter rather than commercial spread—it has a more intense peanut flavor, which is exactly what we want!

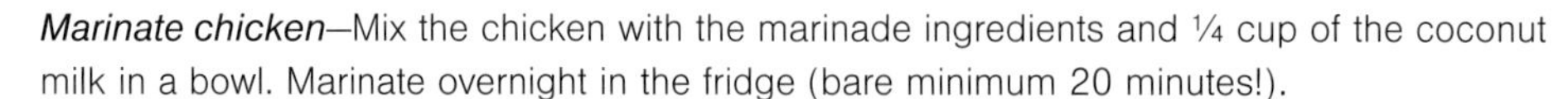

1¼ lb boneless, skinless chicken thighs, cut into ¾ inch pieces[1]

14 fl oz full-fat coconut milk*[2]

13–16 bamboo skewers, 6 inches long[3]

3 tbsp canola oil

**MARINADE**

1 tbsp curry powder[4]

1 tsp sugar

2 tsp red curry paste*

1 tsp kosher salt*

**THAI PEANUT SAUCE**

2 tbsp red curry paste*[5]

¾ cup natural unsweetened peanut butter*[5]

¼ cup sugar

2 tsp dark soy sauce*[6]

1 tsp kosher salt*

2 tbsp apple cider vinegar

¾ cup water

**TO SERVE**

2 tbsp finely chopped unsalted roasted peanuts

Cilantro and sliced red chili* (optional)

Lime wedges (optional)

*Marinate chicken*—Mix the chicken with the marinade ingredients and ¼ cup of the coconut milk in a bowl. Marinate overnight in the fridge (bare minimum 20 minutes!).

*Peanut sauce*[7]—Place the remaining coconut milk and all the peanut sauce ingredients in a small saucepan over medium–low heat. Stir to combine, then simmer, stirring every now and then, for 5 minutes. Adjust the consistency with water—it should be a pourable but thickish sauce. Cover and keep warm while cooking the skewers.

*Prepare skewers*—Thread the chicken onto skewers—I use 4–5 pieces per skewer.

*Cook skewers*—Heat 1½ tablespoon of oil in a large nonstick skillet over medium–high heat. Cook 5–7 skewers at a time for 3 minutes on each side until golden. Transfer to a plate and loosely cover with aluminum foil to keep warm while you cook the remaining skewers.

*Serve*—Pour some peanut sauce into a bowl and sprinkle with a pinch of the finely chopped peanuts. Pile the satay skewers onto a platter, sprinkle with the remaining peanuts and garnish with cilantro, chili, and lime wedges (if using). To eat, dunk the skewers into the sauce and enjoy! Complete your meal with a side of Sesame Ginger Garlic Stir-Fried Vegetables (page 108) and Chinese Fried Rice (page 120). Or serve with Fluffy Coconut Rice (page 337), cucumber, and red onion slices, as pictured.

**NOTES**

1. Chicken breast can also be used but the meat won't be as juicy.
2. Use a good-quality coconut milk as they have a higher percentage of coconut extract (80%+) and therefore better coconut flavor. Economical brands can contain as little as 30% extract and lack fat and flavor.
3. Satay is typically threaded onto short skewers that can conveniently fit in a skillet. If you can only find long skewers, either make giant ones or break/cut the skewers into 6 inch lengths. If you are cooking these on a grill, soak the skewers in water for 2 hours before using to stop them burning.
4. Any general-purpose curry powder is fine. Use hot if you want spicy, otherwise use mild.
5. For gluten-free, ensure the red curry paste, peanut butter, and dark soy sauce you use are gluten free.
6. Adds seasoning and deepens the color of the sauce. Can substitute with light or all-purpose soy sauce but the sauce color will be lighter.
7. Makes more peanut sauce than you will need but it's hard to make less. Keep leftovers for 1 week in the fridge or freezer for 3 months. Serve over rice (pages 334–37), noodles, vegetables (raw or steamed), or as the dressing for The Bangkok—Chicken Satay Noodle Salad (page 183).

LEFTOVERS Fridge 4 days. Not suitable for freezing.

# SAN CHOY BOW (CHINESE LETTUCE WRAPS)

*One of my favorite "happens to be healthy" foods.*

**MAKES: 8 LARGE OR 16 SMALL LETTUCE WRAPS, SERVES 4–5 AS A STARTER I PREP: 15 MINUTES I COOK: 6 MINUTES**

An appetizer mainstay at suburban Chinese restaurants, this is one of my favorite can't-believe-it's-also-healthy dishes! The thing that makes all the difference is a really good sauce for the filling. Get that right and you can make the filling with virtually anything that can be diced and cooked. I've used pork and vegetables here, but it's equally good with chicken, or even entirely meat-free. Serve this with a side of fried rice to fill out the meal and maybe an Asian slaw for extra veggies!

---

**SAUCE**

1 1/4 tsp cornstarch

3 tbsp water

1 1/2 tbsp light soy sauce*

1 tsp dark soy sauce*[1]

2 tbsp oyster sauce

1 tsp sesame oil*

2 tbsp Shaoxing cooking wine*[2]

1 tsp sugar

**FILLING**

1 tbsp peanut oil

1/2 tsp finely minced garlic*

1/2 tsp finely minced ginger*

1/2 yellow onion, finely chopped

10 oz ground pork (or chicken)

1 small carrot, peeled and finely chopped

3 oz canned water chestnuts, drained and finely chopped[3]

5 canned or fresh baby corn,* finely chopped[3]

5 shiitake* or brown mushrooms, finely chopped

**TO SERVE**

12–16 iceberg lettuce leaves, trimmed into 5 inch rounds if desired, or other lettuce leaves[4]

1/4 cup finely chopped unsalted peanuts

1 green onion,* finely sliced

*Sauce*—Mix the cornstarch and water until lump-free, then add the remaining sauce ingredients and stir to combine.

*Cook filling*—Heat the oil in a wok or large nonstick skillet over high heat. Add the garlic and ginger, give it a quick stir, then add the onion. Cook for 1 minute, then add the pork and cook until it turns white. Add all the vegetables and cook for 2 minutes until the carrot is softened and the pork is cooked through. Add the sauce and cook for 1½ minutes or until the sauce thickens and coats the filling ingredients.

*Serve*—Transfer the filling to a serving bowl. Lay out the lettuce leaves, peanuts, and green onion on the side. To eat, spoon some filling into a lettuce leaf, top with peanuts and green onion, bundle it up, and enjoy! To fill out the meal, add a side of Chinese Fried Rice (page 120).

**NOTES**

1. Or more light soy sauce—but note that the sauce will be a lighter color.
2. Can be substituted with mirin* or dry sherry. For nonalcoholic, substitute both the water and Shaoxing cooking wine with low-sodium chicken broth.*
3. Canned water chestnuts and baby corn are widely available these days either in the Asian or canned vegetables aisle of supermarkets. They add delicious texture, so try to include them!
4. You can use any type of lettuce leaves suitable for a wrap or cup, whether crisp or soft. Iceberg lettuce is the type preferred by most Chinese restaurants. If you want to get real fancy, use a cutter to cut out rounds so they are all the same size, as pictured!

LEFTOVERS Filling—fridge 3 days, freezer 3 months.

# SHRIMP TOAST

*Seriously tastes JUST like the real thing!*

**MAKES: 16 PIECES, SERVES 5 AS A STARTER I PREP: 10 MINUTES I COOK: 15 MINUTES**

You'll be amazed how simple this restaurant icon is to make. It tastes authentic, except with even better shrimp flavor because we don't pad it out with bland fillers! It's also fun to assemble (get the kids involved). Just blitz up the shrimp with seasonings, spread onto bread like peanut butter, and cut into triangles. Fry until crisp and serve with sweet chili sauce. Watch them vanish in the blink of eye!

---

8 oz raw shrimp meat,[1] chopped into 1/2 inch pieces

1/4 tsp superfine sugar

1/2 tsp kosher salt*

1 egg white*

3 cups canola oil, plus 1 tsp

1 tsp cornstarch

1/4 tsp finely minced garlic*

1/4 tsp finely minced ginger*

2 tbsp finely sliced green onion*

4 slices white sandwich bread[2]

5 tbsp white sesame seeds

**TO SERVE**

Finely sliced green onion*

Sweet & Sour Sauce (page 327) or store-bought sweet chili sauce

*Puree shrimp meat*—Place the shrimp meat, sugar, and salt in a tall container that fits the head of an immersion blender. Blitz until the shrimp meat is smooth—about 10 seconds. Add the egg white and 1 teaspoon of oil, then blitz for 30 seconds (this lightens the mixture, then add the cornstarch and blitz for another 30 seconds.

*Mix shrimp filling*—Place the shrimp mixture in a bowl, add the garlic, ginger, and green onion and mix to combine.

*Prepare bread*—Remove the crusts from the bread. Spread the shrimp mixture on the bread, covering it from edge to edge. Smooth the surface, then cut each piece diagonally into four. Spread the sesame seeds on a small plate, then press the shrimp side of each piece of bread into the seeds so they stick (aim for full coverage!).

*Fry!*—Heat the oil in a medium saucepan to 355°F[3] over medium-high heat. Place four pieces of shrimp toast, sesame-side down, into the oil and cook for 2½ minutes. Turn, then fry the other side for 1 minute. Drain on a paper towel-lined tray. Repeat with the remaining shrimp toast, making sure that the oil temperature is 355°F before starting the next batch.

*Serve*—Serve sprinkled with green onion, and sweet chili sauce for dipping—the old-school Chinese restaurant way! Serve this as a starter for any Asian-themed meal, or pass them around as canapés at a gathering!

**NOTES**

1. Fresh or frozen and thawed (drain well and pat dry.)
2. Just your everyday soft white sandwich bread. Don't get fancy with crusty artisan sourdough—it's not soft enough!
3. If you don't have an instant read thermometer,* see Oil temperature testing on page 361 of the Glossary.
4. Air-fryer option: Works surprisingly well! Spray the basket and both sides of the shrimp toast generously with canola oil. Place in the basket, sesame-seed side down. Cook for 3 minutes at 400°F, then turn and spray the sesame-seed side with oil again. Cook for a further 4 minutes.

LEFTOVERS Fridge 2 days, but best served fresh. They can be resurrected by reheating in a 350°F oven for 5 minutes! Not suitable for freezing.

# VIETNAMESE RICE PAPER ROLLS

*Delicious and not at all difficult!*

**SERVES: 7 (MAKES 7 ROLLS) | PREP: 20 MINUTES | COOK: NONE**

Vietnamese rice paper rolls are so fresh, clean, and healthy—the perfect light summertime food! Think of them as a blank canvas for any fillings you like. Sometimes I might swap out the shrimp for sliced chicken, shredded omelet, lemongrass* beef, or even tofu. You can also use all sorts of vegetables—think carrots, cabbage, avocado, green onion,* or Asian herbs.

---

11 small (6 oz) cooked shrimp,*[1] peeled

7 butter or oak lettuce leaves (or other soft lettuce)

2 oz dried vermicelli noodles,[2] prepared as per package directions

1 cup bean sprouts

7 x 9 inch round, dried rice paper sheets[3]

14 mint leaves

**PEANUT DIPPING SAUCE**

1 tbsp natural unsweetened peanut butter*

2 tbsp hoisin sauce

1½ tbsp white vinegar (or lime juice)

⅓ cup milk (any fat %), or water

¼ tsp finely minced garlic*

½ tsp sambal oelek* (or other chili paste or sriracha*—for optional spiciness)

*Peanut sauce*—Mix the sauce ingredients in a heat-proof bowl (note—it might not come together properly, but this is okay). Microwave for 30 seconds on High, then mix again until smooth. Set aside to cool. The thickness can be adjusted with water later.

*Shrimp*—Slice in half lengthwise and remove the black vein.

*Lettuce*—Remove the crunchy core of the lettuce leaves—we only want the soft leaves (so it doesn't tear the delicate rice paper).

*Lettuce bundle*—Place some vermicelli noodles and bean sprouts inside a lettuce leaf, then roll the leaf up firmly, crushing the bean sprouts if necessary to make a neat bundle. Finish with the seam side down. Repeat with the remaining lettuce leaves to make seven bundles. This makes it (much!) easier to make the rice paper rolls—no pokey bits of bean sprouts tearing the delicate rice paper!

*Soak rice paper*—Fill a large bowl with warm water. Note which side of the rice paper is the smooth side—this is supposed to be the outside of the roll. Submerge the rice paper in the water for 2 seconds. If your bowl isn't large enough to fit the whole rice paper in one go, that's fine, just rotate it and count 2 seconds for each section you submerge in the water.

*Roll!*[4]—Place the rice paper on a work surface, smooth-side down. Place three shrimp halves with a mint leaf in between on the top third of the rice paper. Place a lettuce bundle in the middle. Starting from the bottom, fold up the rice paper to cover the lettuce bundle, then fold the sides of the rice paper in. Finally, roll the lettuce bundle over to cover the shrimp and mint leaves.

*Serve*—Serve immediately with the peanut dipping sauce.

**NOTES**

1. If using whole cooked shrimp that you peel yourself, look for ones that are around 4 inches long (when straightened, including the head and tail). If cooking yourself, heat a little oil in a nonstick skillet and cook raw peeled and deveined small shrimp for 1 minute on each side. Cool, then cut as per the recipe.
2. Not to be confused with bean thread noodles, which are clear and chewy.
3. Readily available these days in the Asian or noodle aisle of grocery stores.
4. Rolling notes! The rice paper softens and becomes sticky so it will seal itself. If you roll up using the described method, your rice paper roll should look pretty with the shrimp and mint leaves clearly visible on the smooth side of the roll with the paper seam on the side or underside.

LEFTOVERS Best served within 2 hours of making without refrigerating. However, the rolls can be kept for up to 24 hours, wrapped individually in plastic wrap to prevent them from drying out.

# MUM'S GYOZA

*The best in the world. Period.*

**MAKES: 40–45 PIECES, SERVES 5–6 AS A MAIN | PREP: 30 MINUTES | COOK: 20 MINUTES**

I always order a side of gyoza at ramen restaurants (it's the done thing in Japan!). But nobody, not even the best ramen shops, make gyoza as good as my mum! Why are Mum's so ripping good? For one thing, she goes with more pork and less cabbage. I also love how much garlic chives she puts in for that burst of pungent flavor. If you're worried about the wrapping part, don't be. It's really easy! Just watch the recipe video (scan the QR code) and you'll be a gyoza-wrapping master in no time!

---

1 tsp cornstarch, for dusting

40–45 round wonton (gyoza) wrappers (gow gee wrappers)—1½ standard packages[1]

3 tbsp vegetable oil (or other cooking oil)

⅓ cup water per batch, for steaming

**FILLING**

1½ cups very finely chopped[2] green cabbage

1 tsp kosher salt*

1 lb ground pork (the fattier the better[3])

1 cup finely chopped garlic chives*[4]

½ tsp finely minced garlic*

1 tsp finely minced ginger*

1 tsp sesame oil*

1 tbsp cornstarch

2 tsp all-purpose or light soy sauce*[5]

**DIPPING SAUCE**

Soy sauce*

Rice wine vinegar

Rayu (Japanese chili oil)*

*Cabbage*—Toss the cabbage with ½ teaspoon salt, then set aside for 20 minutes to wilt the cabbage slightly. Squeeze out the excess water, then place the cabbage in a medium bowl.

*Filling*—Add the remaining filling ingredients, including the remaining ½ teaspoon salt. Use your hands to mix until combined.

Sprinkle a baking tray with 1 teaspoon of cornstarch.

*Wrap gyoza (Use QR code to watch tutorial video)*—Place one gyoza wrapper in the palm of your left hand (for right-handed people). Dip your finger in water and run it around the edge of half the gyoza wrapper (to seal). Place 1 slightly heaped tablespoon of filling in the middle of the wrapper. Fold the wrapper over and use your right hand, assisted by your left thumb, to create four pleats. Press to seal and place on the tray. Repeat with the remaining wrappers and filling.

*Cook*—Heat 1 tablespoon of oil in a large nonstick skillet with a lid[6] over medium–high heat. Place about 12 gyoza in in the pan, arranging them in rows and so each gyoza is overlapping slightly. Cook for 2 minutes until the underside is light golden. Now pour ⅓ cup of water around the gyoza and cover with the lid.

*Steam*—Allow to steam until the water has completely evaporated (so the golden underside becomes a bit crispy again) and the wrapper is slightly translucent on top, about 3–4 minutes. Use a spatula to transfer the gyoza to a plate. Present the golden side up (i.e. upside down) as is traditional, keeping the rows together as best you can. Cook the remaining gyoza.

*Serve*—Serve the gyoza with the dipping sauce! Let people make their own sauce. I use equal portions of soy sauce and vinegar with a generous splash of chili oil. Serve with a side of Chinese Fried Rice (page 120) or a chopped salad with Asian Sesame Dressing (page 333).

**NOTES**

1. Gyoza wrappers are sold in the Asian section of the refrigerator at large grocery stores these days.
2. To chop the cabbage, cut it into ⅛ inch thick slices, then finely chop it, almost like you're mincing garlic so it blends seamlessly into the pork.
3. When cooking to impress, ask your butcher for ground pork belly. Best flavor!
4. Garlic chives substitute—¾ cup ordinary chives with an extra ½ teaspoon of finely minced garlic.
5. Use a Japanese all-purpose soy sauce, if you can—our family uses Kikkoman. Otherwise, any general-purpose soy sauce or light soy sauce will work just fine. Do not use dark soy sauce or the flavor will be too strong.
6. If you don't have a lid, just place a sheet of aluminum foil across the skillet, then top with a baking tray to keep it in place.

LEFTOVERS Fridge 4 days. Raw gyoza can be frozen for 3 months. Thaw, then cook as per the recipe.

# SPRING ROLLS

*You've never had a spring roll until you've had homemade.*

**MAKES: 15–20 SPRING ROLLS, SERVES 5–6 AS A STARTER | PREP: 25 MINUTES | COOK: 12 MINUTES**

Spring rolls don't have to be the soggy dog-chews filled with pasty mush that you've probably bought and regretted one too many times in your life! A great spring roll is stuffed with juicy meat and fresh vegetables all wrapped with light, crispy pastry that shatters as you bite into it. Have a go at making these yourself and you'll struggle to pay for a spring roll ever again!

---

2 tsp cornstarch

1 tbsp water

15–20 x 8 inch spring roll wrappers or 35–40 small spring roll wrappers,[1] thawed if frozen

3 cups canola oil

1 green onion,* finely sliced diagonally (optional)

**FILLING**

1½ tsp finely minced garlic*

14 oz ground pork (the fattier the better)[2]

1½ cups shredded peeled carrot (1 large or 2 small)

1½ heaped cups bean sprouts

1½ tightly packed cups finely shredded green cabbage[3]

6 dried shiitake mushrooms*[4]

1 tbsp canola oil

1 tsp cornstarch

2 tsp soy sauce* (light or all-purpose is best, dark is also okay)

1½ tbsp oyster sauce

**CHOICE OF DIPPING SAUCE**

Sweet & Sour Sauce (page 327)

Sweet chili sauce, store-bought

*Shiitake mushrooms*—Soak the mushrooms in boiling water for 30 minutes until soft. Drain, squeeze out any excess water, then finely chop into ⅛ inch pieces.

*Filling*—Heat the oil in a large nonstick skillet over high heat. Cook the garlic for 15 seconds until light golden, then add the pork and cook, breaking it up as you go, until it turns white. Add the carrot, bean sprouts, cabbage, and mushrooms and cook for 3 minutes. Add the cornstarch, soy sauce, and oyster sauce and cook for 1 minute until the liquid has evaporated. The filling should not be watery—it should be kind of sticky (watery filling = soggy spring rolls). Transfer to a bowl, cool to room temperature, and refrigerate for 20 minutes.[5]

*Cornstarch water*—Mix the cornstarch and water in a small bowl (for sealing the rolls).

*Wrap spring rolls*—Carefully peel off one spring roll wrapper, keeping the others covered under a damp dish towel. Place the wrapper, smooth-side down, in a diamond orientation. Place 2 tablespoons of filling on the bottom of the diamond. Roll up halfway, fold the sides in, then finish rolling. Use the cornstarch mixture to seal. The rolls should be about 4 inches long and 1 inch thick once wrapped. Repeat with the remaining wrappers and filling.

*Fry*—Pour enough oil into a wok or large saucepan so the depth is double the thickness of the spring rolls. Heat on medium-high to 355°F. Carefully place the spring rolls in the oil (about 4–5 at a time). Fry, turning occasionally, until deep golden and crisp, around 3 minutes. Transfer to paper towels to drain. Repeat with the remaining spring rolls. (See Note 6 for other cooking methods.)

*Serve*—Serve piping hot with your sauce of choice for dipping!

**NOTES**

1. Spring roll wrappers can be found at grocery stores in the fridge or freezer section.
2. Want to go deluxe? Ask your butcher to grind pork belly meat for you!
3. Green cabbage or napa cabbage* is fine here.
4. Dried have a stronger flavor but can be substituted with 8 fresh shiitake mushrooms.
5. The filling must be fully cooled before using otherwise it may make the spring roll wrapper soggy or burst open when frying. Neither scenario is a happy one!
6. Air-fryer option: Works exceptionally well! Spray the spring rolls generously all over with canola oil. Cook at 365°F for 4 minutes, turn, then cook for a further 4 minutes. Baking option: Not as crispy but works quite well! Spray generously with oil, then bake on a rack set over a tray at 400°F for 20–25 minutes until golden and crispy—no need to turn.

LEFTOVERS Best served freshly made. However, leftovers will keep for 3 days in the fridge and can be resurrected by baking in a preheated 425°F oven for 7 minutes. Or, re-fry briefly!

# LAKSA

*The best coconut noodle soup in the world.*

**SERVES: 2 I PREP: 20 MINUTES I COOK: 45 MINUTES**

To say I love laksa would be a massive understatement. Back in my office job days, I was even part of a lunch club whose sole purpose was regularly stalking new laksa joints in search of the best. Yep, laksa is a "thing" for food lovers! Sydney has some truly excellent laksa shops but sadly, where I live, they're all a very long drive away. So I make my own at home for those (frequent!) laksa itches that need scratching. I hope you love this laksa as much as I do!

**CHICKEN BROTH**

2 cups low-sodium chicken broth*

1 cup water

3 chicken drumsticks

**LAKSA CHILI SAUCE**

½ tsp sugar

1½ tsp light soy sauce*

¼ tsp finely minced garlic*

1½ tsp laksa paste[1]

1 tbsp sriracha,* or other chili sauce

1 tbsp sambal oelek,* or more sriracha*

1 tbsp canola oil

**SOUP**

1½ tbsp canola oil

2 garlic cloves,* finely minced

1½ tsp finely minced ginger*

1 lemongrass* stalk, white part only, finely grated

2 bird's eye chilies,*[2] deseeded and finely chopped

½ cup laksa paste[1]

14 fl oz can full-fat coconut milk*

2 tsp fish sauce (or soy sauce*)

1½ cups tofu puffs[3]

2 oz dried vermicelli noodles

3 oz fresh lo mein noodles[4]

**TO SERVE**

1 cup bean sprouts

Fresh cilantro

Crispy fried shallots* (highly recommended)

Finely sliced red chili* (optional)

Lime wedges

*Chicken broth*—Place the broth ingredients in a medium saucepan over high heat. Bring to a boil, then reduce to medium. Let it simmer gently for 25 minutes or until the chicken flesh is falling off the bone and the liquid reduces by about one-third. Remove the chicken from the broth and set the broth aside.

*Shred chicken*—Pull the chicken flesh off the bone, place in a bowl (discard bone), and set aside.

*Laksa chili sauce*—Mix the ingredients together in a small bowl and set aside for 20 minutes.

*Make soup*—Heat the oil in a large saucepan over medium-low heat. Add the garlic and ginger, sauté for 20 seconds, then add the lemongrass and chili. Cook for 1 minute. Add the laksa paste, then turn the heat up to medium and cook for 2 minutes, stirring constantly until fragrant. Add the prepared chicken broth, coconut milk, fish sauce, and 2 teaspoons of the laksa chili sauce. Stir, then place the lid on and simmer for 10 minutes. Adjust the fish sauce to taste. Add the tofu puffs, turn off the heat, then leave on the stove, covered, for 5 minutes, so the tofu puffs absorb the tasty broth.

*Noodles*—Prepare the noodles as per the package directions, then divide between two bowls.

*Assemble*—Top the noodles with the shredded chicken, then pour the broth over. Top with bean sprouts and sprinkle with cilantro, crispy fried shallots, and sliced pepper, if desired.

*Serve*—Serve with the laksa chili sauce on the side and lime wedges for squeezing.

**NOTES**

1. My favorite brand is Por Kwan, which is sold at Asian stores and some independent grocery stores. The laksa paste made by mainstream Westernized Asian brands sold at grocery stores tend to be too sweet and lack depth of flavor.
2. Bird's eye chilies are quite spicy. Laksa is supposed to be a bit spicy but, if you are spice-shy, feel free to reduce or omit, or add at the end so you can control the spice level.
3. Deep-fried tofu has a puffy spongelike texture and soaks up the soup broth so it bursts in your mouth when you bite into it—is one of the signature joys of laksa! Find it in some larger grocery stores and Asian stores in the fridge section.
4. Or 2 oz more dried vermicelli noodles. The better laksa joints use both noodles.
5. Make ahead: Components can be made up to 3 days ahead, stored separately in the fridge.

LEFTOVERS Best eaten right away once assembled! However, leftovers can be kept in the fridge for 3 days, with the noodles separated from the broth.

# CHINESE NOODLE SOUP

*A master recipe that will serve you well!*

**SERVES: 2 I PREP: 5 MINUTES I COOK: 10 MINUTES**

A good, full-flavored, clear Chinese soup broth is something that everyone should know how to make. Once you have a recipe that you like (in case you missed the hint, I am suggesting that this one here is IT!), it will save you on those nights when you're scrambling for a quick meal. Just make the broth and throw in any vegetables you have, then ladle the soup over any noodles. Even spaghetti—yep, been there, done that! Finish with a dash of chili and boom, dinner done!

6 oz fresh thin egg noodles[1]

2 baby bok choy, cut in half lengthwise (or quarters if large) and washed, or other vegetables of choice[2]

1 cup (5 oz) shredded poached chicken (see page 130)

**BROTH**

3 cups low-sodium chicken broth*

2 garlic cloves,* smashed

¾ inch piece of ginger, cut into 3 slices (no need to peel)

1½ tbsp light soy sauce*[3]

2 tsp sugar

1½ tbsp Shaoxing cooking wine*

½ tsp sesame oil*

**GARNISHES (OPTIONAL)**

1 green onion,* finely sliced

Crispy fried shallots*

Chili paste of choice, or chili oil

*Broth*—Place the broth ingredients in a medium saucepan over high heat. Cover, bring to a boil, then reduce to medium and simmer for 8–10 minutes to allow the flavors to infuse.

*Cook noodles*—Meanwhile, cook the noodles according to the package directions. Drain, but do not rinse (no matter what the package says![1]), and divide between two bowls.

*Bok choy*—Add the bok choy to the soup broth and cook for 1 minute.

*Serve*—Pick the garlic and ginger out of the broth. Ladle the broth over the noodles, then top with chicken and bok choy. Sprinkle with green onion and crispy fried shallots (if using). I also always add a big dollop of chili paste!

**NOTES**

1. Or 3 oz dried egg noodles or dried rice noodles, prepared as per package directions—but do not rinse, whatever the package says! This has the effect of diluting the flavor of the broth and cools the noodles—bad!
2. The vegetables are cooked in the broth for convenience, so you can use any vegetables than can be boiled, like carrots, zucchini, or beans.
3. Light soy sauce keeps the broth nice and clear. All-purpose soy sauce can also be used but the broth color will be slightly darker. Do not use dark soy sauce.

LEFTOVERS Broth—fridge 5 days, freezer 3 months. Noodles are best cooked fresh.

# OUR SECRET FAMILY QUICK RAMEN

*Authentic-tasting miso ramen in under an hour? Yes!*

**SERVES: 2 | PREP: 15 MINUTES | COOK: 45 MINUTES**

**This is my family's from-scratch "instant ramen" recipe! Real ramen takes days to prepare, involving mountains of broth bones and slowly simmering big pots of soup. We started making this quick miso ramen recipe instead that tastes uncannily like the real thing but takes a fraction of the time and effort! Ground pork is the secret. It flavors the broth and then doubles as a topping. Aside from pork, you just need a handful of Japanese and Western pantry staples. Customize your ramen toppings however you like. We love to do Sapporo-style miso ramen, complete with soft-boiled egg, sweetcorn, and of course a generous pat of butter!**

1 1/2 tbsp pork lard[1]

1/2 tbsp sesame oil*

7 oz fatty ground pork (pork belly best!)[2]

2 tsp finely minced garlic*

1/2 tsp finely minced ginger*

1 1/2 tbsp cooking sake*

7 oz fresh ramen noodles[3]

**BROTH**

3 cups low-sodium chicken broth*

1/4 cup water

5 dried shiitake mushrooms*

1 small yellow onion, thickly sliced

**RAMEN BROTH**

2 tbsp shiro miso[4] (white miso)

1 tsp sugar

1 tsp light soy sauce*[5]

1 1/4 tsp dashi powder[6]

Pinch of kosher salt*

**PORK SAUCE**

1 tsp canola oil

1/2 tsp sugar

1 tsp light soy sauce*[5]

1/2 tsp dark soy sauce*

1 tbsp cooking sake*

**OTHER TOPPINGS**

1 egg, soft-boiled*

1/3 cup corn kernels (frozen, or canned and drained)

1 1/2 cups bean sprouts

1/4 tsp toasted white sesame seeds*

1 green onion,* finely sliced

1 1/2 tbsp unsalted butter, cut into 2 slices

*Broth*—Place the broth ingredients in a medium saucepan over medium–high heat. Bring to a simmer, then reduce the heat to low. Cover, then simmer gently for 30 minutes. Set aside and keep warm.

*Cook pork*—Place the lard and sesame oil in a large saucepan over medium–high heat. Once the lard melts, add the pork and cook until it changes from pink to white. Add the garlic and ginger, then cook until you get some golden pork bits sticking to the base of the pan (about 2 minutes). Add the sake and cook for another 30 seconds. Remove from the stove.

*Ramen broth*—Strain the broth into the ground pork pot through a fine-mesh strainer, pressing the liquid out of the mushrooms and onion. Discard the onion and reserve the mushrooms for another purpose (add to a stir-fry!). Whisk in the ramen broth ingredients. Return to the stove over medium heat and simmer for 3 minutes.

*Strain*—Strain the ramen broth into another medium saucepan, pressing the liquid out of the pork. Reserve pork. Cover the broth with a lid and keep hot for serving.

*Pork topping*—Heat the 1 teaspoon of oil in a medium nonstick skillet over medium–high heat. Add the reserved ground pork and cook for 1 minute. Add the other pork sauce ingredients and cook for 1 minute until caramelized. Transfer to a bowl and keep warm.

*Corn and bean sprouts*—Warm the corn and bean sprouts for 30 seconds on High in the microwave.

*Noodles*—Cook the noodles as per the package directions but no matter what the package says, do not rinse! This dilutes the flavor of the broth and cools the noodles—both bad things!

*Assemble and serve*—Divide the noodles between two bowls and pour the hot ramen broth on top. Top with the pork, egg, corn, and bean sprouts. Sprinkle with sesame seeds and green onion, then place the butter into the broth. Serve!

**NOTES**

1. Pork fat that can be found at large grocery stores, usually alongside butter. Use leftovers for roasting vegetables—extra flavor!
2. Ask your butcher to grind up pork belly meat for you! If you can only find standard packages of ground pork, add another tablespoon of pork lard.
3. Ramen noodles can be found at Asian grocery stores. Substitute with thin egg noodles.
4. A type of light miso that can be found at large grocery stores and Asian stores.
5. Light soy sauce can be substituted with all-purpose soy sauce.
6. Dashi powder can be found at large grocery stores and Asian stores. It's a fish-based broth powder that is a key ingredient in Japanese cooking.
7. Make ahead: Ramen components can be stored separately for up to 3 days in the fridge, though the noodles should be cooked fresh.

# WONTON SOUP

*The ultimate freezer standby.*

**MAKES: 50 WONTONS, ENOUGH FOR 8–10 BOWLS OF SOUP I PREP: 40 MINUTES I COOK: 15 MINUTES**

Who doesn't love a bowl full of these slippery-tailed little mouthfuls of goodness? My pork and shrimp wontons are lightly flavored with a touch of ginger and sesame oil for extra tastiness. They're delicious with noodles just tossed with oyster sauce and sesame oil, but I love them most in clear soup as in this recipe. Wontons freeze exceptionally well, so I always make extra. Nothing is more handy than pulling out a bag of these plump little dumplings when you can't be bothered cooking. They're the ultimate homemade convenience food!

---

50–60 wonton wrappers[1]

½ green onion,* finely sliced

Chili paste of choice (optional)

**WONTON FILLING**

7 oz ground pork

7 oz raw shrimp,* peeled, deveined and roughly chopped[2]

1 tbsp finely minced ginger*

5 tbsp finely minced green onion* (about 2)

1 tbsp light soy sauce*[3]

2 tbsp Shaoxing cooking wine*[4]

½ tsp kosher salt*

2 tsp sesame oil*

**WONTON SOUP (MAKES 2 BOWLS OF SOUP)**

1 quantity broth from Chinese Noodle Soup (page 242)

3 stems Chinese broccoli,[5] cut into 2½ inch lengths

5 oz fresh egg noodles[6]

*Filling*—Place the filling ingredients in a bowl and use a potato masher to mash until fairly smooth, about 20 mashes. Don't turn the shrimp into a complete paste—small chunks are good.

*Wrap wontons*—Scan the QR code below to watch the tutorial video! Lay five wonton wrappers on a work surface (keep unused wontons in the package so they don't dry out). Place 1 heaped teaspoon of filling on each wonton wrapper (I use a measuring teaspoon and an eating teaspoon to scrape the filling out). Brush two edges of the wrapper with water, then fold into a triangle to seal, pressing out the air. Brush water on one corner and bring the opposite corners together, pressing to seal. Keep the wrapped wontons in a container with a lid as you work so they don't dry out. Repeat with the remaining wontons.

*Wonton soup*—Make the broth as per the directions on page 242. Boil the Chinese broccoli in the broth for 2 minutes to cook through.

*Cook*—Bring a large pot of water to a boil. Cook the noodles as per the package directions. Transfer with tongs to a colander to drain, then divide among bowls. In the same water, cook the wontons for 4 minutes or until they float. Transfer with a slotted spoon straight into serving bowls.

*Serve*—Ladle the broth over the noodles and wontons. Top with the Chinese broccoli and serve sprinkled with green onion and a dollop of chili paste, if desired!

**NOTES**

1. Wonton wrappers are square and are available in large grocery stores in the refrigerated section, usually alongside fresh pasta. The standard packages have 40 sheets, so you will need two packages. There are yellow and white varieties. Use either.
2. If using whole fresh shrimp that you peel yourself, you will need 14 oz. Reserve the shrimp heads and shells and add into the Easy Shrimp Broth (see page 143) to make the most of their intense shrimp flavor!
3. Can be substituted with all-purpose soy sauce, but not dark soy sauce.
4. Can be substituted with low-sodium chicken broth.*
5. Also known as gai lan or kai lan, sold at everyday grocery stores these days. Or use other vegetables of choice that can be cooked in broth.
6. Or 2 oz dried egg or rice noodles.
7. Wontons are excellent for freezing! Freeze uncooked wontons in airtight containers. Cook from frozen for 6–8 minutes as per the recipe directions. IMPORTANT: Do not freeze wontons if you made them with defrosted frozen shrimp.

LEFTOVERS Fridge 4 days, but best made fresh. Uncooked wontons are great for freezing (see Note 7).

# BIGGER THINGS

**For Sunday suppers and impressing friends.**

# TACHIN

*Crispy Persian saffron rice stuffed with spiced lamb. 100% amazing!*

 **SERVES: 6–8 I PREP: 20 MINUTES I COOK: 90 MINUTES**

Tachin is a traditional Persian dish of fluffy, saffron-stained rice baked into an upturned cake. The bottom scorches lightly as the rice cooks in the pan so, when you flip it out, you get a deliciously crispy layer on top, a bit like an upside-down paella. Rice-only versions of tachin are common, but the best ones for me also have delicately spiced, stewed meat sandwiched in the middle. I've used ground lamb here, which works beautifully. You could easily use other meats, though. As if all this wasn't enough, it's also so impressive in appearance—I mean, just look at it!

**BARBERRIES**

1½ tbsp unsalted butter

½ cup dried barberries[1]

1 tsp superfine sugar

Canola oil spray

**PARBOILED RICE**

2 cups basmati rice[2]

1 tbsp kosher salt*

**LAMB FILLING**

1½ tbsp unsalted butter

1 yellow onion, finely chopped

2 garlic cloves,* finely minced

1 lb ground lamb (or beef)

½ tsp each black pepper, allspice, and ground cardamom

1 tsp ground turmeric

1½ tsp ground cinnamon

1¼ tsp kosher salt*

1 cup canned crushed tomatoes

½ cup water

2 tbsp pine nuts, toasted*

**SAFFRON YOGURT MIX**

½ lightly packed tsp saffron threads[3]

2 tbsp boiling water

1 cup plain yogurt

⅓ cup melted ghee* or unsalted butter

3 egg yolks*

¾ tsp kosher salt*

**YOGURT SAUCE**

1½ cups plain yogurt

1½ tbsp lemon juice

1½ tbsp extra-virgin olive oil

⅜ tsp kosher salt*

*Barberries*—Melt the butter in a small skillet over medium–high heat. Add the dried barberries and stir for 1 minute until they plump up. Sprinkle with the sugar and stir to mix together. Transfer to a bowl and set aside.

Preheat the oven to 400°F.

*Parboil rice*—Bring 12 cups of water to a boil in a medium pot. Add the rice and salt then, once the water comes back up to a boil, cook for 5 minutes. Drain in a colander, then set the colander over the pot and leave to steam-dry for 10 minutes.

*Lamb filling*—Melt the butter in a large nonstick skillet over medium–high heat. Cook the onion and garlic for 2 minutes until the edges are tinged with gold. Add the lamb and cook, breaking it up as you go, until you no longer see pink. Add the spices and salt, then cook for 2 minutes. Stir in the tomatoes and water, then adjust the heat so it's simmering gently. Cook for 8 minutes until the liquid mostly evaporates, but the mixture is still juicy. Stir in the pine nuts and one-third of the barberries. Cool for at least 5 minutes before using.

*Saffron yogurt mix*—Grind the saffron threads into a powder using a mortar and pestle.[3] Add the boiling water to the mortar, then stir to dissolve. Pour into a large bowl, then add the yogurt, ghee or butter, egg yolks, and salt. Whisk to combine, then mix in the drained rice.

*Assemble*—Spray a 9½ inch clear glass pie dish[4] with canola oil, then spread with one-third of the rice mixture. Pat down firmly, then smooth the surface (I use an offset spatula). Use one-third of the remaining rice to create a ½ inch thick wall around the inside of the pie dish, right up to the rim, pressing the rice mixture firmly. Fill the rice mold with lamb mixture just to ½ inch from the rim. Sprinkle with half the remaining barberries. Top with the remaining rice and smooth the surface so it's level with the edge of the pie dish (pack it in real good!).

*Bake*—Bake in the oven for 1 hour until the top is golden and crunchy, and the base is golden. Remove from the oven and rest for 5 minutes.

*Yogurt sauce*—Mix the yogurt sauce ingredients in a bowl, then set aside in the fridge for at least 30 minutes, or until required.

*Serve*—Turn the tachin out upside down onto a serving platter.[5] Sprinkle with the remaining barberries and serve with the yogurt sauce. This dish will pair nicely with a side salad of chopped tomatoes, cucumbers, radish, and red onion tossed with Lemon Dressing (page 333), finished with finely chopped cilantro.

**NOTES**

1. A Persian ingredient found at speciality and Middle Eastern stores that taste like sour cranberries and add lovely pops of color. Substitute with dried sour cherries or dried cranberries, roughly chopped.
2. Basmati is the traditional rice used in this dish. However, long-grain or medium-grain white rice can be substituted. Do not use jasmine, paella, risotto, or sushi rice.
3. Saffron gives the rice its striking color and unique flavor. Grinding it releases more flavor and color. Use ¼ teaspoon imitation saffron powder for a more economical alternative. If you don't have a mortar and pestle, just soak the threads in hot water for 5 minutes.
4. Glass works best so you can check the color of the underside. If you don't have glass, just lift the edge of the rice to check. The pie dish I use is 8 inches diameter across the base and 9½ inches at the rim. You can also use a square or rectangle dish.
5. To invert, cover the tachin in the pie dish with a serving plate. While holding them together, firmly flip—swiftly and with confidence!

LEFTOVERS Fridge 3 days, freezer 3 months.

# BEEF WELLINGTON

*Gordon Ramsay, eat your heart out.*

**SERVES: 6–8 I PREP: 2 HOURS + 1 HOUR RESTING + 12–24 HOURS BRINING I COOK: 2 HOURS**

Even professional chefs tell me that beef Wellington gives them nightmares and they've always struggled to nail it. The most common failures are a soggy base and unsightly red juices bleeding out after slicing. Well, I can never resist a challenge! After many attempts (those chefs weren't kidding), I'm proud to say I've cracked the perfect beef Wellington. Of course it involves some neat tricks! Salting the beef ahead locks the juices in so they don't leak out. For a crispy base, a protective layer of prosciutto and crepe around the meat is the key to preventing sogginess. And you need a full 1 hour resting time, so all the beef juices get reabsorbed into the meat. The result? Incredibly juicy, edge-to-edge rosy-pink beef with a 100 percent crispy base! The perfect Wellington.

---

2 lb center-cut beef tenderloin[1] 9–10 inches long, patted dry

2 tsp kosher salt*

2 tbsp extra-virgin olive oil

16 thin slices prosciutto[2]

2 tbsp dijon mustard

1½ lb butter puff pastry[3] (for wrapping plus optional lattice)

All-purpose flour, for dusting

Canola oil spray

**MUSHROOM DUXELLE**

1½ lb portabella mushrooms,[4] cleaned with paper towels, chopped into ½ inch pieces

4 tbsp unsalted butter

4 oz shallots,* finely diced

3 garlic cloves,* finely minced

¼ tsp kosher salt*

⅛ tsp black pepper

**CREPE**

1 large egg*

½ cup all-purpose flour

½ cup milk

Pinch of kosher salt*

2 tsp finely chopped chives (optional)

**EGG WASH**

2 egg yolks* mixed with 2 tsp milk

**TO SERVE**

Red Wine Sauce (page 327) or dijon mustard

*Brine beef*[5]—Sprinkle the salt over the beef, then rub it all over the meat. Put the beef on a rack set over a tray, then refrigerate, uncovered, for 12–24 hours.

*Sear beef*—Heat the olive oil in a cast-iron skillet over high heat until very, very hot. Sear each side of the beef for just 30 seconds, until browned. Transfer to a rack and cool for 30 minutes. Wrap tightly in plastic wrap, twisting the ends tightly to give it a neat cylindrical shape. Refrigerate for 1 hour.

*Crepe*—Whisk together the egg, flour, milk, and salt until smooth. Stir in the chives (if using). Refrigerate for 1 hour (no longer, or it will get too thick).

*Mushroom duxelle*—Place the mushrooms in a large food processor and pulse 5–10 times, scraping the sides as necessary, until the mushrooms are chopped into 1⁄16 inch pieces.

Melt the butter in a large, deep, nonstick skillet (or heavy-based pot) over medium–high heat. Sauté the shallots and garlic for 3 minutes, then add the mushrooms, salt, and pepper. Cook for 20–25 minutes until most of the liquid has evaporated and the mushrooms cook down into a dry paste consistency.[6] When you draw a path across the base of the pan, no liquid should leak out from the mushrooms.

*Mushroom slab*—Lightly spray a baking tray with oil, then line with parchment paper with some overhang (so it can be lifted out later). Lightly spray the paper with oil. Measure the size of your beef,[7] then spread the mushroom duxelle in the tray so it covers an area equal to the surface of the beef—you don't need to be exact. Cover with a piece of parchment paper, then press down firmly with your hands to form a thin slab. Remove the paper and smooth the surface using a small offset spatula. Cool, then refrigerate, uncovered, until required.

*Bake crepe*—Preheat the oven to 350°F.

Spray a rimmed 16 x 12 inch baking tray[8] lightly with oil. Pour the batter in, then tilt to spread it evenly all across the tray. Bake for 6 minutes until just set, then remove from the oven and let it cool on the tray. It should be soft and pliable. Do not refrigerate.

*Prepare crepe wrap*—Measure the length and circumference of your beef again, then trim the crepe to that size plus 2 inches extra (headroom for both length and width!). Lay the crepe on a large sheet of plastic wrap. Cover the crepe with overlapping slices of prosciutto, aiming for full coverage.

*Roll out mushroom slab*—Use the parchment paper overhang to lift the mushroom slab off the tray and place it on a work surface. Cover with another sheet of parchment paper, then roll the slab out to an even ⅛ inch thickness (just like you're rolling out pastry!) so it is large enough to cover the entire surface of the crepe. Remove the top sheet of parchment paper.

*Top crepe with mushroom*—With the mushroom slab still on the paper, flip it upside down, with the paper-side facing up, on top of the prosciutto so it covers the surface area of the crepe.[9] Remove the paper, patch up any cracks as needed using your fingers, then trim off (eat!) any excess mushroom so it lines up with the edges of the crepe.

*Wrap beef in crepe*—Remove the beef from the fridge and unwrap. Brush mustard all over the meat. Place the beef on the lower third of the prepared crepe. Working from the edge closest to you, use the plastic wrap to lift up the crepe firmly (but gently!), rolling the beef up in the crepe as tightly as possible. Finish with the seam side down. Trim the edges with scissors so the crepe is not hanging beyond the end of the beef. Wrap tightly in plastic wrap, then twist the ends tightly to form a neat log shape. Refrigerate on a bed of dish towels as you prepare the puff pastry.

Preheat the oven to 425°F for 30 minutes. Set the oven shelf one-third of the way up from the bottom of the oven.

*Prepare puff layer 1*[10]—Thaw the puff pastry as needed to make it pliable for rolling, then place it on a large sheet of parchment paper sprinkled with flour. Measure the size of your beef roll (it grows!), allowing for enough extra pastry to cover the ends and a 1½ inch overlap at the seam, then trim the pastry to size. (If you intend to do the optional lattice layer—see below—ensure the pastry is no thicker than ⅛ inch[11]. Roll it thinner if necessary.)

*Wrap beef in puff layer*—Brush the long top edge of the pastry with the egg wash. Remove the plastic from the beef. Place the beef on the lower end of the pastry then, working from the edge closest to you, use the parchment paper to help roll it up in the puff pastry. Finish with the pastry seam-side down. Enclose the ends with pastry by trimming, brushing with egg wash, then pressing to seal. Loosely wrap with the used parchment paper, then refrigerate while preparing the lattice layer.

*Lattice layer (optional)*[12]—Lay out a sheet of partially thawed puff pastry on a well-floured sheet of parchment paper. Pressing down firmly, slowly roll a lattice dough cutter lengthwise across the pastry. Separate the lattice gently to ensure the pastry is properly cut through, then transfer the lattice with the paper to an upside-down baking tray. Check the paper is still well floured so the lattice can slide off easily.

Remove the beef from the fridge, unwrap, and place it on a sheet of parchment paper on a baking tray. Brush it all over with egg wash. Gripping the lattice paper and the upside-down tray with one hand, lower it down close to the beef Wellington. Then use your dominant hand to slowly slide the lattice off the paper to cover the beef, controlling how wide the lattice diamonds are spread before it touches the egg wash (once it's on the beef, it is hard to adjust). Tuck the long edges of the lattice under the beef, then trim. Enclose the ends of the beef with the lattice, using the egg wash to seal. Brush the lattice with egg wash (see video for demonstration).

*Cook Wellington*—Insert a cooking thermometer* horizontally through one end of the Wellington so the tip is in the middle of the beef. Leave the beef on the counter until the internal temperature reaches at least 52°F,[13] then place the beef in the oven for 40 minutes or until the internal temperature reads exactly 95°F.

*Rest*—Remove the beef from the oven and immediately transfer to a rack. Leave to rest, uncovered, for 1 hour.[13] The temperature will rise by a whopping 38°F to 133°F as it rests (for medium-rare).

*Serve*—Carve the Wellington into 1 inch thick slices using a serrated knife. Marvel at the blushing pink perfection and crispy base! A tiny amount of red meat juice may leak out. If so, dab with paper towels before putting it on plates. Keep the uncut beef Wellington on the rack to protect the crispy base.

For a truly great, high-end restaurant-worthy experience, serve on a bed of Creamy Mashed Potato (page 338) with Red Wine Sauce (page 327). Otherwise, serve with a dab of dijon mustard. Though honestly, between the ridiculously juicy meat and the mushroom duxelle, you don't really need a sauce! Complete your meal with steamed vegetables lightly dressed with French Dressing (page 333).

Congratulations! You have just made beef Wellington, a feat that even some professional chefs admit they have never conquered. You legend, you!

*See Notes on page 256.*

TRAY-BAKED CREPE

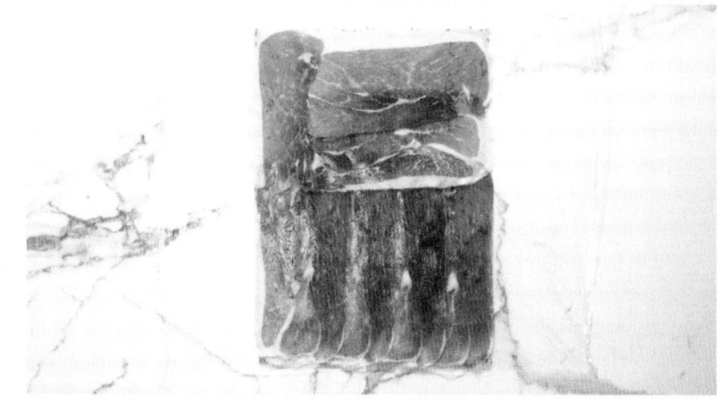

PROSCIUTTO

MUSHROOM DUXELLE “SLAB”

ROLLING UP BEEF IN CREPE

WRAP TIGHTLY IN PLASTIC WRAP

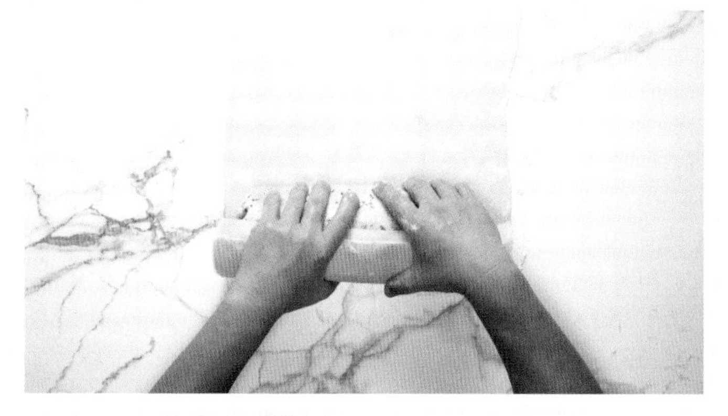

WRAP WITH PUFF PASTRY

OPTIONAL LATTICE

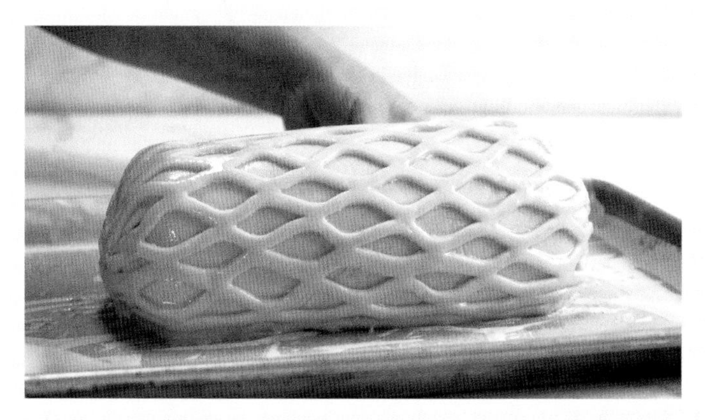

READY TO BAKE!

## NOTES

1. Ask your butcher for "center-cut beef tenderloin." This is a thick cylindrical piece of beef that is uniform in thickness so it cooks evenly. The more economical tenderloin cut–the thinner tapered tail end–will work but it needs to be folded and tied to create a "log" of even thickness.
2. You need enough prosciutto to fully wrap the beef, with each slice overlapping. This provides extra insurance against leakage, to protect the crispy base.
3. It's best to get pastry sheets large enough to wrap the beef Wellington. If you can't, just stick the smaller sheets together to make a big enough pastry sheet using lightly whisked egg to adhere, then "smear" the pastry to hide the seam.
4. Best for great mushroomy flavor but white mushrooms and brown mushrooms work well too.
5. Brining makes all the difference! It helps trap the beef juices in the meat fibers so very little unsightly red meat juice bleeds from the beef. This also keeps the base crisp once cut and seasons the beef all the way through.
6. The duxelle should be dry, yet moist enough so you can roll a 1 inch ball without the mixture sticking to your hands.
7. I use string to determine the circumference, then I use a ruler to measure the string and length of the beef log. Note: The log gets bigger as you progress through the recipe!
8. You need a tray at least the size of the surface area of the beef. If it's larger, that's fine because the crepe batter is thick enough that you can control how far it spreads.
9. If the mushroom slab breaks when you flip it over, just peel the paper off and patch it up.
10. Partially frozen pastry is the easiest to handle for both the first layer and lattice layer. Fully thawed puff pastry can be too sticky and floppy to use. Place it back in the freezer at any point to refreeze to firm it up. If it fully freezes again, don't worry as it only takes minutes to start thawing again.
11. If puff layer 1 is thicker than ⅛ inch and you do the lattice layer on top of it, puff layer 1 will not fully cook through. Roll it out thinner to ⅛ inch on a sheet of parchment paper dusted with flour. However, if you are not doing the lattice layer, then the puff pastry can be thicker as it will cook through.
12. The lattice layer is traditional but 100% optional. Wellington looks great with unadorned puff pastry! To cut the lattice layer, place a sheet of puff pastry on a VERY well dusted sheet of parchment paper. Trim the pastry so the length is 20% longer than the length of the beef, and the height is two-thirds of the circumference (because the lattice gets stretched). Dust the pastry surface lightly with flour, then dust the lattice cutter. Starting from the short end, holding down the edge of the pastry in place with the palm of your hand, apply pressure firmly and roll the cutter along the length of the pastry (I do little backward and forward motions to ensure it is fully cutting through). If it gets sticky, sprinkle with extra flour (don't lift the cutter mid-roll!). Pull the lattice apart to ensure the slits are cut properly. If not, use a small knife and follow the lines. Using the paper, transfer the pastry onto a large upside-down lightweight baking tray (this is the easiest way to slide the lattice onto the beef). Then freeze until partially frozen, if needed.
13. Ensure the beef internal temperature is no lower than 52°F when putting the Wellington in the oven or there may not be enough residual heat for the internal temperature to rise from the pull temperature of 95°F to the target 133°F as it rests (perfect medium-rare). A full 1 hour's resting time is needed to settle the meat and minimize leakage of unsightly red meat juices (plus, a crisp base!). The internal temperature will peak at 133°F at 40 minutes, then decline to 130°F at the 1 hour mark. Don't worry if your beef peaks at higher than 133°F. Even if it reaches 145°F, it will still be pink and juicy! And frankly, even if your beef is not as pink as you desired, it's still going to be juicy thanks to the brining, the tender cut of beef and the enclosed cooking method.
14. If your Wellington only rises to 130°F, that's fine as it is still medium-rare. It's great even at 127°F, which is technically rare but looks and tastes medium-rare in Wellington.
15. Make ahead: The mushroom duxelle slab can be prepared the day before. The beef can be prepared up to the point of wrapping in the crepe or in the puff pastry, then left overnight and finished the next day.

**LEFTOVERS** Best consumed freshly made while the pastry is crispy. However, will keep 4 days in the fridge in a single block–don't slice. Reheat on a tray, covered with aluminum foil, in a 200°F oven (conventional and fan-forced) until the beef is 120°F (still pink) and the pastry is re-crisped. Time will depend on size of Wellington. Not suitable for freezing.

# CHRISTMAS BAKED SALMON

*My readers would have my head if I didn't include this!*

 **SERVES: 8–10 I PREP: 25 MINUTES + COOLING I COOK: 25 MINUTES**

This festive holiday main was an instant hit with my website readers! Many tell me they even make it year-round because it looks so great and pays off so well for minimal effort. Featuring a honey butter glaze, this whole side of salmon is baked in aluminum foil before being slathered with creamy dill sauce and topped with a rubble of colorful festive toppings. It's a celebration of flavors, textures, and the holiday season that's as pretty as a picture!

**CREAMY DILL SAUCE**

1½ cups sour cream (full-fat essential)

½ lightly packed cup finely chopped dill

½ shallot,* finely grated

1½ tbsp lemon zest

½ tsp kosher salt*

**"TAPENADE"**

1 cup orange juice[2]

1 cup dried cranberries

1 cup slivered almonds, toasted[3]

⅓ cup roughly chopped Italian parsley

¼ tsp each kosher salt* and black pepper

1 tbsp extra-virgin olive oil

**SALMON**

2½–3 lb salmon side,[1] skin on, pin-boned

2¼ tsp kosher salt*

1 tsp black pepper

**HONEY BUTTER GLAZE**

10 tbsp unsalted butter

½ cup honey

3 garlic cloves,* finely minced

**TO SERVE**

Seeds from 1 pomegranate*

¼ cup roughly chopped parsley

3 tbsp lemon juice

2 lemons, each cut into 6 wedges

*Creamy dill sauce*—Mix the sauce ingredients in a bowl until smooth. Refrigerate until required.

*"Tapenade"*—Heat the orange juice in a saucepan over high heat until hot, then turn off the heat and add the cranberries. Cover with a lid and stand for 15 minutes so they plump up, then drain (discard liquid) and cool.

Mix the cranberries with the remaining tapenade ingredients. Set aside until required.

Preheat the oven to 350°F.

*Prepare salmon*—Cover a baking tray with two layers of aluminum foil, then top with parchment paper. Place the salmon on the paper, then fold up the foil sides a bit so the glaze won't run onto the tray.

*Honey butter glaze*—Place the glaze ingredients in a small saucepan over medium-high heat. Once the mixture starts foaming, turn the heat down to medium. Let it foam for 2 minutes to thicken, then remove and pour it straight over the salmon.

*Bake salmon*—Sprinkle the salmon with salt and pepper, then cover with a piece of parchment paper, then foil. Crimp to seal the sides to enclose the salmon in a parcel—it doesn't need to be 100 percent tightly sealed. Bake for 15 minutes, then remove from the oven.

*Oven-broil salmon*—Remove and discard the paper and foil on the salmon. Fold the base paper and foil sides down to expose the salmon surface, tucking any exposed paper edges under the foil to ensure it won't catch fire when broiling. Switch the oven to broil on high. Place the salmon on a shelf 12 inches from the heat source and cook for 7–10 minutes until you get caramelization mostly on the edges and a bit on top (keep an eye on it). Check to ensure the salmon is cooked—the target internal temperature (see page 351) is 125°F for perfect medium-rare[4] (the flesh should flake easily).

*Cool*—Use the foil overhang to transfer the salmon from the tray to a serving platter straight away (otherwise it keeps cooking). Slide the foil, then the paper out from under the salmon, allowing the juices to pool on the platter (this stuff is gold!). Loosely cover with foil, then leave to cool for at least 15 minutes, up to 2 hours. This dish is great served warm or at room temperature.

*Assemble*—Spoon big dollops of the creamy dill sauce across the salmon surface, then thickly spread (about ¼ inch thick). Pile the tapenade over the top, scatter generously with pomegranate seeds and parsley, then drizzle with lemon juice.

*Serve*—To serve, cut the salmon into pieces. I use a cake cutter. Serve with lemon wedges so people can add more to taste. Encourage people to squidge the salmon into the honey butter sauce that will be mixed with the semi-melted creamy dill sauce—it's so good! Serve with a big bowl of tomato, cucumber, and red onion chunks tossed with Lemon Dressing (page 333).

**NOTES**

1. Get a whole side of salmon with the skin on, for ease of handling. The recipe also works well on a smaller scale for salmon fillets.
2. Use store-bought pure orange juice with no added sugar, or squeeze your own.
3. To toast almonds: Preheat a small skillet over medium heat (no oil). Add the almonds, then stir for 2 minutes or until lightly browned. Keep them moving as they burn easily! Transfer to a bowl straight away to cool.
4. Though 125°F is the target pull temperature for optimum juiciness, it can go as high as 140°F (even slightly over) and the flesh will still be juicy as salmon is an oily fish.
5. Make ahead: Prepare the glaze, tapenade, and creamy dill sauce in advance, but cook the salmon on the day.

LEFTOVERS Fridge 3 days, but best served immediately once assembled. Not suitable for freezing.

# LAMB SHANKS IN RED WINE SAUCE

*Magnificent, yet a cinch to make.*

 **SERVES: 4 | PREP: 20 MINUTES + 24 HOURS MARINATING | COOK: 3 HOURS**

Tough cuts of meat slow-cooked into tender submission are the safest and easiest way to make luscious dishes that are both economical and impressive, and lamb shanks are among my absolute favorites. The meat is rich and meltingly good when properly cooked, and I love how each shank makes just the right size as a portion. Be sure to use salt-reduced broth, otherwise the sauce will be too salty at the end. Better yet, make your own broth!

---

4 x 12–14 oz lamb shanks[1]

½ tsp kosher salt*

1 tsp black pepper

3 tbsp extra-virgin olive oil

3 garlic cloves,* finely minced

2 tbsp tomato paste

4 cups low-sodium beef broth*[2]

1 cup water

Finely chopped parsley, to serve (optional)

**RED WINE MARINADE**

1 yellow onion, finely diced

1 carrot, finely diced

1 celery stalk, finely diced

3 cups pinot noir red wine*[3]

5 thyme sprigs

2 fresh bay leaves*

**SAUCE THICKENER**

6 tsp cornstarch mixed with 2 tbsp water

2 tbsp cold unsalted butter, cut into ½ inch cubes

*Marinate*—Place the shanks in a bowl with the red wine marinade ingredients, arranging them so the meat end is as submerged as possible in the wine. Cover and refrigerate for 24 hours.

Preheat the oven to 350°F.

*Strain and reduce wine*—Strain the shanks in a colander, reserving the red wine. Transfer the shanks to a plate—leave the vegetables and herbs in the colander. Reduce the wine in a medium saucepan over medium–high heat, simmering rapidly for 15 minutes until reduced by half. Scoop off and discard any scum that rises to the surface.

*Sear shanks*—Pat the shanks dry with paper towels, then sprinkle with salt and pepper. Heat 2 tablespoons of olive oil in a large, heavy-based ovenproof pot over high heat. Sear two shanks, rotating with tongs, until brown all over—around 5 minutes. Transfer the shanks to a plate, then repeat with the remaining shanks. Drain the excess fat from the pot and scrape out any loose burned bits.

*Sauté aromatics*—Turn the heat down to medium–low. Heat the remaining 1 tablespoon of olive oil in the same pot. Add the vegetables and herbs in the colander, and the garlic, then cook for 5 minutes. Add the tomato paste and cook for 2 minutes.

*Braising liquid*—Add the red wine, broth, and water to the pot, then stir. Arrange the shanks in the pot so the meat ends are as submerged as possible.[4]

*Slow-cook*—Turn the heat up to bring the liquid to a simmer. Cover, then transfer to the oven for 2 hours 20 minutes, or until the meat is fork-tender, just barely holding onto the bone. Remove from the oven and carefully transfer the lamb to a plate using a slotted spoon and tongs. Cover loosely with aluminum foil to keep warm.

*Optional restaurant-style lamb shank presentation*—see Note 5 for technique.

*Reduce sauce*—Strain the sauce into a bowl through a fine strainer, but do not press the juices out of the vegetables (makes the sauce grainy). Discard the vegetables. Pour the sauce back into the pot, then simmer rapidly over medium heat until reduced to 2 cups, about 10–15 minutes.

*Thicken sauce*—If using store-bought broth, add all the sauce thickener, stir, then simmer for 2 minutes until it is a thin syrupy consistency. If using homemade broth, start with one-third of the sauce thickener, simmer, then add more only if needed.[6] Remove the pot from the stove, then whisk in the butter until melted. Taste the sauce and add more salt if needed (you will need an extra ½ teaspoon of salt if using homemade beef broth).

*Serve*—Place the lamb shanks on a bed of Creamy Mashed Potato (page 338). Spoon over the red wine sauce, sprinkle with parsley (if using), and serve! Mixed baby leaf greens tossed with French Dressing (page 333) would make a lovely side dish here.

*See Notes on page 262.*

## NOTES

1. Use lamb foreshanks, not hindshanks (too giant!).
2. While this recipe is terrific with store-bought beef broth, homemade Beef Broth (page 348) catapults it to fine-dining level.
3. Pinot noir gives the sauce a lovely rounded flavor, but any dry red wine will work. The sauce does not taste "winey" as it is slow-cooked for so long, leaving an elegant, savory flavor in the sauce. There's no need to use expensive wine—see Wine in the Glossary (page 363) for my (firm) views on this! Sadly, there is no nonalcoholic substitute for this recipe as the wine is key for the sauce flavor.
4. If you're struggling to fit the shanks in, just do your best to arrange them so the meat is submerged as much as possible. They will shrink while cooking, so you can rearrange them part-way through the slow-cook.
5. Restaurant-style lamb shank presentation (so the shank meat has a nice neat shape when served—100% optional!): Once cooked, wrap the meat end of the shanks tightly in plastic wrap and push the meat down the bone to give them a nice round shape and expose more bone. Rest on the counter while reducing the sauce (it will hold its shape), or cool, then refrigerate until ready to serve.
6. Gelatin from the bones in homemade broth will naturally thicken the sauce so you will not need as much of the sauce thickener.

LEFTOVERS Fridge 4 days, freezer 3 months. To reheat, thaw then either warm in the microwave (fast option) or place the shanks only in a dish covered with aluminum foil and reheat at 350°F for 45 minutes until the meat is warmed through. Microwave the sauce—adjust the thickness with water.

SCANPAN

# SLOW-COOKED BEEF RIBS IN KOREAN BBQ SAUCE

*Dump-and-bake fall-apart incredibleness. (Is that a word? It is now!)*

**SERVES: 8 I PREP: 10 MINUTES I COOK: 5 HOURS**

One for spicy food lovers! These beef ribs are slowly braised in a sweet and deeply savory Korean BBQ sauce with a solid chili kick for the fun factor. Simply mix the sauce up, pour it over the ribs, and bake until the meat is slipping off the bone. The succulent beef ribs come out swimming in what I call a "kapow" sauce—guaranteed to blow away your tastebuds with flavor! Serve with rice or make DIY lettuce wraps stuffed with rice and this beef!

---

8 x 10–12 oz (about 6 lb in total) beef short ribs[1]

**KOREAN BBQ SAUCE**

2 tbsp canola oil

2 tbsp finely minced garlic* (5–6 cloves)

1 cup gochujang,[2] mild

¾ cup mirin*

¾ cup rice vinegar

3 tbsp light soy sauce*

⅓ cup sugar

¾ cup ketchup

1½ cups water

**TO SERVE**

Green onion,* finely sliced diagonally[3]

Preheat the oven to 350°F.

*Korean BBQ sauce*—Mix the ingredients in a bowl, then pour into a 13 x 9 inch metal or ceramic roasting pan. Add the beef ribs, turn to coat in the sauce, then position meat-side down in the sauce (bone facing up). Cover tightly with aluminum foil.

*Slow-cook ribs*—Transfer the ribs to the oven and bake for 4 hours. Remove the foil and bake, uncovered, for 30 minutes. Turn the ribs so the meat side is facing up. Spoon the sauce over the ribs and bake for a further 30 minutes until the surface of the ribs is caramelized and the meat is fall-apart tender.

*Finish sauce*—Skim off any excess fat from the surface of the sauce in the pan, then mix until smooth.

*Serve*—Transfer the ribs to a serving platter and pour the sauce over. Sprinkle with the green onion, then serve with White Rice (page 335) and a refreshing side salad of cucumber slices drizzled with Ginger Dressing (page 333).

**NOTES**

1. Beef ribs come in a variety of cuts. For this recipe you want what is called beef short ribs, which are chunky rectangular blocks with the bone in where they are cut with one bone per piece.
2. Gochujang is a sweet Korean rice and soy bean-based chili paste. I used mild (spice level 3). It adds a ton of umami (savory flavor) and a decent amount of spice to anything! You can find it in some large grocery stores (Asian aisle), or Asian/Korean grocery stores. It lasts "forever" in the fridge. This dish is fairly spicy, but not blow-your-head-off spicy. The spiciness of gochujang reduces as a result of slow-cooking and is also diluted by the other ingredients in the sauce as well as the meat juices that leach out of the beef. You can reduce the gochujang a bit if you want to reduce spiciness, but this will compromise the flavor of the sauce.
3. To make the green onion curly, as pictured, place the finely sliced onion in a bowl of water in the fridge for 15 minutes or so.

LEFTOVERS Fridge 4 days, freezer 3 months.

# PORK RIBS WITH BBQ SAUCE

*I'd be disowned if this wasn't in the cookbook!*

**SERVES: 4–5 NORMAL PEOPLE, 3 HUNGRY AUSSIE BLOKES OR 1 DOZER I PREP: 15 MINUTES + 20 MINUTES (OR OVERNIGHT MARINATING) I COOK: 2 HOURS**

My oven-baked pork ribs have always been a smash with website readers, friends, and family alike! I rub the ribs with a classic seasoning before popping them in the oven to slow-cook until beautifully tender. They're then given a good brush with a rich, dark, molasses-infused barbecue sauce for an irresistibly sweet and sticky finishing glaze. Pile the sliced ribs high on a plate with more barbecue sauce to pass, and let your guests dig in. Make sure you've got plenty of napkins to go around!

---

5 lb meaty pork ribs[1] (2 racks)

3/4 cup alcoholic apple cider or apple juice[2]

1 tbsp extra-virgin olive oil

**RUB**

2 1/2 tsp paprika

2 tsp garlic powder

1 1/2 tsp each dried thyme, oregano, and onion powder

1 tsp cayenne pepper (omit for less spice)

1 1/2 tsp kosher salt*

1/2 tsp black pepper

**BARBECUE SAUCE**

1/2 cup apple cider vinegar

1 1/2 cups ketchup

1/2 cup alcoholic apple cider[2] or apple juice

1/3 tightly packed cup brown sugar

1 1/2 tbsp molasses* (original, not blackstrap)

2 tsp Worcestershire sauce

1 tsp Tabasco (optional)

2 tsp mustard powder

1 1/2 tsp garlic powder

1 tsp kosher salt*

1 tsp black pepper

*Rub*—Mix the rub ingredients in a small bowl, then rub the mixture onto both sides of the ribs (most on the meaty side). Set aside to marinate for 20 minutes (or overnight).

Preheat the oven to 325°F.

*Slow-cook ribs*—Place the ribs on a rimmed baking tray[3] in a single layer. Pour the cider underneath the ribs, cover with aluminum foil, then bake for 1 1/2 hours or until the meat is pretty tender but not "falling off the bone."[4]

*Barbecue sauce*—Place all the barbecue sauce ingredients in a saucepan and simmer for 45 minutes over medium heat, stirring occasionally, or until thickened to a thick syrup consistency. Set aside.

*Brown ribs*—Remove the foil from the ribs, drizzle with olive oil, then bake for 15 minutes until the rub becomes nice and crusty. Remove the ribs from the oven and turn the heat up to 400°F.

*Glaze*—Line a new baking tray with aluminum foil, then parchment paper (you'll thank me later!). Transfer the ribs to the new tray. Pour any juices from the first tray over the ribs.

Flip the ribs so the bonier side is facing up. Brush generously with the barbecue sauce, then bake for 10 minutes. Remove from the oven, turn the ribs over so the meaty side is up, slather generously with sauce, and bake for 5 minutes. Repeat two or three times (slather, then oven 5 minutes) until you've got a gorgeous barbecue glaze on the ribs.

*Serve*—Cut the ribs into individual or multiple rib portions and serve with the remaining barbecue sauce on the side. Complete your feast with Cornbread Muffins (page 342), steamed corn cobs, and finish with My Forever Chocolate Cake (page 302)!

**NOTES**

1. Look for meaty pork ribs that are nice and fatty, 1 inch+ thick (including bone).
2. Using an alcoholic cider adds extra depth of flavor. Pale beers (ordinary lager, pale ale, etc.) and other fruit ciders also work really well.
3. Use a baking tray with a rim high enough so the apple cider doesn't slosh over the edge. It doesn't need to be that high as there isn't that much liquid.
4. This recipe is forgiving so don't fret about exact timing here! At 1 1/2 hours, use two forks to check if you can pry the meat apart with little effort (but it shouldn't yet be "falling off the bone with a touch"). Remember, the ribs will get another 30–40 minutes in the oven.

LEFTOVERS Fridge 4 days. Not suitable for freezing.

# THE BEST EVER LAMB SHOULDER . . .

## . . . is slow-cooked for 12 hours!

 **SERVES: 5–6 | PREP: 10 MINUTES + 2–24 HOURS MARINATING (OPTIONAL) | COOK: 12½ HOURS**

I have a recipe for 3-hour roasted lamb shoulder for those days when I'm short on time and need to knock out a tasty roast without too much fuss. It's wickedly good and always a hit. When I really want to impress though, this is the lamb I make! The slow-cooking over 12 hours results in incredibly juicy meat that collapses at just the touch of a fork, with the added bonus that it reheats 100 percent perfectly so it's ideal for making ahead. I guarantee this is truly the most amazing, mouth-watering lamb roast you'll ever make!

---

3½–5 lb bone-in lamb shoulder[1]

1 yellow onion, unpeeled, cut into 6 wedges

2 cups water

**MARINADE**

2½ tsp finely chopped fresh rosemary leaves[2]

1 tbsp dried oregano

2 garlic cloves* (big!), finely minced

1 tsp kosher salt*

½ tsp black pepper

¼ cup extra-virgin olive oil

**LAMB JUS**

1 tsp cornstarch

¼ cup water

¼ tsp kosher salt*

*Marinate lamb*—Mix the marinade ingredients in a small bowl. Rub the mixture all over the lamb, getting it right into all the cracks and crevices! If time permits, marinate for 2 hours on the counter in a roasting pan, or up to 24 hours in the fridge. (I skip this more often than not!)

Preheat the oven to 450°F.

*Roast lamb over high heat*—Place the onion in the roasting pan under the lamb. Pour the water into the pan. Roast, uncovered, for 45 minutes.

*Slow-roast lamb*[3]—Turn the oven down to 200°F. Cover the lamb with parchment paper, then a double layer of aluminum foil, and seal very tightly to avoid water evaporation. Roast for 12 hours (I do this overnight). Test the side of the lamb with two forks to ensure the meat is fall-apart tender. If not, cover and return to the oven, checking every 15 minutes.

*Rest*—Transfer the lamb to a large dish (reserve the liquid in the roasting pan). Cover loosely with foil and rest for at least 10 minutes before serving (it will stay warm for 2–3 hours).

*Lamb jus*—Strain all the liquid in the roasting pan into a medium saucepan (there should be around 3–4 cups). Bring to a boil, then simmer rapidly on medium–high until it reduces down to 1 cup. Mix the cornstarch and water together, then pour this in slowly in a thin stream while stirring continuously. Cook for 2 minutes over medium heat, stirring every now and then, until it thickens to a syrupy consistency. Add salt to taste and transfer to a gravy boat.

*Serve*—Use tongs for tearing the meat off the bone—no knife for carving needed! Serve with the jus, a side of Garlic Roast Potatoes (page 339), and steamed vegetables tossed with Mediterranean Dressing (page 333). For dessert, I see Apple Crumble (page 301) on your table!

**NOTES**

1. If your shoulder is much smaller, reduce the roasting time—start checking at the 10 hour mark. Don't fret about overcooking—shoulder is a well-marbled cut of meat and the low oven temperature is extremely forgiving.
2. Substitute with 1¼ tsp finely chopped dried rosemary.
3. I do the lamb shoulder overnight. With the low oven temperature and all the liquid in the pan (you end up with about 3–4 cups once finished!), I am not concerned about any burning while sleeping with the oven on.
4. Make ahead: Cook the lamb as per the recipe. Cover loosely with aluminum foil and let it cool completely to room temperature, around 4 hours. Refrigerate until required. Remove from the fridge 2 hours prior, then reheat, covered with foil, in a 300°F oven for 1 hour. Or microwave, if it's an emergency (it happens!).

LEFTOVERS Fridge 4 days, freezer 3 months.

# JUICIEST, EASIEST ROAST CHICKEN EVER

*A new fuss-free method with exceptional results!*

 **SERVES: 4 | PREP: 10 MINUTES | COOK: 70 MINUTES**

A little-known secret is that pot-roasting is hands-down the best way to roast a chicken. A covered pot keeps all the moisture locked in, while uncovering it later ensures golden skin. I also rest the chicken, breast-side down, so the juices settle into the breast meat. The result? Literally juices running everywhere with every bite you take. It will blow your mind! I like to use a simple spice rub, but you can make this chicken your own. Try herb butter under the skin, harissa paste, or a barbecue sauce baste. Or just go plain—it's really that good!

---

3½ lb whole chicken

14 oz russet potatoes,[1] peeled and cut into ¾ inch cubes

10 oz carrots (about 2 large carrots), peeled and cut into 1 inch chunks

5 tbsp unsalted butter, melted

¼ tsp each kosher salt* and black pepper

**SEASONING**

¼ tsp onion powder

½ tsp dried thyme, crushed with fingers until a bit powdery

½ tsp garlic powder

½ tsp paprika

½ tsp black pepper

2½ tsp kosher salt*

*Seasoning*—Mix the ingredients together in a small bowl.

*Prepare chicken*—Dry the chicken skin by patting it with paper towels. Sprinkle ½ teaspoon of the seasoning inside the chicken cavity, ¼ teaspoon on the underside, and rub the remainder on the top and sides. Tie the drumsticks together and tuck the wings under the chicken. Leave the chicken on the counter for 2 hours.[2]

Preheat the oven to 400°F. Leave a 9½–11 inch cast-iron pot in the oven as it heats up (no lid).

*Prepare vegetables*—Place the potato and carrot in a bowl and drizzle with the melted butter plus the salt and pepper. Toss.

*Roast covered*—Remove the hot pot from the oven. Place the potato and carrot in the base of the pot, then put the chicken on top. Loosely cover the pot with aluminum foil and bake for 30 minutes.

*Baste*—Remove the pot from the oven. Remove the foil and baste the chicken with the juices in the pot, shuffling the veggies aside to get to it (use a spoon, though a turkey baster is super handy if you have one!).

*Roast uncovered*—Return to the oven and roast for 40 minutes, uncovered, basting twice more with the pot juices until the internal temperature in the joint between the thigh and leg is 160°F.[3] Do not fret if you are a bit over as this recipe is very forgiving!

*Baste and rest*—Prop the chicken up on the side of the pot, legs up, breast-side down (as pictured).[4] Baste again with the pot juices, then rest for 15 minutes.

*Serve*—Carve the chicken and prepare yourself for the extraordinary amount of juices you will see, especially in the breast. It's going to blow your mind! Pile the chicken pieces on a platter with the vegetables. Pour the leftover sauce into a gravy boat and serve with the chicken.

**NOTES**

1. Any potato can be used for this recipe, whether starchy or waxy.
2. This takes the fridge-chill out of the chicken so it cooks through more evenly, rather than an overcooked outer layer by the time the fridge-cold center cooks through.
3. The internal temperature of cooked chicken breast is 155°F and chicken thigh is 160°F. By the time the chicken thighs reach 160°F, the chicken breast will be higher than 155°F which usually means the breast is a bit dried out. But not in this recipe!
4. Resting the chicken in this position makes the chicken juices settle in the breast so it's extraordinarily juicy. I promise, you are going to be amazed!

LEFTOVERS Fridge 4 days, freezer 3 months.

# BEEF BRISKET WITH BBQ SAUCE

*So lip-smackingly good yet completely effortless!*

 **SERVES: 6–8 | PREP: 10 MINUTES + 30 MINUTES (OR OVERNIGHT) MARINATING (OPTIONAL) | COOK: 8–10 HOURS**

This is the beef brisket version of the pork ribs on page 266. My friends love it so much that I couldn't not include it! (It's also insanely popular with my website readers.) I've given a few methods of cooking, but all result in amazingly moist (not stringy!), sliceable brisket that pulls apart with just a tug—just the way great beef brisket should be. Serve as a meal with steamed corn cobs and Cornbread Muffins, or pile high onto rolls with coleslaw as sliders.

---

3–4 lb beef brisket[1]

1 tbsp canola oil

**RUB**

1 tightly packed tbsp brown sugar

2 tsp paprika

1 tsp onion powder

1 tsp garlic powder

½ tsp ground cumin

¾ tsp mustard powder

2 tsp kosher salt*

½ tsp black pepper

**BARBECUE SAUCE**

4 garlic cloves,* finely minced

1 cup apple cider vinegar

3 cups ketchup

1 tightly packed cup brown sugar

4 tsp each black pepper, onion powder, and mustard powder

2 tsp cayenne pepper (reduce for less spice)

2 tbsp Worcestershire sauce

*Rub*—Mix the rub ingredients in a small bowl, then rub the mixture all over the brisket. Leave to marinate for 30 minutes. If time permits, leave overnight in the fridge, but I rarely do this.

*Slow-cook brisket*—Place the barbecue sauce ingredients in a slow-cooker and mix to combine. Add the brisket—squish it in to fit if needed. It won't be fully submerged. Cook on Low for 8 hours for a 3 lb brisket, or 10 hours for a 4 lb brisket. After this time the beef should be tender enough to easily pry apart the fibers with forks, but not collapsing (we want to slice it!). (See Note 2 for other cooking methods.)

*Finish sauce*—Transfer the brisket to a tray. Pour the liquid from the slow-cooker into a medium saucepan. Simmer over medium-high heat for 25 minutes until the sauce thickens to a syrupy consistency.

Preheat the oven to 425°F.

*Glaze*—Drizzle the brisket with the oil. Roast in the oven for 15 minutes until brown spots appear. Remove from the oven, baste generously with the barbecue sauce, then return to the oven for 5 minutes. Repeat once or twice more (baste, then oven for 5 minutes) until the surface is beautifully glazed and caramelized.

*Serve*—Slice the brisket thinly across the grain and serve with the remaining barbecue sauce. Complete your feast with Taco Slaw (page 222), soft rolls or Cornbread Muffins (page 342), steamed corn cobs, and finish with My Forever Chocolate Cake (page 302)!

**NOTES**

1. This recipe works best with brisket because it holds its shape even after slow-cooking until "fall-apart tender" so it can be sliced. No other slow-cooking cuts of beef have this unique quality. Look for thick pieces rather than thin rolled cuts. For smaller briskets, the cooking time will not reduce much because the meat fibers need a minimum amount of time to become tender.
2. Other cooking methods:
   - Slow-cooker on High: Same recipe, 4.5 hours for 3 lb, 5 hours for 4 lb.
   - Pressure cooker: Same recipe, 1 hr 15 minutes for 3 lb, 1½ hours for 4 lb. Let it depressurize naturally, or wait 15 minutes, then quick release.
   - Oven: Sprinkle the rub over brisket as per the recipe, then place in a roasting pan with the barbecue sauce ingredients. Add 2 cups water, then roast, tightly covered with aluminum foil, at 325°F for 4 hours or until fork-tender. Transfer the pan juices to a saucepan to add to the barbecue sauce. Bake and baste as per the recipe.
3. Make ahead: Cook the brisket but do not glaze. Refrigerate for up to 3 days. Remove from the fridge 1 hour prior to cooking, then warm the brisket for 30 minutes, wrapped with aluminum foil, in a 325°F oven, finishing with 10 minutes uncovered. Then glaze with the barbecue sauce as per the recipe.

LEFTOVERS Fridge 4 days, freezer 3 months.

# ULTRA-CRISPY SLOW-ROASTED PORK BELLY

*With sliceable yet fall-apart tender meat.*

 **SERVES: 4–6 | PREP: 10 MINUTES + 12–24 HOURS FRIDGE-DRYING (OPTIONAL) | COOK: 3 HOURS**

Perfect roasted pork belly has lusciously slow-cooked meat, buttery layers of melt-in-your-mouth fat, and superbly crispy edge-to-edge crackling. Turning wishes into reality though takes more than just whacking the meat in the oven and a prayer to the kitchen gods! Most recipes that promise awesome pork belly are frankly baloney. But I've honed my pork belly recipe to deliver the goods flawlessly, every single time. It really comes down to just a handful of easy techniques and tricks. Follow these and on your table will land the most spectacular pork belly you've been dreaming about all your life! Serve with a simple creamy mustard sauce—it pairs fantastically well with pork.

**PORK BELLY**

2 lb pork belly, skin on, not scored[1]

1 ½ tsp extra-virgin olive oil

1 tsp kosher salt*

¼ tsp black pepper

½ tsp ground fennel (optional)

**CREAMY MUSTARD SAUCE**

⅓ cup pork belly roasting juices[2]

½ cup low-sodium chicken broth*

⅓ cup heavy cream*

1 tbsp wholegrain mustard

*Dry skin overnight*—If time permits, place the pork belly on a plate, pat the skin dry with paper towels, then leave, uncovered, in the fridge for 12–24 hours to dry out the skin. (This is a crispy crackling insurance step.)

Preheat the oven to 275°F.

*Prepare pork*—Drizzle the flesh (not skin) with 1 teaspoon of the oil. Sprinkle over ½ teaspoon salt, all the pepper and fennel, then rub over the flesh, including the sides.

*Aluminum foil box*—Place two pieces of aluminum foil on a baking tray. Put the pork belly in the middle of the foil, skin-side up. Fold the sides in to enclose the belly, forming an open box, pinching the corners to seal them tightly and fit the belly as snugly as possible. The sides should come up around as high as the belly.

*Season skin*—Pat the skin dry with paper towels. Rub with the remaining ½ teaspoon of oil, then sprinkle the remaining ½ teaspoon salt over the skin. Rub the salt in with your fingers, being sure that the salt is dispersed evenly across the skin from edge to edge.

*Cook pork*—Place in the oven and roast for 2½ hours. After 1½ hours, remove and tighten the foil box (the pork will have shrunk), then continue cooking. (This keeps the pork fat/juice level as high as possible and the flesh protected, so it stays moist.)

Remove the pork from the oven. Increase the heat to 475°F.

*Level pork skin (key crackling step!)*[2]—Remove the pork from the foil (reserve the pork juices in the foil box) and place on a rack set over a tray. Make scrunched-up balls of foil using clean foil. Place them under the pork belly to prop up as needed so the skin surface is as level as possible.

*Crackling time!*—Place the pork back in the hot oven for 30 minutes, rotating the tray after 15 minutes, until the crackling is deep golden, puffy, and crispy all over. If some patches are browning faster, protect them with foil patches.

*Rest*—Remove the pork from the oven, then rest on the rack for 10 minutes.

*Make sauce*—Pour the reserved pork juices into a jar and skim off the fat. Measure out ⅓ cup of the pork belly juices.[3] Pour into a small saucepan, along with the remaining sauce ingredients, and whisk to combine. Simmer for 10 minutes over medium heat, whisking every now and then, until it reduces down to a thin syrup.

*Serve*—Carve the pork into ¾ inch slices using a serrated knife and serve with the sauce, Creamy Mashed Cauliflower (page 338), and arugula dressed with Balsamic Dressing (page 333).

**NOTES**

1. To achieve the best crackling, seek out pork belly with flat unwrinkled skin that has not been scored, and is not sold in a vacuum pack. If your pork belly is vac-packed (which means the skin is juice-soaked), the overnight drying step is highly recommended to ensure the skin is well dried. Why not scored? Because I've made pork belly so many times to know for a fact that you do NOT need to score for perfect crackling! Also, all too often butchers (or home cooks) accidentally pierce through the fat into the flesh, which causes meat juices to bubble up onto the skin, resulting in rubbery patches.
2. Even distribution of heat across the pork skin yields the best crackling. Higher areas get more heat so they crackle better than lower areas, so make the pork skin as horizontal as possible using the aluminum foil balls.
3. If you are short on pork juices, top up with extra chicken broth.

LEFTOVERS Fridge 4 days. To reheat leftovers, separate the crackling from the meat. Reheat the meat in a microwave and the crackling in a 400°F oven to retain crispiness. Not suitable for freezing.

# MUSHROOM LASAGNE

*This is my pick of the chapter. It's that good!*

**SERVES: 8–10 NORMAL PEOPLE, OR 1 NAGI + 1 DOZER | PREP: 45 MINUTES + 30 MINUTES RESTING | COOK: 70 MINUTES**

Here's a mushroom lasagne that plays no second fiddle to beef lasagne! It still has everything we love about the classic: a deeply savory ragu, creamy béchamel, and edge-to-edge bubbling cheese, all in the right proportions to the pasta for the perfect bite. It's the ideal comfort food for a mixed group of carnivores and vegetarians—nobody is going to miss the meat I can promise you!

13 oz fresh lasagne sheets[1]

24 slices (13 oz) Swiss cheese[2]

1 cup (4 oz) shredded* mozzarella

½ cup (2 oz) shredded parmesan,* using a box grater

**MUSHROOM RAGU**

1½ oz dried porcini mushrooms[3]

1½ cups chardonnay wine*[4]

2 lb white button mushrooms, cleaned[5] and stems trimmed

¼ cup extra-virgin olive oil

1½ tbsp unsalted butter

3 garlic cloves,* finely minced

1 large yellow onion, finely diced

1 large carrot, peeled and grated using a box grater[6]

2 celery stalks, grated using a box grater[6]

3½ tbsp tomato paste

1 tbsp finely chopped fresh oregano[7]

1½ tsp finely chopped fresh rosemary[7]

2½ tbsp all-purpose flour

1 cup low-sodium vegetable or chicken broth*

14 oz can crushed tomatoes

2 fresh bay leaves*

2½ tsp kosher salt*

1 tsp black pepper

**BÉCHAMEL SAUCE**

7 tbsp unsalted butter

⅔ cup all-purpose flour

4 cups hot milk

1 tsp kosher salt*

⅛ tsp white pepper

⅛ tsp ground nutmeg

*Soak porcini mushrooms*—Soak the dried porcini mushrooms in the wine for 30 minutes. Remove the porcini mushrooms (reserve the wine), squeeze out the excess wine (reserve this too), then finely chop the mushrooms. Set aside.

*Blitz mushrooms*—Cut the white button mushrooms into fourths (large ones into eighths). Pulse 4–5 times in a food processor, scraping the sides as needed, until finely chopped into ⅛ inch pieces.

*Mushroom ragu*—Heat the olive oil and melt the butter in a large heavy-based pot over medium–high heat. Add the garlic, onion, carrot, and celery, then cook for 3 minutes. Add the tomato paste and cook for 1 minute. Add the white mushrooms, oregano, and rosemary, then cook for 6 minutes until the water comes out of the mushrooms and begins to evaporate. Add the porcini mushrooms and reserved white wine. Stir, bring to a boil, then leave to simmer rapidly for 3 minutes until the wine is mostly evaporated.

*Simmer*—Mix in the flour and stir for 1 minute. Add the broth and boil for 5 minutes to partially reduce the mixture. Add the tomatoes, bay leaves, salt, and pepper, bring to a boil, then lower the heat and simmer for 15 minutes until it reduces to a thick ragu.

Preheat the oven to 400°F.

*Béchamel sauce*—Melt the butter in a large saucepan over medium heat. Reduce the heat to low, add the flour, and stir it into the butter (this is called a roux). Cook, stirring regularly, for 5 minutes. Don't let the roux brown—we want a white sauce! Switch to a whisk. While whisking constantly, slowly pour in half the milk. Once the roux dissolves into the milk, you will notice it thickens rather quickly. Pour in the remaining milk, then add the salt, pepper, and nutmeg and whisk until lump-free. Cook for 8 minutes, stirring regularly with a wooden spoon, until the sauce coats the back of the wooden spoon thickly. Remove from the stove and leave, uncovered, to cool to room temperature. It will be spreadable like soft butter, which makes it easy to spread on the lasagne layers.

*Assemble*—Smear a bit of ragu across the base of a 13 x 9 x 3 inch baking dish. Cover the base with lasagne sheets, cutting the sheets to fit, as needed. Spread with one-fourth of the mushroom ragu, ¾ cup of the béchamel sauce (using a spatula), then cover with six slices of Swiss cheese. Repeat three more times (a total of five lasagne sheet layers with four layers of ragu). Finish by spreading the last lasagne sheet with the remaining béchamel sauce and sprinkle with the mozzarella then the parmesan.

*Cook lasagne*—Bake in the oven for 35 minutes until the cheese is melted and has some golden spots.

*Serve*—Rest for 30 minutes before cutting and serving with a side salad of baby spinach leaves and finely sliced red onion tossed with Italian Dressing (page 333).

*See Notes on page 278.*

**NOTES**

1. I urge you to use fresh lasagne sheets from the fridge section of the supermarket rather than dried, as it is much more pleasant to eat! But if you are using dried lasagne sheets (the no pre-cooking required type), add 1 cup extra chicken broth into the mushroom ragu. It needs to be more watery as the dried lasagne sheets will absorb the liquid to cook.
2. I use the standard store-bought pre-sliced squares of Swiss cheese because they're easy to layer. The alternative is to shred, then sprinkle cheese on each layer. You will need 3¾ cups (13 oz). You can substitute with other cheese slices of choice.
3. Dried porcini mushrooms are fairly accessible these days at large grocery stores and independent produce stores. They bring a stronger mushroom flavor to the ragu. Substitute with dried shiitake mushrooms.*
4. Substitute with any other dry white wine that's not too sweet or woody. For nonalcoholic, use low-sodium chicken broth.
5. Wipe the mushrooms clean with paper towels. If they are extremely dirty, wash them under water, then dry thoroughly.
6. Cut the celery into three pieces for easier handling. Hold the carrot and celery almost perpendicular to the box grater so the shredded pieces are very short (rather than holding them on an angle to grate long strands).
7. Substitute with half the amount if using dried.
8. Make ahead: Cool all the components before using (otherwise they sweat and go watery). Assemble, then refrigerate (up to 3 days) or freeze (up to 3 months) before baking. Thaw and bake, covered, for 15 minutes, then uncover and bake as per the recipe.

LEFTOVERS Fridge 3 days, freezer 3 months.

# CHICKEN RAGU

*Rich and luscious—a pasta dream come true!*

**SERVES: 8 I PREP: 20 MINUTES I COOK: 2 HOURS**

I'm told Italians never put chicken in pasta, which is honestly strange to me because I think chicken and pasta are delicious together (I've got at least a couple of recipes in this book!). This recipe is based on a rich beef and red wine ragu, except it's made with chicken. Searing the chicken and the layers of ingredients in this ragu are the key to getting the same depth of flavor as with a beef ragu. I'm super-proud of the result, and think it makes for a more affordable but equally tasty alternative to beef!

---

3 lb bone-in, skin-on chicken thighs[1]

1 tsp kosher salt*

½ tsp black pepper

2–3 tbsp extra-virgin olive oil

1¼ lb dried pappardelle pasta[2] (or other pasta of choice)

Parmigiano Reggiano or parmesan,* freshly grated

**RAGU**

4 oz bacon lardons (or speck or pancetta), cut into small batons ⅛ inch wide[3]

3 garlic cloves,* finely minced

1 yellow onion, finely diced

1 carrot, peeled and grated using a box grater[4]

1 celery stalk, grated using a box grater[3]

3 tbsp tomato paste

1½ cups tomato passata*

3 cups pinot noir red wine*[5]

3 cups low-sodium beef broth*[6]

1 fresh bay leaf*

3 thyme sprigs

¼ tsp kosher salt*

¼ tsp black pepper

**SAUCE THICKENER[7]**

2½ tbsp all-purpose flour

1½ tbsp unsalted butter, softened

Preheat the oven to 350°F.

*Season chicken*—Dry the chicken by patting it with paper towels. Sprinkle with salt and pepper.

*Sear chicken*—Heat the oil in a large heavy-based pot over high heat. Place the chicken into the pot, skin-side down, and cook for 2 minutes or until the skin is golden brown. Turn and cook the flesh side for 1 minute, then transfer to a plate.

*Cook bacon*—Discard all but 1 tablespoon of fat in the pot. Add the bacon and cook until light golden, then transfer with a slotted spoon to the chicken plate.

*Sauté aromatics*—If there's less than 1½ tablespoons of fat in the pot, top up with more olive oil. Reduce the heat to medium, then add the garlic, onion, carrot, and celery. Cook, stirring regularly, for 5 minutes until the onion is translucent and sweet—but don't let it become golden. Turn the heat back up to medium–high, add the tomato paste, and cook for 1 minute. Add the passata and cook for 5 minutes, stirring constantly, until it reduces by half and darkens in color.

*Make sauce*—Add the wine, stir, then leave to simmer rapidly for 10 minutes until reduced by half. Add the beef broth, bay leaf, thyme, salt, and pepper, then stir.

*Slow-cook chicken*—Return the bacon and chicken to the pot. Bring the liquid up to a simmer, cover, then transfer to the oven for 1 hour 15 minutes, or until the chicken flesh shreds very easily.

*Shred chicken*—Transfer the chicken from the ragu into a large roasting pan. Remove the skin, then shred the flesh using two forks—some finely, some in larger chunks. Discard the skin and bones. Cover and keep warm.

*Finish ragu*—Set the pot over medium heat. In a small bowl mix together the flour and softened butter until a smooth paste forms. Add it to the pot and stir until it melts. Simmer the ragu for 5 minutes until it becomes a thin syrup that coats the back of the spoon. Stir in the chicken. Taste the ragu and add more salt if desired. Stand back and admire your big pot of chicken ragu! Keep it warm while you cook the pasta.

*Cook pasta*—Cook the pappardelle in a large pot of salted water as per the package directions minus 1 minute. Just before draining the pasta, scoop out a big mugful of pasta cooking water, then drain the pasta in a colander.

*Toss ragu with pasta*—Add the pasta into the pot of sauce with a splash of the pasta cooking water. Toss well with two wooden spoons until the sauce stains the pasta red and is clinging to the pappardelle, rather than pooled in the base of the pot.

*Serve*—Divide into warmed pasta bowls, sprinkle with Parmigiano Reggiano, and serve immediately! Mixed baby leaf greens drizzled with Italian Dressing (page 333) would pair well with this dish.

*See Notes on page 292.*

**NOTES**

1. This recipe needs to be made with bone-in chicken thighs so they are still nice and juicy after the required cooking time. Breast will dry out!
2. Allow 3 oz pasta and 1 cup of sauce per serving.
3. Biting into small chunks of bacon is part of the awesomeness of this dish, so try to find bacon, speck, or pancetta in block form so you can cut it into batons. Otherwise, use thick bacon slices.
4. Cut the celery into three pieces for easier handling. Hold the carrot and celery almost perpendicular to the box grater so the shredded pieces are very short (rather than holding them on an angle to grate long strands).
5. Or other dry red wine. Wine is a key ingredient in this ragu so, if you are unable to consume alcohol, this recipe is not recommended. The best substitute in this book is to use My Forever Spaghetti Bolognese recipe (page 168) but, instead of cooking ground beef, stir in shredded chicken toward the end of the sauce simmer time.
6. Though it may sound counterintuitive, beef is better than chicken broth in this recipe for richer flavor and deeper color.
7. Also called a beurre manié.* Refer to the Glossary (page 357) for how to convert to gluten-free.
8. For gluten-free, ensure the broth is gluten-free (not all brands are), use a gluten-free flour for the sauce thickener and use gluten-free pasta or serve over rice.

LEFTOVERS Fridge 4 days, freezer 3 months. Once tossed with the pasta, it is best eaten fresh, though leftovers will keep for 3 days.

# STUFFED BUTTERNUT SQUASH

*It's a vegetarian roast!*

 **SERVES: 7–8 | PREP: 20 MINUTES + 20 MINUTES COOLING | COOK: 1½ HOURS**

The idea for this dish arose when I thought how cool it would be to create an epic "roast" centerpiece, fit for special occasions that everyone can enjoy, including vegans! A whole butternut squash gets stuffed with a medley of vegetables, lentils, nuts, and herbs. Just like a roast, it's then trussed and slow-roasted until gorgeously tender. Finally it's brought to the table (to much applause, of course!), then served cut into thick slices. Give this a try at your next meat-free banquet. Your guests will devour it!

---

4 lb butternut squash[1]

2 tbsp extra-virgin olive oil

¾ tsp kosher salt*

Yogurt Sauce (page 251), to serve

**STUFFING**

2 tbsp extra-virgin olive oil

2 garlic cloves,* finely minced

1 red onion, finely chopped

4 oz white button mushrooms, finely chopped

⅓ cup dried French green lentils[2]

½ cup dried cranberries[3]

½ tsp each fresh rosemary and thyme leaves,[4] finely chopped

½ tsp ground nutmeg

⅓ cup pinot noir red wine*[5]

¾ cup low-sodium vegetable broth*

1¼ cups cooked Brown Rice (page 335)

1 tightly packed cup roughly chopped baby spinach[6]

¼ cup finely chopped pistachio nuts

¼ cup finely chopped roasted unsalted cashews[7]

¼ cup finely chopped roasted almonds[7]

¾ tsp kosher salt*

½ tsp black pepper

Preheat the oven to 400°F.

*Roast squash*—Cut the squash in half lengthwise.[8] Scoop the seeds out using a spoon and discard or save for another purpose. Rub the squash flesh and skin with oil, then sprinkle with ½ teaspoon salt. Bake on a baking tray for 1 hour, or until the center can be easily pierced with a knife with little resistance (a bit on the firm side is okay). Remove from the oven and cool for 15 minutes.

*Make stuffing*—Heat the oil in a medium saucepan over medium heat. Cook the garlic, onion, and mushrooms for 4 minutes. Add the lentils, cranberries, rosemary, thyme, nutmeg, wine, and broth. Simmer on low heat for 30 minutes, or until the liquid is all absorbed (tilt the saucepan to check). Turn the stove off. Stir in the rice and set aside for 10 minutes, then stir in the spinach, nuts, salt, and pepper.

*Stuff squash*—Scoop out the squash flesh from each half (reserve), leaving a ¾ inch thick wall of flesh.[9] Use a dish towel to squeeze the excess water out of the reserved flesh, by gathering it up and wringing firmly.[10] Stir all the reserved flesh into the stuffing mix.

Sprinkle the flesh of the scooped-out squash shell with ¼ teaspoon salt. Pile the stuffing into one half of the squash, overfilling it so it mounds up. Place the other half of the squash on top—the stuffing should fill the lid. Tie the two halves together by trussing with kitchen string (as pictured left) every 1¼ inches to hold the squash in a nice shape.

*Bake squash*—Bake for 40 minutes until the filling is hot in the middle (check with a knife).

*Rest*—Remove the squash from the oven and rest for 10 minutes.

*Serve*—Cut the squash into 1 inch thick slices and place on a plate. Serve with the yogurt sauce.

*See Notes on page 286.*

**NOTES**

1. Look for a nice-shaped one, not too squat and not long and skinny.
2. Also known as "puy lentils," these are the little dark lentils. Substitute with dried green or brown lentils. Canned lentils are softer than ideal but will work. Simmer to reduce the liquid by half before adding 1 cup canned lentils (drained). Cook down until the liquid is evaporated, then proceed as per the recipe.
3. Substitute with dried sour cherries.
4. Or use half the amount of dried rosemary and thyme.
5. Or other dry red wine. See Wine in the Glossary (page 363) for more information. Substitute with more vegetable broth.
6. Substitute with any leafy greens like kale* or English spinach.
7. Cashews can be substituted with more almonds, or almonds can be substituted with more cashews. Macadamias and walnuts are also suitable.
8. I find the easiest way to cut a butternut in half is with a big sturdy knife. With the squash lying on its side, hold it steady, then insert the knife vertically through the top of the squash, in the middle. Then gently bring the knife down toward you to cut through the first half. Rotate and repeat on the other side.
9. Don't make the wall too thin or it might compromise the structural integrity of your grand roast!
10. To do this, I bundle half the flesh in the dish towel like a money bag, twisting the top as tightly as I can to squeeze out the water. Once done, the flesh should resemble a soft ball of dough!

LEFTOVERS Fridge 3 days. Not suitable for freezing.

# SPANISH SEAFOOD STEW

*Zarzuela de mariscos (good luck pronouncing that!)*

**SERVES: 4 I PREP: 30 MINUTES I COOK: 20 MINUTES**

I honestly can't think of a better way to celebrate excellent-quality seafood than this Spanish stew. It's a cliché, but this one really is all about letting the ingredients' natural flavors shine through. That's not to say it's short on taste, though. The shellfish drop plenty of intense seafoody juice into the broth—no fish broth required! Stirring in the garlicky picada at the end takes it over the top. Dish it out and mop up that sauce with crusty bread. I can eat bowls of this stew!

1 lb skinless, boneless snapper or other firm white fish fillets,[1] 3/4 inch thick

1/2 tsp kosher salt*

1/4 tsp black pepper

1 1/2 tbsp all-purpose flour

1/4 cup extra-virgin olive oil, plus extra for drizzling

7–8 oz whole medium raw shrimp* (about 8), bodies peeled[2] and deveined, heads and tails left in place

2 lb mussels,* scrubbed and beards removed[3]

2/3 cup chardonnay or other dry white wine*[4]

1 1/2 yellow onions, finely diced

1 x 7 oz whole squid, sliced into 1/4 inch thick rings

2 tbsp roughly chopped Italian parsley

2 lemons, cut into wedges

**TOMATO PUREE**

6 tomatoes, cut into fourths, then 3 chunks

3/4 tsp sugar

3/4 tsp kosher salt*

**PICADA**

15 whole blanched almonds[5]

1/2 cup cubed white bread

3 garlic cloves, peeled

1/4 cup roughly chopped Italian parsley

1/4 tsp black pepper

1 1/2 tbsp extra-virgin olive oil

1 1/2 tbsp water

*Tomato puree*—Puree the ingredients in a blender, food processor, or with an immersion blender until smooth. Set aside until required.

Preheat the oven to 350°F.

*Picada*—Spread the almonds on a small baking tray, then place in the oven for 5 minutes. Add the bread to the same tray and bake for a further 6 minutes until the bread is fully crisp but not golden. Place the almonds in a mortar and pestle.[6] Add the garlic and pound into a paste. Add the bread, parsley, and pepper, then pound to crush the bread into crumbs. Add the olive oil and water and continue pounding to form a pesto-like paste. Set aside.

*Sear fish*—Pat the fish dry using paper towels. Sprinkle both sides with salt and pepper, then dust with flour, shaking off the excess. Heat 2 tablespoons of oil in a large, deep 12 inch skillet[7] over medium–high heat. Sear each side of the fish for 1–1½ minutes until light golden, then transfer to a plate. It will still be raw inside.

*Sear shrimp*—Heat 1 tablespoon of oil in the same pan. Sear the shrimp for 45 seconds on each side, then add to the plate with the fish.

*Steam mussels*—Turn the heat to high. Pour the mussels and wine into the pan, cover with a lid, and cook for 2 minutes just until the mussels open (which indicates they are cooked). Strain the mussels into a bowl and reserve the cooking liquid—this is free seafood broth! Remove and reserve the meat from half the mussels, discarding the shells. Keep the remaining mussels intact. (Note: mussels that remain closed do not need to be discarded. It does not mean they are off! Just pry them open with a butter knife.)

*Make sauce*—Add the remaining oil to the pan over medium–high heat. Cook the onion for 4 minutes until softened. Pour the tomato puree in (careful, it will splutter!), stir, then let it simmer on medium heat until it thickens enough so you can almost draw a path across the base of the pan. Add the picada and reserved mussel broth. Stir and simmer for 1½ minutes.

*Combine seafood and sauce*—Add the fish to the sauce, and the shrimp around the fish. Scatter the squid across the surface, then pour over the mussels and mussel meat. Place the lid on and leave to cook (on medium–low) for 2 minutes or until the fish is just cooked.[8]

*Serve*—Remove the pan from the stove and remove the lid. Drizzle the stew with olive oil and sprinkle with parsley. Serve in the pan with lemon wedges and Easy Crusty Artisan Bread (page 341) or No-yeast Rolls (page 344).

**NOTES**

1. Any firm white fish fillets can be used. See Fish in the Glossary (page 359) for an extensive list. Salmon could also be used. Try to get fish that is even in thickness as it's best for even cooking.
2. Peeling the shrimp is optional. Large pre-peeled shrimp can also be used.
3. See Mussels in the Glossary (page 360) for more information.
4. If you can't consume alcohol, use nonalcoholic white wine.
5. Almonds with skin removed, so they are cream-colored.
6. If you don't have a mortar and pestle, place all the picada ingredients, except the parsley, in a tall jar with 2 tablespoons of water. Blitz into a chunky paste using an immersion blender. Add the parsley and blitz until very finely chopped. It should look like pesto, not a green smoothie!
7. You will need a cooking vessel that is 12 inches wide and 3 inches deep, or a very large pot.
8. Internal temperature 130°F, or check that the flesh flakes easily. See Internal Cooked Temperatures chart (page 351) for more information.

LEFTOVERS Fridge 2 days but best made fresh.

# SHEPHERD'S PIE & COTTAGE PIE

*What, you mean nobody told you they are exactly the same recipe?*

**SERVES: 8 I PREP: 20 MINUTES + 2 HOURS COOLING (OR OVERNIGHT REFRIGERATION—OPTIONAL) I COOK: 1 HOUR 45 MINUTES**

Ever wondered what the difference between shepherd's pie and cottage pie is? Shepherd's pie is made from lamb, while cottage pie is made from beef! (Think of shepherds herding sheep and you'll remember which is which.) Here's a recipe for, well, both—just pick your meat! This is my straight-up version, packing plenty of flavor with no fancy bells and whistles, which everyone should know how to make.

**FILLING**

1½ tbsp extra-virgin olive oil

2 garlic cloves,* finely minced

1 yellow onion, finely chopped

1 carrot, peeled and finely chopped

1 celery stalk, finely chopped

¾ tsp each dried thyme and rosemary

1½ lb ground lamb (shepherd's pie) or ground beef (cottage pie)

¼ cup all-purpose flour[1]

¼ cup tomato paste

2 cups low-sodium beef broth*[1]

½ cup pinot noir red wine*[2]

1 beef bouillon cube,* crumbled

1 tbsp Worcestershire sauce[1]

2 bay leaves*

1 cup frozen peas

¾ tsp kosher salt*

½ tsp black pepper

**MASHED POTATO TOPPING**

2½ lb russet potatoes,[3] peeled and cut into 1 inch cubes

2 tbsp unsalted butter

⅔ cup milk

1 tsp kosher salt*

¼ tsp white pepper

**TOPPING**

3 tbsp finely shredded parmesan*

2 tbsp unsalted butter, melted

Chopped parsley, to serve (optional)

*Filling*—Heat the oil in a very large skillet over medium-high heat. Cook the garlic and onion for 1 minute. Add the carrot, celery, thyme, and rosemary, and cook for 3 minutes.

Turn the heat to high. Add the ground meat and cook, breaking it up as you go, until browned. Mix in the flour and cook for 1 minute. Stir in the tomato paste, broth, red wine, bouillon cube, Worcestershire sauce, and bay leaves.

*Simmer*—When the mixture starts bubbling, reduce the heat to medium-low so it's simmering gently. Cook for 30 minutes, stirring occasionally so the base doesn't burn, until it reduces down to a thick gravy consistency suitable for your pie filling[4].

*Cool*—Stir in the peas, salt, and pepper, then transfer to a 1½ quart casserole dish. Cool to room temperature for at least 2 hours (or up to 3 days in the fridge).

Preheat the oven to 400°F.

*Mashed potato topping*—Place the potato in a large pot of cold water, then bring to a boil. Cook for 10 minutes or until soft. Drain well, then return to the pot. Add the butter, milk, salt, and pepper. Mash until the potato is smooth and spreadable, adjusting with more milk if required.

*Assemble and bake*—Spread the hot mashed potato on top of the filling. Use a fork to draw squiggles over the surface (creates crunchy ridges!). Sprinkle with parmesan and drizzle with butter. Bake for 40 minutes or until the surface is golden brown.

*Serve*—Stand for 5 minutes before serving, garnished with parsley, if desired.

**NOTES**

1. For a gluten-free option, skip the flour and use 2 tablespoons cornstarch mixed with a splash of water—stir into the sauce at the end and simmer until thickened. Be sure to use gluten-free Worcestershire sauce and beef broth too.
2. Pinot noir gives the sauce a lovely rounded flavor, but any dry red wine will work. No need to use expensive wine—see Wine for cooking* in the Glossary (page 363). Substitute with nonalcoholic red wine or more beef broth (same quantity).
3. Use any floury or all-purpose potatoes that you ordinarily use for mashed potatoes.
4. The sauce will not thicken further in the oven, so get the thickness right at this stage.
5. Make ahead: Assemble but don't bake it. Once cool, either refrigerate for 4 days or freeze for 3 months. Thaw if frozen, then bake, covered with aluminum foil, for 15 minutes then uncovered as per the recipe.

LEFTOVERS Fridge 4 days, freezer 3 months.

# GUINNESS STEW

*Can you think of anything better for a cold winter day? (Your answer is no!)*

**SERVES: 5–6 I PREP: 20 MINUTES + 24 HOURS RESTING (OPTIONAL) I COOK: 3 HOURS**

Guinness stew is a fantastic option for changing up your regular rotation of casseroles in the colder months. The stout really gives a unique and wonderful depth to the stew, richer than the usual! Don't worry that it will be bitter or overly beery as the Guinness cooks out by the time the stew is done and leaves just the mellow, malty notes in the sauce. Beef is the classic meat choice for this Irish stew, but you can also use lamb. I like to add smoky bacon for extra tastiness, but you can leave it out.

---

2½ lb beef chuck steak,[1] cut into 2 inch pieces

¾ tsp kosher salt*

¾ tsp black pepper

2 tbsp extra-virgin olive oil

**STEW**

3 garlic cloves,* finely minced

2 yellow onions, finely chopped

6 oz thick-cut bacon, cut into ¾ x ½ inch pieces

3 carrots, peeled and cut into ½ inch thick pieces

2 large celery stalks, cut into ¾ inch pieces

3 tbsp all-purpose flour

15 fl oz Guinness[2]

3 cups low-sodium chicken broth*[3]

¼ cup tomato paste

2 bay leaves*

3 thyme sprigs

½ tsp black pepper

Kosher salt,* to taste, if needed

*Season beef*—Pat the beef dry with paper towels, then sprinkle with salt and pepper.

*Brown beef*—Heat the oil in a large heavy-based pot over high heat. Add one-third of the beef and sear to brown the beef well on all sides, around 4 minutes. Transfer to a bowl and repeat with the remaining beef.

*Cook aromatics*—Lower the heat to medium. If the pot is looking dry, add a bit more oil. Cook the garlic and onion for 3 minutes until softened, then add the bacon. Cook until the bacon is golden, then stir in the carrot and celery to coat them in the bacon fat. Add the flour and stir for 1 minute.

*Cook stew*—Add the Guinness, chicken broth, tomato paste, bay leaves, thyme, and pepper. Mix well so the flour dissolves into the liquid. Return the beef to the pot (including any pooled juices) and stir gently—the liquid level should just cover the beef.

*Slow-cook*—Cover with a lid, then reduce the heat to low so the surface is barely rippling, with a small bubble appearing every 3 seconds or so. Cook for 2 hours—the beef should be pretty tender by now.

*Reduce sauce*—Remove the lid, then simmer for a further 30–45 minutes, stirring every now and then, until the beef falls apart at a touch and the sauce has reduced and thickened into a thin syrupy consistency. Skim the excess fat off the surface, if desired. Adjust the salt to taste (the bacon provides a decent amount of salt so I don't add more). Remove the bay leaves and thyme.

*Rest overnight (optional)*—At this stage, you can serve immediately. However, for the absolute best results, leave until the next day to let the flavors develop further. To do this, put the lid on the pot and let it cool to room temperature (about 4 hours), then refrigerate overnight.

*Serve*—Before serving, reheat the stew in a 350°F oven for 40 minutes. It can also be done on a low stove, but be very careful when stirring so as not to break up those fragile beef pieces! Serve with Creamy Mashed Potato (page 338) on the side.

**NOTES**

1. Boneless short ribs can also be used.
2. Guinness brings a dark rich flavor to the sauce. It can be substituted with other dark beer and stouts. Unfortunately, there is no suitable nonalcoholic substitute to achieve the same flavor. But if you use beef broth* instead you will still end up with a really great, flavorful stew. It just won't be an Irish one!
3. If you're wondering why chicken broth in a beef stew, the answer is that it lets the Guinness flavor come through more because chicken broth is milder than beef broth. I really love being able to taste the rich Guinness flavor here. However, beef broth can be used in a pinch.

LEFTOVERS Fridge 4 days, freezer 3 months.

# BEEF LASAGNE

*One of my all-time top five foods.*

**SERVES: 10 I PREP: 20 MINUTES I COOK: 3½ HOURS (AND WORTH EVERY SECOND!)**

**If you know someone who doesn't like lasagne, you should stop being friends with them. Lasagne, as far as I'm concerned, is something we should all agree is one of mankind's greatest inventions! A good lasagne, though, is easier said than done. Too much pasta and it's unsatisfying. Too much sauce or meat and it falls apart. Not enough cheese, well, we won't even go there. This recipe is my idea of the perfect lasagne!**

12 oz fresh lasagne sheets[1]

1 ½ cups (5 oz) shredded* mozzarella

½ cup (2 oz) shredded parmesan,* using a box grater

**RAGU BOLOGNESE**

1 tbsp extra-virgin olive oil

2 garlic cloves,* finely minced

1 yellow onion, finely chopped

1 carrot, peeled and finely diced

1 celery stalk, finely diced

1 ½ lb ground beef[2]

8 oz ground pork (or more beef)[2]

28 oz can crushed tomatoes

¼ cup tomato paste

1 cup pinot noir red wine*[3]

3 beef bouillon cubes,* crumbled

2 fresh bay leaves*

½ tsp each dried thyme and oregano

2 tsp Worcestershire sauce

½ tsp kosher salt*

⅛ tsp white pepper

1 tsp sugar (if needed)[4]

**CHEESE SAUCE**

4 cups whole milk, hot

7 tbsp unsalted butter

⅔ cup all-purpose flour

¾ tsp kosher salt*

¼ tsp black pepper

⅛ tsp ground nutmeg

2 cups (7 oz) shredded* gruyere or other cheese[5]

*Make ragu*—Heat the oil in a large heavy-based pot over medium heat. Add the garlic, onion, carrot, and celery. Cook for 10 minutes until softened and sweet—they should not become golden. Turn the heat to high. Add the beef and pork, then cook, breaking it up as you go. Once the beef is no longer red, add the remaining ragu ingredients, EXCEPT the sugar. Stir, then lower the heat so it is simmering very gently—aim for just one or two small slow bubbles on the surface at a time. Place the lid on and slow-cook for 2 hours, stirring every now and then.

*Simmer*—Taste and add sugar if needed (economical canned tomatoes can be sour). Simmer for a further 30 minutes without the lid. The meat should be really tender and the sauce should be a thick, rich consistency. Taste and add more salt and pepper, if desired.

*Cheese sauce*—Make the béchamel sauce as per the Mushroom Lasagne recipe on page 278. Stir in the nutmeg and gruyere at the end until it melts. Cover and allow to cool for 30 minutes until it becomes spreadable like soft butter once cooled, which is our goal.

Preheat the oven to 400°F.

*Assemble lasagne*—Smear a bit of ragu[6] across the base of a 13 x 9 x 3 inch baking dish, then cover with lasagne sheets. Trim the sheets to fit, as needed. Spread with one-fourth of the ragu, then spread with one-fifth (about ¾ cup) of the cheese sauce. Smooth the surface using a small offset or rubber spatula. Cover with lasagne sheets, then repeat three more times so you have four layers of ragu and five layers of lasagne sheets. Top the fifth layer of lasagne sheets with the remaining cheese sauce. Smooth the surface, then sprinkle with mozzarella followed by parmesan.

*Cook lasagne*—Bake for 35 minutes until the cheese is melted and has some golden spots.

*Serve*—Stand for 30 minutes before cutting and serving. Accompany with a big bowl of arugula lightly dressed with Balsamic Dressing (page 333), sprinkled with grated parmesan.

**NOTES**

1. Fresh lasagne sheets are best. If using dried lasagne sheets (the no pre-cooking type), add ¾ cup water to the ragu at the end. It needs to be more watery as the dried lasagne sheets will absorb the liquid to cook.
2. A combination of both beef and pork makes a richer, more luscious ragu than just using ground beef as ground pork is fattier and more tender—but beef brings the flavor.
3. Or other dry red wine. Can be substituted with low-sodium beef broth.*
4. A touch of sugar can go a long way to take the edge off the sourness of more economical brands of canned tomatoes.
5. Gruyere is best for flavor and melting qualities when you're cooking to impress. Otherwise, use cheddar, colby, or monterey jack cheese.
6. This stops the lasagne sheets from sliding around, which is so irritating!
7. Make ahead: Assemble the lasagne, then fully cool. Cover tightly with plastic wrap and refrigerate for up to 4 days, or freeze for 3 months. To reheat, fully thaw in the fridge for 36–48 hours. Cover with aluminum foil, then bake in a 400°F oven for 25 minutes. Uncover and bake for a further 25 minutes.

LEFTOVERS Fridge 4 days, freezer 3 months.

# EGGPLANT PARMIGIANA

*So good that I can't find the words to do it justice.*

**SERVES: 8–10 | PREP: 40 MINUTES | COOK: 1 HOUR 40 MINUTES**

A great Italian classic that I think everybody should know. What's not to love about layers of meltingly soft eggplant with rich tomato sauce, all bound with loads of cheesy goodness? This is one of my go-to meatless dishes when I'm feeding a mixed crowd of meat-lovers and vegetarians. It's so good, I know that everybody will be happy!

---

5 x 12 oz (4 lb) eggplants, sliced lengthwise 1/4 inch thick, skin left on

1/3 cup extra-virgin olive oil

1 2/3 cups (6 oz) finely grated parmesan*

2 lightly packed cups basil leaves, stalks reserved

1 1/2 cups (5 oz) shredded* mozzarella

**PARMIGIANA SAUCE**

2 tbsp extra-virgin olive oil

1 yellow onion, finely chopped

5 garlic cloves,* minced

2 1/2 cups tomato passata*

14 oz can crushed tomatoes

1 1/2 tsp sugar

1 1/2 tbsp finely chopped fresh oregano[1]

1 cup water

3/4 tsp kosher salt*

1/4 tsp black pepper

Reserved basil stalks (see above)

Preheat the oven to 425°F. Line three or four large baking trays with parchment paper.

*Bake eggplant*[2]—Brush each side of the eggplant slices with oil. Arrange in a single layer on the trays and bake for 40 minutes or until lightly browned, flipping the eggplants halfway. Remove the trays from the oven, then leave the eggplant on the trays to cool.

*Parmigiana sauce*—Heat the olive oil in a large skillet over medium–high heat. Sauté the onion and garlic for 3 minutes until softened. Add the remaining ingredients, except the basil stalks, then stir and bring to a simmer. Reduce the heat so it's simmering gently, then cook, uncovered, for 30 minutes, stirring occasionally until thickened, adding the reserved basil stalks in the last 10 minutes. The sauce should be quite thick—thicker than your usual pasta sauce. Discard the basil stalks. Keep the sauce warm until required.

*Assemble and bake*—Reduce the oven to 350°F. Smear a little sauce on the base of a 13 x 9 inch baking dish. For layer one, cover the base with one-third of the eggplant, laying the slices so they overlap slightly. Spread with one-third of the remaining sauce. Drizzle with a little olive oil, sprinkle with one-third of the parmesan, then one-third of the basil leaves. For layer two, repeat with another one-third each of eggplant, sauce, olive oil, parmesan, and basil.

For the final layer, repeat again with the remaining eggplant, tomato sauce, and some olive oil. Do not put the basil on the top layer (we will garnish after baking). Scatter with the remaining parmesan, then top with all the mozzarella. Bake for 25 minutes until bubbling and golden.

*Serve*—Remove from the oven and let it rest for 10 minutes (makes it easier to slice). Scatter over the remaining fresh basil leaves, cut like lasagne and serve!

**NOTES**

1. Fresh oregano can be substituted with ½ teaspoon dried oregano or 1 fresh basil sprig.
2. I put a tray on the top and middle shelf, and one tray on the floor of the oven. As each tray finishes, I remove the tray and move the others up.
3. Make ahead: Assemble but do not bake. Cover with plastic wrap and refrigerate for 3 days or freeze for up to 3 months. Thaw, then bake, uncovered, for 35 minutes at 350°F. Or bake from frozen, covered, for 40 minutes, then uncovered for 20 minutes.

LEFTOVERS Fridge 3 days. Not suitable for freezing once baked.

# SWEET ENDINGS

**Funny how I *always* have room for dessert . . .**

# APPLE CRUMBLE

*The great apple crumble—done right!*

**SERVES: 5–6 | PREP: 15 MINUTES + 10 MINUTES STANDING | COOK: 35 MINUTES**

A great apple crumble is pretty hard to beat as a way to round off a tasty home-cooked meal. I'm not even fussed if I'm served one that's less than perfect. Like pizza, even when they're average they're still damned good! But here are two tricks that'll give your crumble the edge. Adding a touch of flour to the filling so it thickens the apple juices slightly produces a lovely syrup rather than watery juices. Also, a little baking powder in the topping will magically lighten it so it's not rock hard. Shh! Keep these little tips our secret!

---

**APPLE FILLING**

2 lb granny smith apples,[1] peeled and cut into 1/2 inch cubes

1 tbsp all-purpose flour

1/2 cup granulated sugar

1/2 tsp ground cinnamon

2 tbsp lemon juice (or water)

**TOPPING**

1 cup old-fashioned rolled oats

1 cup all-purpose flour

1 lightly packed cup brown sugar

1/2 tsp baking powder*

1 tsp ground cinnamon

8 tbsp unsalted butter, melted

Pinch of kosher salt*

**TO SERVE**

Vanilla ice cream

Preheat the oven to 350°F.

*Filling*—Place the apple in a bowl, sprinkle with flour, sugar, and cinnamon, then toss to combine. Pour over the lemon juice, then toss again. Spread out evenly in a 1½ quart baking dish.

*Topping*—Place the ingredients in a bowl and mix with a wooden spoon until clumps form, like wet sand. Spread the topping over the apple, using your fingers to make it crumble, if required.

*Bake*—Bake for 35 minutes or until golden brown. Remove from the oven, cover loosely with aluminum foil to keep warm and let stand for 10 minutes before serving (this lets the sauce in the filling thicken slightly).

*Serve*—Serve warm with vanilla ice cream (of course)!

**NOTE**

1. Weigh before peeling. Other apple types work well too but, if they are sweeter apples, you may want to halve the sugar in the filling.

LEFTOVERS Fridge 3 days but best made fresh. Not suitable for freezing.

# MY FOREVER CHOCOLATE CAKE

*Great chocolate flavor. Moist, tender crumb. Just one bowl and a wooden spoon.*

**SERVES: 12 | PREP: 15 MINUTES + 10 MINUTES COOLING | COOK: 35 MINUTES**

I've tried many, many different chocolate cake recipes in my time but this is the one I keep coming back to. It's because this cake truly tastes like chocolate (surprisingly few do!), has a beautifully tender and moist crumb, and keeps very well. It's also crazy easy to make—you don't even need beaters! Use this recipe to make a single-layer rectangular cake, layered round cakes, or bundt cakes. Frost it with fluffy buttercream or simply with whipped cream.

---

1¾ cups all-purpose flour

¾ cup unsweetened cocoa powder[1]

1½ tsp baking powder*[2]

1½ tsp baking soda*[2]

2 cups sugar

1 tsp kosher salt*

2 large eggs*

1 cup milk (whole or low-fat)

½ cup canola oil

2 tsp vanilla extract

2 tsp instant coffee powder[3] OR substitute the boiling water with freshly brewed coffee

1 cup boiling water

**FROSTING**

1 quantity Chocolate Buttercream (page 307)

Sprinkles, to decorate (optional)

Preheat the oven to 350°F. Place a shelf in the middle of the oven. Grease a 13 x 9 x 2 inch rectangular cake pan (see Note 4 for other pans) with butter, then line the base with parchment paper.

*Batter*—Sift the flour, cocoa, baking powder, and baking soda into a large bowl. Add the sugar and salt and whisk briefly to combine. Add the eggs, milk, oil, and vanilla and whisk well to combine until lump-free—about 30 seconds. Add the coffee and boiling water, then whisk to incorporate. The batter will be very thin!

*Bake*—Pour the batter into the cake pan. Bake for 45 minutes or until a wooden skewer inserted into the center comes out clean.

*Cool*—Cool for 10 minutes, then turn out upside down onto wire racks.[5]

*Frost and serve*—Cool completely before frosting, then serve, decorated with sprinkles, if desired.

**NOTES**

1. I use regular cocoa powder but Dutch processed also works and will give the cake a slightly richer color and more intense chocolate flavor.
2. Baking powder and baking soda have different cake-raising characteristics so, for best results, it's safest to use both. However, if you only have baking powder, you can substitute the baking soda with an extra 4½ teaspoons of baking powder. The cake will rise marginally less but it's still excellent. Tip: Dead baking powder is a common baking fail—expiry dates on jars are misleading! See Baking powder testing in the Glossary (page 357) to check if yours is still good.
3. An increasingly well-known trick to bring out the chocolate flavor in cakes is to add a touch of coffee. You can't taste the coffee once baked, it just enhances the chocolate flavor. Either add instant coffee powder, or substitute the water with freshly brewed coffee.
4. Other pan sizes and cooking times: bundt pan—50 minutes; single 9 inch round pan—45 minutes; two 9 inch round pans—35 minutes; three 8 inch round pans—25 minutes. It's best not to use a springform pan if you can avoid it because the batter is very thin and there may be a small amount of leakage. However, if that's all you have, minimize leakage by plugging the creases with softened butter.
5. Use the base as the top of the cake as it is perfectly flat. Also, by cooling it upside down, the weight of the cake should flatten out any slight dome, making the cake layers almost completely level.

LEFTOVERS Keeps near perfectly for 5 days! Store in the fridge but be sure to bring to room temperature before serving (nobody likes cold cake!).

# MY PERFECT VANILLA CAKE

*"Plush" is the best word to describe this gorgeous cake!*

**SERVES: 12 | PREP: 20 MINUTES + 15 MINUTES COOLING | COOK: 35 MINUTES**

This recipe has rocketed into the top 10 on my website since I published it two years ago and has stayed there ever since! It's a classic vanilla butter cake but with Japanese techniques applied to produce the moistest and softest cake you've ever eaten. It's a true professional bakery-quality cake, which also stays fresh for 4 days—unheard of! This cake is the ultimate blank canvas for your cake-making imagination: from layer cakes to birthday cakes, Victoria sponge to strawberry shortcake . . . the possibilities are endless!

**BATTER**

2 cups all-purpose flour[1]

2½ tsp baking powder[2]

¼ tsp kosher salt*

4 large eggs,* at room temperature

1½ cups superfine sugar[3]

8 tablespoons unsalted butter, cut into ½ inch cubes

1 cup whole milk

3 tsp vanilla extract[4]

3 tsp canola oil[5]

**FROSTING**

Buttercream Frosting of your choice (page 307) or whipped cream and berries/jam

Preheat the oven to 350°F for 20 minutes before starting the batter. Place the shelf in the middle of the oven. Grease two 8 inch[6] cake pans with butter, then line with parchment paper.

*Dry ingredients*—Whisk the flour, baking powder, and salt in a large bowl. Set aside.

*Fluff eggs*—Beat the eggs for 30 seconds on medium–high (speed 6 of 10) in a stand mixer fitted with the whisk attachment, or use handheld electric beaters. With the beaters still going, slowly pour the sugar in over 45 seconds, then beat for 7 minutes on high (speed 8), or until tripled in volume and white in color.

*Heat butter and milk*—While the egg is beating, place the butter and milk in a heatproof jar and microwave for 2 minutes on High to melt the butter (or use the stove). Do not let the milk bubble and boil (foaming is okay).

*Add dry ingredients*—When the egg is whipped, scatter one-third of the flour mixture across the surface, then beat on speed 1 for 5 seconds. Add half the remaining flour mixture, then mix again for 5 seconds. Add the remaining flour, then mix for 5–10 seconds until the flour is just mixed in. Once you can't see any flour, stop straight away.

*Hot milk mixture*—Pour the hot milk mixture, vanilla, and oil into the now-empty flour bowl. Add about 1½ cups of the egg mixture (no need to be exact) into the hot milk mixture, then use a whisk to mix until smooth—you can be vigorous. It will be foamy.

*Combine batter*—Turn the beaters back on to the lowest speed (speed 1), then slowly pour the hot milk mixture back into the egg mixture over 15 seconds, then turn the beaters off.

*Finish batter*—Scrape down the side and base of the bowl and beat on speed 1 for 10 seconds—the batter should now be smooth and pourable.

*Bake*—Pour the batter into the prepared pans. Bang each cake pan on the counter three times to knock out any large bubbles. Bake for 30 minutes or until golden and a toothpick inserted into the center of the cake comes out clean.

*Cool*—Remove the cakes from the oven. Cool in the pans for 15 minutes, then gently turn out onto wire racks. If using as layer cakes, cool upside down—the slight dome will flatten perfectly. Level cake = neat layers.

*Decorate and serve*—Decorate with the frosting of your choice, or cream and fresh berries, or jam. Though honestly, the cake is so moist, you can eat it plain!

**NOTES**

1. Cake flour also works fine but it doesn't improve the texture or shelf life so it's unnecessary!
2. Dead baking powder is a common baking fail—expiry dates on jars are misleading! See Baking powder testing in the Glossary (page 357).
3. Granulated sugar works fine too, but you may get some tiny brown spots on the base (larger grains don't dissolve as well).
4. Use the best vanilla extract you can afford, for great vanilla flavor. Give imitation vanilla essence a miss.
5. Or vegetable or grapeseed oil, or other neutral-flavored oil.
6. It's best to use a pan without a loose base as the batter is quite thin so there may be slight leakage. If you only have a springform pan, plug the crack with softened butter. Other cake pan sizes: three 8 inch cake pans—23 minutes; two 9 inch cake pans—27 minutes; three 9 inch cake pans—20 minutes; two 6 inch cake pans—halve the recipe, 25 minutes' bake time; 12 cup bundt pan (grease and dust with flour)—bake 1 hour; 9 x 13 inch rectangular pan—30 minutes.

   For cupcakes, halve the batch of batter, line a 12-hole muffin pan with cupcake liners. Fill the holes two-thirds of the way (no more) and bake for 22 minutes.

LEFTOVERS Store unfrosted cake in an airtight container in a cool pantry. It will stay near fresh for 5 days, which is a special feature of this cake! Or freeze for 3 months. If decorated with cream or buttercream-based frosting it should be kept in the fridge. Always bring the cake to room temperature before serving!

# Buttercream Frosting—10 Flavors!

*One master buttercream frosting, infinite possibilities!*

Everyone needs an excellent buttercream frosting in their sweets-baking toolbox. A bad frosting sticks out like a sore thumb and will cripple even the most impeccably baked cake! My buttercream is creamy and fluffy with the perfect texture for frosting sky-high or slathering onto cakes. Use this master recipe and go wild dreaming up your own flavors—there's a universe of options out there! Meanwhile, I've included ten scrumptious ideas to get you started.

# BASE BUTTERCREAM FROSTING

MAKES ENOUGH FROSTING FOR: TWO 8–9 INCH LAYER CAKES (SIDES, TOP, AND MIDDLE) | 12 CUPCAKES, PIPED INTO TALL SWIRLS | 24 CUPCAKES, SMEARED ON GENEROUSLY WITH A BUTTER KNIFE | TOP OF A 13 X 9 INCH RECTANGULAR CAKE | PREP: 12 MINUTES | COOK: NONE

2 sticks unsalted butter,* at room temperature[1]

4 cups confectioners' sugar, sifted

Flavoring of choice (choose from opposite page)

*Cream butter*—Beat the butter in a stand mixer fitted with the paddle attachment, or with handheld electric beaters, for 3 minutes on the highest speed until it changes from yellow to almost white, scraping down the bowl once or twice. The butter should be smooth and creamy.

*Confectioners' sugar*—Add the confectioners' sugar in three lots. Start beating slowly (to avoid a powder storm), then increase speed gradually. With each addition, once the confectioners' sugar is mostly incorporated, add more confectioners' sugar and repeat. When all the confectioners' sugar has been added, beat on high for a full 3 minutes until fluffy.

*Flavor it!*—Add your flavoring of choice, then beat for a further 30 seconds or until incorporated. If the buttercream is too thick, use milk to make it soft and creamy but it should still hold its form for frosting. If it's too loose, use extra confectioners' sugar to thicken.

*Frost*—Use the frosting immediately! See Death by Chocolate Caramel Cake directions (pages 311–12) for the easy way to frost cakes.

**NOTES**

1. The butter should be soft enough that a dent remains when touched with your finger but not so soft that it leaves a shiny slick of grease on your finger. If you want to get technical, the temperature should be 65°F! If it is too soft, your buttercream may end up too sloppy. See Butter in the Glossary (page 357) for a fast, reliable way to soften fridge-cold butter.
2. Use coconut cream* if you happen to have a bit left over (for example, if a cookbook author irritatingly calls for part of a can in, say, a Satay Dressing recipe—page 183!). Otherwise just use cow's milk*—it doesn't matter because most of the coconut flavor comes from the extract.
3. Mint chocolate frosting—Take care not to overmix as it will break the chocolate. If piping the frosting, chill your hands or the chocolate may melt in the piping bag and bleed into the green frosting.
4. Make ahead: The frosting can be made up to 2 days ahead. Keep in the fridge with plastic wrap touching the surface (to prevent a crust forming). Bring to room temperature, then beat on high speed for 1–2 minutes to make it fluffy and creamy again.

LEFTOVERS Buttercream needs to be used immediately. Frosted cakes and cupcakes should be kept in the fridge. But always bring to room temperature before eating because buttercream goes hard in the fridge—it should be soft and creamy!

VANILLA
3 tsp vanilla extract
⅛ tsp table salt*
1-2 tbsp milk, as needed
COCONUT
4 tbsp coconut cream*[2]
1½ tsp coconut extract
¼ tsp table salt*
LEMON
3 tsp lemon zest
1 tsp lemon extract
4 tbsp lemon juice
⅛ tsp yellow food coloring (optional)
CHOCOLATE
½ cup unsweetened cocoa powder, sifted
1 tsp vanilla extract
⅛ tsp table salt*
5 tbsp milk
NUTELLA
1¼ cups Nutella
¼ tsp table salt*
1–2 tbsp milk, as needed
SALTED CARAMEL
See page 311.
BAILEY'S IRISH CREAM!
3 tbsp Bailey's Irish Cream
½ tsp vanilla extract
PEANUT BUTTER
6 tbsp natural unsweetened peanut butter*
¼ tsp table salt*
2 tbsp milk
MINT CHOCOLATE[3]
2 tsp peppermint extract
¼ tsp green food coloring
1 tbsp milk
½ cup (1¾ oz) finely chopped dark chocolate (70% cocoa)—place in fridge for 30 minutes, then gently stir in at the end
MARGARITA!
2½ tsp lime zest
5 tsp lime juice
2½ tbsp tequila
¼ tsp table salt*

# DEATH BY CHOCOLATE CARAMEL CAKE

*Decadently rich, yet even sweet-averse people love it!*

 **SERVES: 12–16 I PREP: 40 MINUTES + 5 HOURS CHILING (ACROSS VARIOUS STEPS) I COOK: 45 MINUTES**

This cake combines my chocolate cake with a double-punch of salted caramel frosting and drizzle for the most indulgent cake I think I've ever made. Rich as it is, there's something magical about salt in the caramel that cuts through the richness, so even people who declare they don't like "sweet desserts" can't stop eating it, eyeing off a second, possibly even third slice (I'm looking at you, Mum!). It truly is a dangerous cake. I guess that's why I named it Death by Chocolate Caramel Cake. But I say, what a way to go!

---

1 quantity My Forever Chocolate Cake (page 302) baked using three 8 inch cake pans

2 tbsp finely chopped dark chocolate (70% cocoa)

**SALTED CARAMEL**

1 1/4 cups superfine sugar

1/4 tsp table salt*

5 tbsp unsalted butter, cut into 1/2 inch cubes

3/4 cup + 2 tbsp heavy cream,* warmed (must be full-fat)

**SALTED CARAMEL BUTTERCREAM FROSTING**

2 sticks + 4 tbsp unsalted butter,* at room temperature

4 cups confectioners' sugar

1 cup salted caramel (see above)

1/2 tsp table salt*

*Cake*—Make the cakes as per the directions on page 302. Cool them upside down on wire racks. Wrap in plastic wrap and refrigerate for 1 hour[1] (or until you're ready to frost, keeps for 5 days).

### SALTED CARAMEL

*Melt sugar*—Spread one-fourth of the sugar across the base of a medium saucepan and let it melt over medium–high heat, stirring occasionally if needed to help it melt evenly. Once the sugar has melted and is a light golden color, add another fourth of the sugar. Stir briefly, then once fully melted again, repeat twice more with the remaining sugar. Once all the sugar is melted, leave on the stove for another 2–3 minutes or until it becomes an amber caramel color. Keep a close eye on it so it doesn't burn—don't walk away!

*Add butter and cream*—Remove from the heat, then whisk in the salt and butter until melted. Slowly pour in one-third of the cream (the caramel will bubble a bit), pause, and let the bubbles subside, then slowly pour in the remaining cream. Whisk to combine. Put the saucepan back over medium–high heat. Once bubbles appear on the surface, let it boil for 1 minute, scraping down the side of the saucepan as needed.

*Cool*—Pour the caramel into a bowl, then cover with plastic wrap touching the surface of the caramel. Cool on the counter for 1 hour, then refrigerate for at least 4 hours,[2] preferably overnight. You should have about 1½ cups of salted caramel sauce.

Measure out 1 cup of the salted caramel for the frosting. Reserve the rest for decorating. Keep in the fridge until required.

### SALTED CARAMEL BUTTERCREAM FROSTING

*Buttercream*—Cream the butter and confectioners' sugar following the recipe on page 308.

Add the 1 cup salted caramel and salt and beat for 30 seconds on high until incorporated. Transfer to an piping bag fitted with a ⅜ inch round nozzle (for ease of frosting).

### DECORATING!

*Caramel drizzle*—Warm the reserved salted caramel until runny. Allow to cool but ensure it is still drizzle-able (if that's not a word, it is now!).

*Frost and drizzle!*—(See page 312 for step photos.) Place one fridge-cold cake upside down[3] on a turntable or serving platter. Pipe a coil of frosting on the surface,[4] then spread with a small offset spatula. Drizzle with 1 tablespoon of salted caramel. Place a layer of cake on top, then repeat with frosting/salted caramel. Place the final layer of cake on top, then pipe and spread with frosting. Pipe frosting around the side of the cake as well and spread to cover.

Drizzle the top casually with the salted caramel, using as much or as little as you want, in whatever pattern you want. Sprinkle with chopped chocolate. Stand back and admire your masterpiece!

*Serve*—Rest the cake on the counter for 30 minutes. Use a hot, sharp knife[5] to cut neat slices and watch how quickly it is devoured! *See Notes on page 312.*

**NOTES**

1. Fridge-cold cakes are firmer than freshly made room-temperature cakes so they are easier to handle for frosting.
2. It's important to fully chill the caramel before adding to the frosting, otherwise the frosting will be too loose.
3. The base of the cake is nice and flat so use that as the upper face.
4. Piping coils of frosting onto the cake is a quick and easy way to spread even layers of frosting. If you don't have a round nozzle, just snip ½ inch off the end of the piping bag, which will make a ⅜ inch wide round opening.
5. I fill a tall jar with hot tap water. Dunk the knife in, then wipe dry on a dish towel. Cut, then dunk in hot water and repeat.
6. Serving tip: The best way to cut the cake is to refrigerate it for 2 hours after decorating. Cut it when it's fridge-cold (you get really neat slices this way) but then leave the cake slices for 30 minutes to come to room temperature so the frosting becomes creamy.

LEFTOVERS Store the cake in the fridge, but be sure to bring to room temperature before serving. Keeps perfectly for 5 days in an airtight container, though bear in mind that once cut the exposed cake surface will dry out a bit.

**THE EASY WAY TO FROST A CAKE**

# SIMPLE STRAWBERRIES & CREAM

*Just five basic ingredients!*

 **SERVES: 4 | PREP: 10 MINUTES | COOK: 10 MINUTES**

Simple is never the same as boring! The magic behind the world's greatest food pairings lies in their simplicity: basil and tomato, bacon and eggs, butter and popcorn . . . and strawberries and cream. You just need five basic ingredients to make a head-turning version of this classic duo that's light, elegant, and modern. It'd be at home on the menu of any fine-dining restaurant! It's also a great one to prepare ahead for dinner parties—see Note 4.

---

**STRAWBERRY SYRUP**

1 cup strawberries, hulled and cut into 1/2 inch cubes

1/3 cup water

1/3 cup superfine sugar[1]

1/2 tsp lemon juice (optional)

1/2 tbsp very finely sliced mint leaves (optional)

**CANDIED ALMONDS**

1/4 cup slivered almonds,[2] chopped

2 tbsp superfine sugar[1]

**CHANTILLY CREAM**

1 1/2 cups heavy cream*

1 tsp vanilla bean paste[3] (or vanilla extract)

1 1/2 tbsp superfine sugar[1]

**TO SERVE**

14 strawberries, same size, tops trimmed flat (so they sit straight), cut in half

12 small mint sprigs (optional)

*Strawberry syrup*—Place the ingredients, except the mint leaves (if using), in a small saucepan and bring to a simmer over medium heat. Simmer gently for 10 minutes, then transfer to a tall container or jar large enough to fit the head of an immersion blender. Blitz for 5 seconds until smooth. It will seem watery but will thicken into a syrup as it cools. Allow to cool on the counter, then refrigerate for 30 minutes until cold. Stir in the mint leaves, if using, just before serving.

*Candied almonds*—Place the almonds and sugar in a small skillet over medium heat. Once the sugar melts and becomes a little golden (about 1½ minutes), turn the heat down to medium-low and keep stirring until the sugar crystallizes and coats the almonds, about 2 minutes. Transfer to a bowl and let the almonds fully cool. Roughly chop half the almonds, but keep the rest whole.

*Chantilly cream*—Make this just before serving. Place the ingredients in a bowl and beat on high with handheld electric beaters for 2–3 minutes or until soft peaks form. Transfer the cream to a piping bag fitted with a large star-shaped nozzle.

*Assemble*—Arrange seven strawberry halves upside down in a circle in a shallow bowl. Pipe a swirl of cream inside. Spoon 2½–3 tablespoons of the strawberry syrup around the strawberries. Sprinkle the almonds on the cream and garnish with mint if desired.

*Serve*—Serve with a flourish and enjoy!

**NOTES**

1. Superfine sugar works better because it dissolves more easily. However, granulated sugar will work fine too.
2. Or roughly chopped unsalted roasted whole almonds.
3. Or better yet, the seeds of 1 vanilla bean!
4. Make ahead: The strawberry syrup can be made up to 5 days in advance (store in the fridge). The candied almonds can be made up to at least a week in advance, probably much longer (store in an airtight container in the pantry). The fresh strawberries can be cut the day before and kept in an airtight container. To make the cream ahead, make a stabilized cream instead by substituting one-third of the cream for mascarpone. Whip together as per the recipe, then transfer to a piping bag and store in the fridge for up to 24 hours. The cream will stay fluffy and aerated, ready to pipe when required.

LEFTOVERS Once assembled, best served straight away.

# LIME PROSECCO GRANITA

*INCREDIBLY easy dessert that's a hit with everyone!*

  **SERVES: 5–6 I PREP: 5 MINUTES + 1 HOUR REFRIGERATING + 4 HOURS (OR MORE) FREEZING I COOK: NONE**

This is THE sweet finish you pull out for hot summer days, to end rich meals, or when you simply do not have the time (or inclination) to make a labor-intensive dessert. It's as simple as pouring everything into a pan, then whacking it in the freezer. No need to scrape the granita regularly, like most recipes call for, because the alcohol keeps it from freezing solid. Beautifully refreshing, sweet enough, and tangy enough, everybody loves it! Using prosecco is ideal because—a) it's a bit sweet, b) it doesn't taste boozy once frozen, c) the kids can't have any so this is ALL for the grown-ups!

---

1 cup granulated sugar

1 cup water

3 cups cold prosecco[1]

1 tsp lime zest

6 tbsp lime juice

**TO SERVE**

Lime wedges

Grated lime zest

Mint leaves (optional)

*Sugar syrup*—Put the sugar and water in a small saucepan, bring to a boil, and stir until the sugar is dissolved. Pour into a large jar, cool to room temperature, then refrigerate for at least 1 hour until cold.

*Mix and freeze*—Add the remaining ingredients to the jar, then stir. Taste and adjust the flavor, if desired. Pour into two 13 x 9 inch ceramic, plastic, or glass dishes or containers so the liquid is no more than ¾ inch deep.

Cover with a lid or plastic wrap and place in the freezer for 4+ hours (you can make this days in advance!). There is no need to scrape periodically as the alcohol prevents the mixture from freezing solid.

*Serve*—Scrape the mixture with a fork to create granular flakes. Spoon into pretty little bowls or glasses and serve garnished with lime wedges and zest, and mint leaves, if desired!

**NOTE**

1. Prosecco is a sparkling/semi-sparkling white wine from Italy. It is typically sweeter than French champagne and most sparkling wines, which makes it ideal to use in granita. While you can substitute with other types of sparkling wine or champagne, you will probably need to add more sugar and possibly less lime juice.

LEFTOVERS Keeps in the freezer for 3 months!

# BLUEBERRY TART WITH ALMOND FILLING

*Classic, timeless flavor combination.*

**SERVES: 12 | PREP: 45 MINUTES + 4 HOURS COOLING AND CHILING (ACROSS VARIOUS STEPS) | COOK: 1 HOUR**

The appeal of this tart is its casual charm. Rustic yet chic, the combination of berries with a classic almond cream filling in a buttery tart crust is a patisserie favorite. Here, I'm using my go-to sweet French tart crust, *pâte sucrée*, which I think is superior to regular shortcrust pastry both in flavor and ease of working. Experiment with different fruits! Try mangoes, peach slices, halved figs, apricots, or other berries (except strawberries, they're a bit too watery).

**SWEET TART CRUST**

1½ cups all-purpose flour, plus extra for dusting

6½ tbsp confectioners' sugar

¼ tsp kosher salt*

2½ tbsp almond meal[1]

7 tbsp cold unsalted butter, cut into ½ inch cubes

1 large egg,* at room temperature

**ALMOND PASTRY CREAM**

7 tbsp unsalted butter, softened

½ cup sugar

1 cup almond meal[1]

½ tsp almond essence

2 large eggs,* at room temperature

1 tbsp all-purpose flour

**TOPPING**

2 cups blueberries

Confectioners' sugar, for dusting

*Sweet tart crust*—Whisk the flour, confectioners' sugar, salt, and almond meal in a bowl. Rub the cold butter in with your fingertips until it resembles bread crumbs. Add the egg and mix with a rubber spatula until it becomes too hard to stir anymore, then use your hands to bring it together into a dough. Knead to bring it together into a smooth ball. Flatten into a ¾ inch thick disk, wrap with plastic wrap, then refrigerate for 30 minutes, or up to 2 days.[2]

*Line tart pan (See Note 3 for hot weather warning!)*—Unwrap the chilled dough. Roll out into a 13 inch wide, ⅛ inch thick circle on a lightly floured work surface. Roll the pastry lightly onto the rolling pin, then unroll it gently over a 9 x 1 inch tart pan. Fit the pastry in the pan, pressing it into the sides, taking care not to stretch it.[4] Roll the rolling pin over the tart pan to trim the excess dough. Prick the base 25 times with a fork,[4] cover with plastic wrap, then freeze for 2 hours,[5] or up to 1 month. If not using immediately, it can be frozen for up to 1 month.

Preheat the oven to 400°F. Remove the tart from the freezer, unwrap, then cover with two large sheets of parchment paper arranged in a cross, with some overhang. Fill to the brim with baking beads.[4]

*Par-bake (blind bake)*—Bake for 20 minutes. Use the overhanging paper to transfer the baking beads to a bowl. Return the uncovered tart to the oven for 5 minutes, then cool for 1 hour before filling.

*Almond pastry cream*—Beat the butter and sugar with handheld electric beaters on low speed for 15 seconds or until combined. Beat in the almond meal and almond essence just until incorporated. Add the eggs one at a time, beating in between until incorporated. Add the flour and beat just until incorporated. Refrigerate for 30 minutes.

Preheat the oven to 400°F.

*Assemble and bake*—Spread the pastry cream into the tart shell and smooth the surface. Scatter two-thirds of the blueberries across the surface. Bake for 15 minutes, then remove from the oven. Reduce the heat to 350°F. Top with the remaining blueberries and bake for a further 20–25 minutes or until the surface is golden around the edges and light golden in the center.

*Serve*—Cool for 1 hour. Dust with confectioners' sugar, cut generous slices, and serve!

**NOTES**

1. Not to be confused with almond flour, which is finer.
2. If the dough is in the fridge for much longer than 1 hour, leave it on the counter to soften slightly before rolling out.
3. Hot weather is not a friend of tart pastry! So, if it's warm in your kitchen, place ice packs on your work surface to cool it before rolling out the pastry. This will ensure your pastry does not break when you are working with it.
4. Stretching and pulling the pastry causes shrinkage during baking. Pricking helps prevent the base from puffing up during par-baking. Freezing the pastry is a trick to prevent shrinkage. If you are pressed for time, though, you can skip this and just bake immediately, but expect a bit of shrinkage. Baking beads also prevent shrinkage by keeping the pressure on the base and walls of the tart shell. No baking beads? Use dried rice or beans instead (fill to the rim). Save and re-use!

LEFTOVERS Fridge 5 days, though it's best on the first 2 days. Unfilled tart shell can be kept in an airtight container for 2 days.

# LEMON CHEESECAKE

*That color! That creamy filling! That stunning lemon flavor!*

**MAKES: 10–12 PIECES, SERVES 10–12 | PREP: 15 MINUTES + 6 HOURS COOLING | COOK: 45 MINUTES**

**There's lemon cheesecakes, then there's this lemon cheesecake. Created with the assistance of French pastry chef Jennifer Pogmore, who found herself in the unlikely position as my mentor for all things pastry, this is truly exceptional—because she wouldn't settle for anything less! It strikes that perfect balance of tang, sweetness, and luxurious richness without being overly heavy, with the most incredible lemon flavor. And that lemon curd topping is something else!**

**BASE**

5 oz whole graham crackers[1]

7 tbsp unsalted butter, melted

2 tbsp superfine sugar

**CHEESECAKE FILLING**

1 lb block of cream cheese,[2] well softened

1 tbsp lemon zest[3]

2 tbsp lemon juice[3]

1 tsp vanilla extract

¾ cup superfine sugar

2 large eggs,* at room temperature

**LEMON CURD**

2 tbsp lemon zest[3]

½ cup lemon juice[3]

½ cup + 1 tbsp superfine sugar

2 large eggs*

2½ tbsp unsalted butter

**TO SERVE**

Confectioners' sugar, to dust

Lemon slices (optional)

Whipped cream (optional)

Fresh raspberries (optional)

Mint sprigs (optional)

Preheat the oven to 275°F. Place a shelf in the middle of the oven. Lightly grease and line an 8 inch square pan with parchment paper with a 2 inch overhang.[4]

*Base*—Break the cookies roughly by hand into a food processor. Blitz for 10 seconds on low, or until fine crumbs form. Add the butter and sugar, then blitz to combine—the mixture should look like wet sand. Pour into the prepared pan and use something with a flat bottom to press the batter into the base. Set aside on the counter.

*Filling*—Place all the filling ingredients, except the eggs, in a bowl. Using handheld electric beaters or a stand mixer fitted with the whisk attachment, beat on medium-high (speed 7) until smooth and lump-free, around 15 seconds. Add the eggs and beat just until incorporated.

*Bake*—Bang the bowl firmly three times on the counter to remove any air bubbles. Pour the filling over the base in the pan, then smooth the surface with an offset spatula. Bake for 40 minutes. Meanwhile, prepare the lemon curd.

*Lemon curd*—Put all the lemon curd ingredients in a medium saucepan and whisk over medium-low heat. Whisk constantly (though leisurely!) especially as the butter is melting, to ensure it doesn't split and the eggs don't scramble. When the mixture starts heating up it will begin to thicken (about 3 minutes). Once bubbles start to appear, remove from the stove and strain into a bowl using a fine-mesh strainer (it's fine if most of the zest gets strained out). Cover with plastic wrap touching the surface. Set aside.

*Top with curd*—After 40 minutes, remove the cheesecake from the oven and let it rest for 10 minutes (to deflate and make the surface flat[5]). Spread the curd over the top of the cheesecake, smoothing the surface as well as you can using a small offset spatula, then bake for a further 5 minutes.

*Cool in oven*[6]—Turn the oven off, open the door 8 inches and let the cheesecake cool slowly for 2 hours in the oven (this prevents the surface from cracking), then cool on the counter for a further 1 hour before refrigerating for at least 5 hours.

*Serve*—To serve, cut the cheesecake into squares or bars using a hot[7] knife. They can be eaten on the go by hand or, for a more elegant plating option, cut into rectangles and serve with a small lemon slice and a dusting of confectioners' sugar. If you like, add a dollop of cream, a raspberry, and a mint sprig.

**NOTES**

1. Any plain sweet cookies or crackers will work here—or flavored, if you want!
2. Cream cheese in tubs also works. Whatever you use, make sure it is well softened so it's easy to beat until smooth, making it easier to blend with the other ingredients to make a lump-free filling.
3. You will need 4 big lemons or 6 medium lemons for this cheesecake.
4. So you can hold the overhang paper to lift the cheesecake out to slice.
5. The cheesecake puffs up in the oven. By letting it rest for 10 minutes, the surface levels out so you get a nice even lemon curd layer across the whole surface, rather than pooling more thickly on the border.
6. Cooling in the oven is an important step! It changes the curd so it is more set, less sharp and makes it a brighter yellow—all good things!
7. Run a knife under hot tap water, dry, then cut. Repeat between each slice for neater slices. Cut while the cheesecake is fridge-cold, then serve straight away or leave out for 20 minutes first, to take the chill out of it slightly (you may need to dab condensation off the lemon curd surface).

LEFTOVERS Fridge 5 days. Surprisingly, it freezes really well! Thaw overnight in the fridge.

# EVERYTHING ELSE YOU NEED

# Sauces

**Here's a collection of my favorite sauces that make everything more delicious! Use for dousing, mopping, drizzling, and simmering.**

# CREAMY MUSHROOM SAUCE

**MAKES: 3 CUPS, 4–5 SERVINGS I PREP: 5 MINUTES I COOK: 10 MINUTES**

Serve over steak, chicken, pork, lamb, roast-anything, meatballs, schnitzel, baked potato, mashed potato, pasta, or steamed greens! See, I meant it. It really is a sauce for everything!

---

½ tbsp extra-virgin olive oil

2 tbsp unsalted butter

10 oz button mushrooms, finely sliced

2 garlic cloves,* finely minced

Pinch of salt and freshly ground black pepper

¼ cup chardonnay or other dry white wine*[1]

½ cup low-sodium chicken broth* (or vegetable broth*)

1 cup heavy cream*

½ tightly packed cup (2 oz) finely grated parmesan*[2]

1 tsp fresh thyme leaves (or ¼ tsp dried)

Heat the oil and butter in a large nonstick skillet over high heat. Cook the mushrooms for 5 minutes until golden brown. Just before they're done, add the garlic and salt and pepper, and cook for 2 minutes until the garlic is light golden.

Add the wine—it will sizzle! Stir, scraping the bottom of the skillet, for 1 minute or until mostly evaporated. Add the broth, cream, and parmesan. Stir, then lower the heat to medium so the sauce is simmering—do not boil rapidly or the cream may split.

Simmer the sauce for 2–3 minutes, stirring occasionally, until it thickens. Stir in the thyme and adjust salt and pepper to taste. Remove from the stove and serve.

**NOTES**

1. You can substitute with nonalcoholic white wine.
2. Be sure to finely grate your own parmesan. Pre-grated store-bought won't melt into the sauce properly.

LEFTOVERS Fridge 3 days—warm gently. Not suitable for freezing.

# GRAVY

**MAKES: 2 CUPS, ENOUGH TO DOUSE PROTEIN, MASHED POTATOES, AND STEAMED VEGETABLES FOR 4 PEOPLE I PREP: 1 MINUTE I COOK: 5 MINUTES**

The best way to make a really great gravy in 3 minutes flat? Pan-fry a meat, then, while it's resting, make the gravy in the same pan. All those golden bits left in the pan are free sauce flavor! Try this with any of the proteins in the What I Do with a Piece of . . . chapter.

---

2 tbsp unsalted butter

3 tbsp all-purpose flour

2 cups low-sodium beef broth*

1/8 tsp kosher salt*

1/4 tsp freshly ground black pepper (or more!)

Cook your meat of choice in a skillet (such as chicken breast on page 128, sausages, or steak). Transfer to a plate to rest and, meanwhile, make this gravy in the same pan. Discard any excess fat from the pan, remove any loose bits, and make sure there are no large burned patches on the base of the pan. (If there are, scrape them off and discard.)

Melt the butter over medium–low heat in the same pan, then add the flour. Cook for 2 minutes, stirring regularly.

While stirring constantly, slowly pour in half the beef broth. The gravy will thicken fairly quickly. Once the flour mixture is incorporated into the liquid, stir in the remaining broth. If you have lumps, just do a bit of swishing with a whisk to dissolve them.

Add salt and pepper and simmer for a further 1½ minutes, stirring regularly, until the sauce thickens into a gravy consistency. Serve immediately!

**NOTE**

1. To make this gluten-free, omit the flour. Mix together 1½ tablespoons of cornstarch with a splash of the beef broth in a bowl. Once lump-free, add the remaining beef broth. Follow the recipe as written.

# HONEY GARLIC SAUCE

**MAKES: 1/3 CUP, ENOUGH TO GLAZE 1 LB PROTEIN I PREP: 3 MINUTES I COOK: 2 MINUTES**

An exceptional sauce to serve with pan-seared proteins with high returns for low effort. It's very popular with my website readers! Excellent with chicken, pork, shrimp, and salmon. Make it in the same pan as the meat, while it's resting.

---

1 tbsp unsalted butter (or 1 tbsp olive oil)

2 garlic cloves,* finely minced

1½ tbsp apple cider vinegar (or other clear vinegar)

1 tbsp light soy sauce*

1/3 cup honey (or maple syrup)

Cook your protein of choice in a skillet (such as chicken breast on page 128), then transfer to a plate. Make this sauce in the same pan while the protein is resting.

Discard any excess fat and remove any loose bits from the pan.

Return the pan to medium heat. Add the butter and, once melted, add the garlic and stir for 10 seconds until fragrant. Add the remaining ingredients and stir to combine. Once the sauce comes to a simmer, let it bubble for 1 minute or until thickened into a syrupy consistency.

Return the protein to the pan and turn to coat in the sauce. Serve immediately!

# RED WINE SAUCE

 **MAKES: ⅔ CUP, 4–5 SERVINGS | PREP: 5 MINUTES | COOK: 1 HOUR 45 MINUTES**

A rich, elegant, classic red wine jus to serve with steak (see page 136) and Beef Wellington (page 252) for a bona fide fine-dining experience at home! Truly a sauce you can't buy in a bottle. Important note: This sauce must be made with homemade broth. It will not work with store-bought broth (see Note 2).

---

- 3 cups cabernet sauvignon*[1]
- 1 large shallot,* finely sliced
- 1 fresh bay leaf* (substitute dried)
- 4 cups homemade Beef Broth (page 348)
- 2 tbsp cold unsalted butter, cut into ¼ inch cubes
- ½ tsp superfine sugar
- ½ tsp kosher salt*

Rapidly simmer the wine, shallot, and bay leaf in a medium saucepan over medium–high heat for 30 minutes until reduced by three-quarters to ¾ cup.

Add the broth, then continue to simmer rapidly on medium heat for a further 45 minutes to 1 hour, skimming scum off as needed, until it reduces down to ⅔ cups and thickens into a thin syrup consistency.

Reduce the heat to low, then add the butter pieces, one by one, while whisking constantly. Once all the butter is melted, stir in the sugar and salt. The final consistency should be a thin syrup that pools on a plate without bleeding.

Strain through a fine-mesh strainer into a serving bowl.

**NOTES**

1. A traditional wine of choice for classic French red wine sauce. Merlot is the next best alternative. Do not attempt this sauce with nonalcoholic wine!
2. Jus cannot be made with store-bought broth as it requires the gelatin in homemade broth to thicken. Also, store-bought broth will be far too salty by the time it has reduced to the concentration required.

LEFTOVERS Fridge 5 days (it will thicken when cold), freezer 3 months. Thaw, then reheat on a very low heat until pourable again.

# SWEET & SOUR SAUCE

 **MAKES: ¾ CUP | PREP: 3 MINUTES | COOK: 5 MINUTES**

Quick, easy, and the perfect dipping sauce for homemade Spring Rolls (page 238), Shrimp Toast (page 232), or Crunchy Baked Chicken Tenders (page 29)!

---

- 2 tsp cornstarch
- 2 tbsp water
- ½ cup apple cider vinegar
- ⅓ packed cup brown sugar
- 2 tbsp ketchup
- 2 tsp soy sauce,* light or all-purpose

Place all the ingredients in a small saucepan over medium heat. Bring to simmer, stirring regularly, then cook until it thickens to a syrupy consistency, 3–5 minutes.

LEFTOVERS Fridge 5 days, freezer 3 months.

# WHITE WINE SAUCE

 **MAKES: 1½ CUPS, ENOUGH TO SERVE WITH 4 PIECES OF PROTEIN I PREP: 1 MINUTE I COOK: 2 MINUTES**

Particularly beautiful with fish and chicken, but also excellent with shrimp, scallops, and pork chops. You'll love how quick and easy this luxurious sauce is to make!

---

1¼ cups chardonnay or other dry white wine*[1]

1 shallot,* roughly chopped (about ⅓ cup)

1 tsp lemon juice

1 tsp white wine vinegar (or other clear vinegar)

⅛ tsp kosher salt*

1 pinch of white pepper

1 pinch of sugar

1 cup heavy cream*

2 tbsp cold unsalted butter, cut into ¼ inch cubes

Simmer the wine, shallot, lemon juice, vinegar, salt, pepper, and sugar in a medium saucepan over medium–high heat until the liquid is almost completely evaporated and you're left with the shallots in just a little liquid, around 5 minutes.

Add the cream, bring to a simmer, then reduce the heat to medium. Simmer for 3 minutes or until the sauce is a thin syrupy consistency.

Reduce the heat to low and add the butter pieces, one at a time, while constantly mixing with a wooden spoon. Once the butter is incorporated, it will become glossy and thicken.

Strain the sauce through a fine-mesh strainer, then pour it back into a clean saucepan. Spoon over your protein of choice!

**NOTE**

1. Unfortunately (given the name of the sauce!) this can't be made with nonalcoholic wine.

LEFTOVERS Fridge 5 days. Reheat gently in the microwave or on the stove, whisking until smooth.

# BROWN BUTTER & LEMON BUTTER SAUCE

 **MAKES: ¼ CUP, ENOUGH TO SERVE WITH 2 PIECES OF CHICKEN, STEAK, OR OTHER PROTEIN OF CHOICE I PREP: 1 MINUTE I COOK: 2 MINUTES**

The better butter in 2 minutes, with one ingredient! This goes brilliantly with fish, shrimp, and other shellfish, chicken, steak, pork chops, potatoes, or steamed or roasted vegetables. Add a splash of lemon to transform it into lemon butter sauce—one of the best sauces to pair with any seafood!

---

4 tbsp salted butter, cut into ¾ inch cubes

1 tbsp lemon juice, if making Lemon Butter Sauce

Cook your protein of choice in a skillet and make the sauce while it's resting (see chapter What I Do With a Piece of . . . ).

Discard any excess fat and wipe the pan roughly with a paper towel, ensuring there are no big burned patches in the pan. Allow the pan to cool for 2 minutes (or the butter will burn immediately on contact!).

Return the pan to medium heat and add the butter. Once it melts and becomes foamy, stir leisurely for another 30 seconds or until the butter turns golden brown and smells nutty.

Immediately pour into a small bowl (to stop it cooking further), scraping all the little golden bits out of the pan (extra flavor!). Add the lemon juice (if using). Spoon over your protein of choice!

LEFTOVERS Fridge 5 days, freezer 3 months. Melt, then use as per the recipe.

BLUE CHEESE SAUCE

WHITE WINE SAUCE

BROWN BUTTER SAUCE

CHIMICHURRI

HONEY MUSTARD SAUCE

GRAVY

SWEET & SOUR SAUCE

RED WINE SAUCE

BÉARNAISE SAUCE

# CHIMICHURRI

**MAKES: 3/4 CUP, ENOUGH TO SERVE WITH 4 PIECES OF PROTEIN | PREP: 1 MINUTE + 1 HOUR RESTING | COOK: NONE**

A South American sauce that's a ripper with any steak! Also great with chicken, lamb, pork, fish, and shrimp.

---

1 tightly packed cup parsley leaves, finely minced

1 tightly packed tbsp fresh oregano leaves, finely minced (optional)

2 tsp finely minced garlic*

1 tsp dried chili flakes (optional—adjust to taste)

1/4 cup red wine vinegar[1]

1/2 tsp kosher salt*

1/8 tsp freshly ground black pepper

1/2 cup extra-virgin olive oil[2]

Place all the ingredients in a small bowl and stir gently to combine. Set aside for 1 hour before use—overnight is even better!

Serve in bowls alongside grilled meats so people can help themselves.

**NOTES**

1. Substitute with lemon juice, white wine vinegar, or sherry vinegar.
2. If you double the recipe (as I often do for gatherings!), only scale up the olive oil by around half. Also, for larger batches, you will be able to blitz the parsley in a food processor rather than chopping by hand.

LEFTOVERS Fridge 3 days.

# MY FAVORITE BLUE CHEESE SAUCE

**MAKES: 1 CUP, 4 SERVINGS | PREP: 1 MINUTE | COOK: 10 MINUTES**

Exceptionally great with steak, crispy chicken thighs, roast chicken, steamed vegetables (asparagus!), iceberg lettuce wedges, and using as a dip for hunks of bread, veggie sticks, or tortilla chips!

---

1 tbsp unsalted butter

1 garlic clove,* finely minced

2 rosemary sprigs

1/4 cup chardonnay or other dry white wine*[1]

1 cup heavy cream*

3 oz gorgonzola piccante,[2] crumbled

1/4 tsp kosher salt*

Pinch of white pepper

2 tsp lemon juice

Melt the butter in a medium saucepan over medium heat. Add the garlic and rosemary, then cook for 1 minute until the garlic is light golden. Add the wine and simmer for 3 minutes until mostly evaporated. Add the cream, bring it back to a simmer, then reduce the heat to medium-low and simmer gently for 5 minutes until it thickens to a thin syrupy consistency.

Remove from the heat and stir in the cheese until it melts and the sauce becomes smooth.

Strain the sauce through a fine-mesh strainer into a jar, pressing all the liquid out. You should end up with 1 cup—if you have much more, reduce it further on the stove (or the flavor will be too diluted). Stir in the salt, pepper, and lemon juice and serve warm!

**NOTES**

1. Substitute with nonalcoholic white wine.
2. My favorite blue cheese for this sauce, for flavor and melting qualities. However, any soft blue cheese will work fine here—just don't get the hard, crumbly ones.

LEFTOVERS Fridge 5 days—warm gently. Not suitable for freezing.

# BÉARNAISE SAUCE

**MAKES: 1 CUP, 4 SERVINGS | PREP: 5 MINUTES + 10 MINUTES COOLING | COOK: 2 MINUTES**

This up-market restaurant staple is what I pull out to impress (with minimal effort). Traditionally, it's whisked by hand and there's plenty of ways to mess it up. But the method I use is fast, safe, and indistinguishable from handmade béarnaise. Brilliant and classically served over steak but, with salmon, it's also off-the-charts stunning.

---

8 tbsp unsalted butter, cut into ½ inch cubes

3 egg yolks,* at room temperature

¼ tsp kosher salt*

1 tbsp water

½ tbsp finely chopped tarragon[1]

½ tbsp finely chopped chervil[1]

**INFUSED VINEGAR**

1½ tbsp chardonnay or other dry white wine*[2]

1½ tbsp white wine vinegar (or apple cider vinegar)

¼ tsp freshly ground black pepper

1 small shallot,* finely sliced

2 tarragon sprigs[1]

Simmer the infused vinegar ingredients in a very small saucepan over medium–low heat for 2 minutes. Remove from the stove and stand for 5 minutes. Strain through a fine-mesh strainer—you should have about 1 tablespoon of liquid.

Melt the butter in the microwave in a jar, or on the stove over medium heat, then stand for 30 seconds until the milky whites settle at the bottom (milk solids) and clarified butter (golden part) sits above it. Pour off and measure out ¾ cup of the clarified butter (use while hot), discarding the milk solids.

Place the egg yolks, infused vinegar, and salt in a tall, narrow container that an immersion blender fits in. Blitz briefly to combine. Ensure the clarified butter is still hot then, with the immersion blender on high, gradually drizzle in the clarified butter over about a minute. Once all the butter is in, blitz for a further 10 seconds.

Add the water, then blitz to incorporate. Add more water as needed, 1 teaspoon at a time, until the sauce is thick but loose enough to ooze across a steak, coating it thickly. Stir the tarragon and chervil through the sauce.

Use around 2 tablespoons of sauce per 7–10 oz piece of protein.

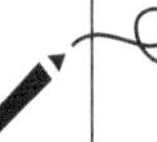

**NOTES**

1. Tarragon is the signature herb in béarnaise, so you really can't substitute this! However, chervil can be substituted with parsley.
2. Though not quite the same, nonalcoholic white wine can be substituted.
3. Béarnaise can be used warm or at room temperature (the heat of the cooked protein will warm it up), it just needs to be a thick, pourable sauce. Once made, cover, then keep in a warm place and it will hold for 20 minutes or so. If not using immediately, store in a thermos and it will remain pourable for 8 hours. Just give it a quick mix before using. Not recommended to refrigerate—once cooled, it will solidify and reheating is highly risky so I recommend avoiding it!

# HONEY MUSTARD SAUCE

**MAKES: ½ CUP | PREP: 3 MINUTES | COOK: NONE**

An excellent and simple sauce that's as good for dipping as it is for spooning over a seared or poached chicken breast (pages 129 and 130), or Smoky Pork Chops (page 145).

---

⅓ cup mayonnaise*

1 tbsp dijon mustard

2 tbsp honey

1½ tsp lemon juice or apple cider vinegar

Mix all the ingredients together in a small bowl until combined. It's ready for use!

LEFTOVERS Fridge 7 days.

# Dressings

**For the following dressings, simply shake all the ingredients in a jar. Makes enough to dress a side salad for 4–5 servings. *Tip*: It's worth investing in good-quality vinegar and olive oil. It makes all the difference with dressings!**

**EVERYDAY SALAD DRESSING**

1 tbsp apple cider vinegar

3 tbsp extra-virgin olive oil

1/4 tsp dijon mustard

1/4 tsp finely minced garlic* (optional)

1/4 tsp kosher salt*

1/8 tsp freshly ground black pepper

**LEMON DRESSING**

3/4 tsp lemon zest

1 tbsp lemon juice

3 tbsp extra-virgin olive oil

1/4 tsp dijon mustard (optional)

1/4 tsp finely minced garlic*

1/4 tsp kosher salt*

1/8 tsp freshly ground black pepper

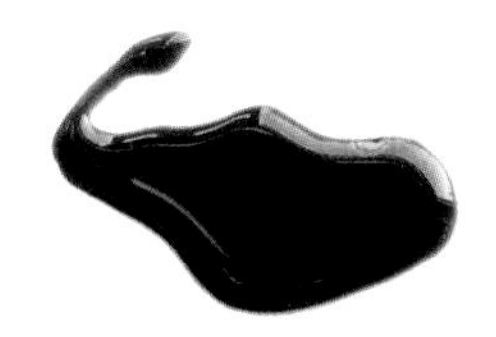

**BALSAMIC DRESSING**

1 1/2 tbsp balsamic vinegar

3 1/2 tbsp extra-virgin olive oil

1/4 tsp kosher salt*

1/8 tsp freshly ground black pepper

**GINGER DRESSING**

1 1/2 tsp finely grated ginger*

1 tbsp light or all-purpose soy sauce*

1 1/2 tbsp sesame oil*

2 tbsp rice vinegar

1/2 tsp superfine sugar

**FRENCH DRESSING**

1 1/2 tbsp white wine vinegar

3 1/2 tbsp extra-virgin olive oil

1/2 tsp dijon mustard

1/4 tsp kosher salt*

Pinch of freshly ground black pepper

**ITALIAN DRESSING**

1 tbsp finely grated parmesan*

1 1/2 tbsp red wine vinegar

3 1/2 tbsp extra-virgin olive oil

1/4 tsp superfine sugar

1/4 tsp finely minced garlic*

1/4 tsp each dried red pepper flakes, basil, parsley, and oregano

1/4 tsp kosher salt*

**MEDITERRANEAN DRESSING**

1 1/2 tbsp red wine vinegar

3 1/2 tbsp extra-virgin olive oil

3/4 tsp dried oregano

1/2 tsp finely minced garlic*

1/2 tsp kosher salt*

1/8 tsp freshly ground black pepper

**ASIAN SESAME DRESSING**

1 tbsp light or all-purpose soy sauce*

1 1/2 tbsp white vinegar

1 1/2 tbsp sesame oil*

2 tsp extra-virgin olive oil

1/2 tsp superfine sugar

## Makes enough dressing for . . .

- 5 heaped cups leafy greens (5–7 oz, depending on variety)
- 4 heaped cups chopped vegetables, raw or cooked (such as cucumbers, tomatoes, snow peas)
- 3 tightly packed cups finely shredded cabbage and other vegetables

# Rice

Knowing how to make rice properly on the stove is a life essential!

# WHITE RICE

**MAKES: 3 CUPS, SERVES 2–3 | PREP: 1 MINUTE | COOK: 25 MINUTES**

1 cup white rice—long-grain and medium-grain

1½ cups water

Place the water and rice in a medium saucepan over medium–high heat. Once the water is bubbling all across the surface, place the lid on, reduce the heat to medium–low, and cook for 13 minutes (no peeking, no stirring!) or until all the water is absorbed.

Remove the saucepan from the stove and leave to rest for 10 minutes with the lid on.

Using a rice paddle or rubber spatula, turn the rice over and fluff it up. Let it steam-dry for a minute or two (no lid), then serve!

# BROWN RICE

**MAKES: 2¾ CUPS, SERVES 2–3 | PREP: 1 MINUTE | COOK: 35 MINUTES**

Despite what most rice packages say, skip the absorption method for brown rice. A boil-and-drain method works much better. I cooked a LOT of brown rice to confirm this!

2 quarts water

1 cup brown rice—medium-grain, long-grain, and basmati

Bring the water to a boil in a medium saucepan over high heat. Add the rice, then boil until the rice is just cooked. For medium and long-grain brown rice cook for 30 minutes. For brown basmati, cook for 14 minutes (but check at 12 minutes).

Drain the rice in a colander and thoroughly shake the excess water out from the pot. Return the rice to the pot, cover, and place it on the turned-off stove to rest for 10 minutes. Fluff and serve!

## My tips for guaranteed fluffy stovetop rice every single time!

*Uncooked to cooked rice ratio:* 1 cup uncooked rice = 3 cups cooked and serves 2–3 as a side

*Cups of raw rice and cooking vessel size:* 1–2 cups in a medium saucepan | 3–4 cups in a large saucepan or small pot | 6–8 cups in a large pot

1. NEVER stir the rice or lift the lid while cooking. That is the path to mushy rice!
2. Never, ever, ever skip resting rice! The rice finishes cooking during this time.
3. No need to rinse rice purchased in packages from grocery stores. This doesn't make rice fluffy; the correct water to rice ratio does. But if you do rinse (for cleanliness or if you just can't break the habit), reduce the water by ¼ cup for each cup of rice, to account for water-logging.
4. Cooking vessel size matters! Too much rice in a small saucepan = mushy rice. See above for the right saucepan size.

LEFTOVERS Fridge 3 days, freezer 3 months. Reheat from frozen in the microwave, 1½ minutes on High, covered, per 1 cup cooked rice.

# JASMINE RICE

 MAKES: 2¾ CUPS, SERVES 2–3 I PREP: 1 MINUTE I COOK: 25 MINUTES

---

1 cup jasmine rice

1¼ cups water

Use the same cooking method as for White Rice (page 335). The only difference is that less water is used for jasmine rice because it is a softer variety.

# BASMATI RICE

 MAKES: 3 CUPS, SERVES 2–3 I PREP: 1 MINUTE I COOK: 25 MINUTES

---

1 cup white basmati rice

1½ cups water

Use the same method as for White Rice (page 335). Fluff gently so you don't break the long basmati rice grains!

# CAULIFLOWER RICE

 MAKES: 6–8 CUPS, SERVES 5–6 PEOPLE I PREP: 10 MINUTES I COOK: 15 MINUTES

Is it the same as real rice, in all its carb-laden glory? No! But when made well, it's a very good consolation for all those times we're going "low-carb."

---

1 head cauliflower, broken into florets

1 tbsp olive oil

Push the cauliflower florets through the feeding tube of a food processor fitted with the grating disk, with the motor running on low. The cauliflower will blitz into little rice-shaped bits! Alternative: Cut the cauliflower into quarters, then grate by hand using a box grater.

Preheat the oven to 425°F.

Spread 6–8 cups (1 lb 5 oz–1¾ lb) of the cauliflower rice on a large baking tray. Drizzle with the olive oil and toss to coat. Bake for 15 minutes, tossing halfway, until still a bit firm. Don't overcook, as it goes watery and soggy!

Use as a substitute for any dish served with rice, such as stir-fries.

LEFTOVERS Fridge 3 days, cooked or raw.

# FLUFFY COCONUT RICE

**MAKES: 6 CUPS, SERVES 5–6 | PREP: 5 MINUTES + 1 HOUR SOAKING | COOK: 45 MINUTES**

The secret to truly excellent coconut rice? Use the oven rather than the stove. Fluffy rice and no scorched pot, every single time!

---

2 cups jasmine rice[1]

14 fl oz can good-quality coconut milk*[2]

1 cup water

5 tsp sugar

½ tsp kosher salt*

1 pandan leaf,*[3] knotted, or 2 kaffir lime leaves,*[3] crushed (optional)

Rinse the rice by placing it in a large bowl, then filling the bowl with water and swishing it around with your hands for 5 seconds. Drain off the milky water, leaving the rice in the bowl, then repeat three more times. Fill the bowl with water, then leave the rice to soak for 1 hour. Drain in a colander and leave the rice in the colander for 5 minutes to drain well.

Preheat the oven to 400°F.

Place the coconut milk, water, sugar, and salt in a small saucepan over high heat. Bring to a boil, then stir to dissolve the sugar.

Place the rice and pandan leaf or kaffir lime leaves in a roughly 8 inch square pan (metal or ceramic).[4] Pour the hot coconut milk in and give it a quick stir to spread the rice out evenly. Working quickly, cover the pan tightly with a double layer of aluminum foil, then bake in the oven for 40 minutes.

Remove the rice from the oven and leave to rest, with the foil on, for 15 minutes. Remove the foil (there will be a layer of reduced coconut milk on the surface), turn out into a bowl and gently fluff with a rice paddle or rubber spatula. Serve!

**NOTES**

1. This recipe will also work with long-grain and medium-grain white rice and basmati rice.
2. Be sure to use a good-quality coconut milk made with at least 50% coconut extract (check the ingredient label on the can). Cheaper brands use less, which means less coconut flavor.
3. Either a pandan leaf or kaffir lime leaves will add a touch of real South-East Asian restaurant flavor to your coconut rice, but it is still absolutely delicious without! Pandan leaves are sold fresh and frozen in Asian stores and some produce stores. To prepare for use, tie the pandan leaves into a knot (like a rope!) to hold them together to fit in the pan and release their flavor. For the kaffir lime leaves,* crush them in your fist a couple of times to release their flavor.
4. You may get faint tinges of golden on the edges or sides of the rice, depending on the pan you use. Once mixed through, though, it's barely noticeable.

# Other starchy vehicles

As a bed for saucy stews, a side for juicy steaks, or with your Sunday roast chicken!

## CREAMY MASHED POTATO

SERVES: 5–6 AS A SIDE | PREP: 10 MINUTES | COOK: 20 MINUTES

2 lb russet[1] potatoes, peeled and cut into 1 inch cubes

1 tbsp plus ½ tsp kosher salt*

3 tbsp unsalted butter, cut into ¾ inch cubes (plus extra optional melted butter)

¼ cup milk

Finely chopped parsley, to serve (optional)

Place the potato in a small pot with 1 tablespoon salt and fill the pot with water until 4 inches above the potato. Bring to a boil over high heat, then reduce to medium–high and simmer rapidly for 15 minutes until the potato is very soft.

Drain well. Turn off the heat and return the potatoes to the empty pot. Add the butter, milk, and ½ teaspoon salt. Mash with a potato masher until smooth.

Serve with a drizzle of extra melted butter and a pinch of parsley, if you want to get fancy!

**NOTE**

1. Or any other all-purpose or floury potato.

## CREAMY MASHED CAULIFLOWER (PUREE)

SERVES: 4–5 AS A SIDE | PREP: 5 MINUTES | COOK: 15 MINUTES

Not just a low-carb alternative to potato, cauliflower puree is a favorite of upscale restaurants to serve alongside rich mains like Ultra-Crispy Slow-Roasted Pork Belly (page 274).

2 lb cauliflower florets (from 2 medium heads)

2 garlic cloves, peeled

2 tbsp unsalted butter

¼ cup (1 oz) finely grated parmesan*

¼ cup sour cream

½ tsp kosher salt*

⅛ tsp freshly ground black pepper

1–3 tbsp reserved water from cooking the cauliflower

Boil the cauliflower and garlic in a large pot of water for 10 minutes until very soft. Reserve a cup of cooking water, then drain.

Blitz the cauliflower and garlic in a food processor (or use an immersion blender) with the remaining ingredients until smooth. Adjust the thickness with the reserved water—sometimes I like it a little thicker, like mashed potato, other times I want it to be a puree.

Serve as a side with anything you'd usually serve mashed potato with!

# GARLIC ROAST POTATOES

**SERVES: 5–6 AS A SIDE | PREP: 5 MINUTES | COOK: 40 MINUTES**

There are many ways to roast potatoes, some more involved than others. But for everyday purposes, these are the potatoes I turn to. No need to fuss with par-boiling or even peeling. Just great, well-seasoned, golden roast potatoes you will make over and over again.



---

- 2 lb baby potatoes, cut in half
- 2 tbsp extra-virgin olive oil
- 1 tsp kosher salt*
- ½ tsp black pepper
- 5 garlic cloves,* smashed
- 5 thyme sprigs
- 3 rosemary sprigs

Preheat a large baking tray in a 425°F oven.

Toss all the ingredients together, then spread the potatoes on the hot tray, cut-side up.

Roast for 40 minutes. Halfway through cooking, rotate the tray and flip the potatoes so they are cut-side down.

Remove from the oven and serve!

# Breads

Bread is life.

# EASY CRUSTY ARTISAN BREAD

**MAKES: 1 LOAF, SERVES 6 I PREP: 5 MINUTES + 3 HOURS RISING I COOK: 45 MINUTES**

This is a wildly popular bread based on a simple no-knead method made famous by the *New York Times*. With a thick, crispy crust and a crumb with authentically large irregular holes, it's easy enough for first-timers, yet has artisan-like characteristics that even bread connoisseurs appreciate!

---

3 cups bread flour,[1] plus 2 tbsp extra for dusting

2 tsp instant/rapid-rise yeast[2]

2 tsp kosher salt*

1½ cups very warm tap water (95–105°F)

Mix the flour, yeast, and salt in a bowl, then add the water and stir with the handle of a wooden spoon. The dough should be too sticky to knead. However, if it's runny like a batter, add more flour. Cover with plastic wrap and rest in a warm (75–85°F) place for 2–3 hours[3] until doubled in volume and the surface is bubbly and jiggles when you shake it.

Preheat a 9½–10 inch cast-iron pot[4] with lid on in a 450°F oven for 30 minutes.

Scrape the dough onto a floured work surface and sprinkle the dough with the extra flour. Fold the sides in using a scraper (or large knife, cake cutter, or spatula), then flip the dough upside down onto a sheet of parchment paper. Shape into a rough round—no need to get too meticulous about a neat shape, this is a rustic loaf!

Using the paper to help lift the dough, transfer the dough and the paper into the HOT pot. Bake with the lid on for 30 minutes, then with the lid off for 15 minutes, until deep golden. Cool for 10 minutes on a wire rack before cutting.

**NOTES**

1. Can substitute with all-purpose flour.
2. If using normal active dry yeast (not instant)—dissolve the yeast in the water, then add flour and salt and mix (no need to foam). Proceed with the recipe.
3. If the weather is hot, the dough may rise in 45 minutes. If it's cold, it may take hours (which is fine!), otherwise move it to a warmer place to speed up the process.
4. The purpose of the cast-iron pot is to create a home version of a professional bakery bread steamer oven environment. Don't have one? Bake your bread on a baking tray and place an 8 inch square pan filled with boiling water on the shelf directly underneath.

# EASY FLATBREAD

**MAKES: 6 | PREP: 15 MINUTES | COOK: 15 MINUTES**

You never knew you could make such incredible flatbreads so easily. And no yeast either! Use for all your flatbread needs, including Greek Chicken Gyros (page 24), Chicken Shawarma (page 46), and lunch wraps. I also use these flatbreads as naan for dunking into curries when I don't have the time to make naan the proper way with yeast.

---

$3\frac{1}{2}$ tbsp unsalted butter

$\frac{3}{4}$ cup milk

2 cups all-purpose flour, plus 2–3 tbsp extra for dusting

$\frac{1}{2}$ tsp kosher salt*

Put the butter and milk in a heatproof jar and microwave for 1 minute or until the butter is melted. (Or do this on the stove over medium heat.)

Put the flour and salt in a bowl and pour in the milk mixture. Mix with a wooden spoon until it mostly comes together into a shaggy dough.

Sprinkle a work surface with half the extra flour, then turn the dough out. Knead for 3 minutes until it becomes a smooth dough. Add extra flour if it's too sticky (but try to keep the flour to a minimum, otherwise the flatbread will be dry). Shape into a ball, put back in the bowl, cover with plastic wrap, and leave on the counter for 30 minutes.

Sprinkle another work area with a bit of extra flour. Cut the dough into six pieces and roll them into balls with your hands. Roll each ball out into 8 inch wide circles, about $\frac{1}{8}$ inch thick.

Heat a medium nonstick skillet over high heat. Cook one flatbread at a time for $1\frac{1}{2}$ minutes on the first side until it puffs up dramatically and the underside has lots of golden splotches. Flip and cook the other side for 45 seconds to 1 minute until the underside has golden spots and it puffs up again.

Transfer to a clean dish towel and loosely wrap the flatbread to keep it warm. This also makes the flatbread soft (rather than crispy), which is what we want. Repeat with the remaining flatbreads.

# CORNBREAD MUFFINS

**MAKES: 12 | PREP: 10 MINUTES | COOK: 25 MINUTES**

Traditionally, cornbread is made in a cast-iron skillet and cut into squares for serving, but I love it in muffin form. More crispy golden surface area! Serve alongside all things Southern—Pork Ribs with BBQ Sauce (page 266) and Beef Brisket with BBQ Sauce (page 273), or for dunking into Chilli Con Carne (page 157).

---

1 tbsp melted butter, for greasing

**DRY INGREDIENTS**

$\frac{3}{4}$ cup yellow cornmeal, fine or medium-ground

$1\frac{1}{2}$ cups all-purpose flour

1 tbsp baking powder*

$\frac{1}{2}$ cup sugar

$\frac{1}{4}$ tsp kosher salt*

**WET INGREDIENTS**

1 stick butter, melted

2 large eggs*

$\frac{3}{4}$ cup milk

1 cup canned creamed corn

Preheat the oven to 400°F. Brush a 12-hole standard muffin pan with the melted butter.

Whisk the dry ingredients in a large bowl. Whisk the wet ingredients in a separate bowl. Pour the wet ingredients into the dry ingredients, then whisk until combined. Divide the mixture into the holes of the muffin pan, using all the batter.

Bake the muffins for 20 minutes until the surface is golden brown. Rest in the pan for 5 minutes, then turn out onto a cooling rack. Cool for at least another 5 minutes before serving.

**EASY FLATBREAD**

**NO-YEAST ROLLS**

**CORNBREAD MUFFINS**

**EASY CRUSTY ARTISAN BREAD**

# NO-YEAST ROLLS

**MAKES: 4 | PREP: 10 MINUTES | COOK: 25 MINUTES**

Here are some exceptional bread rolls made without yeast! Crusty on the outside, fluffy on the inside. They're incredibly easy to make. Slather with butter and dunk into your favorite soups and stews!

---

1⅔ cups all-purpose flour,[1] plus 3 tbsp extra for dusting

3½ tsp baking powder*[1]

½ tsp kosher salt*

½ tsp sugar

¾ cup warm whole milk[2]

Preheat a 9½ inch (or larger) cast-iron pot[3] with the lid on in a 425°F oven for 30 minutes.

Mix the flour, baking powder, salt, and sugar in a bowl. Slowly add the milk while stirring with the handle of a wooden spoon. Mix until it comes together into a sticky dough.

Dust a work surface with 1 tablespoon of flour, turn the dough out, then sprinkle the surface of the dough with another 1 tablespoon of flour. Knead for 5 minutes or until the dough becomes pretty smooth, using the remaining flour only if required to make it kneadable without sticking all over your hands (try to minimize flour usage).

Cut the dough into four pieces, roughly shape each into a ball. Stretch the surface of each ball and tuck it under to make the surface smooth. Roll again into balls. Make two parallel slashes ¾ inch deep and 1¼ inches long across the surface of the rolls using a serrated knife.

Remove the hot pot from the oven and place the balls in the pot. Cover with a lid and bake for 20 minutes, then remove the lid and bake for a further 5 minutes until the surface is crusty and light golden.

Remove the bread rolls from the pot and cool for at least 10 minutes before devouring!

**NOTES**

1. Or 1⅔ cups self-rising flour instead of all-purpose flour and baking powder.
2. Microwave in a heatproof jar for 30 seconds. It should be around 95°F.
3. See Note 4, Easy Crusty Artisan Bread (page 341).

# Homemade broths

Good restaurants always make their own broths, and this is the secret to why their dishes often have that richer, deeper, "restaurant-quality" taste to them! Store-bought broth simply does not compare to homemade. If you truly want the best, making your own broth really is worth it!

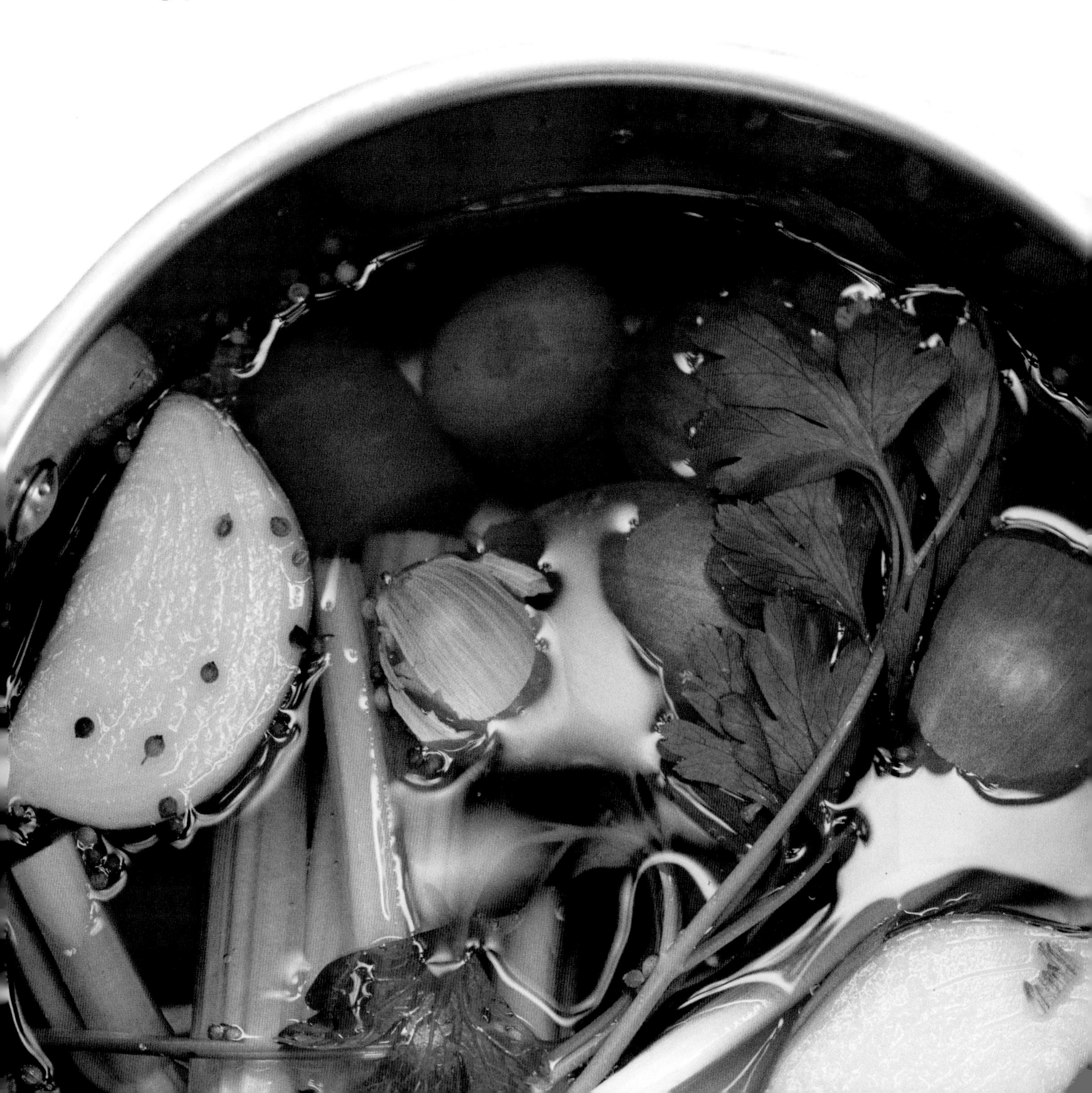

# VEGETABLE BROTH

 **MAKES: 4 CUPS | PREP: 5 MINUTES | COOK: 2 HOURS**

---

8 cups cold tap water

2 carrots, unpeeled, cut into 3 equal pieces

1 yellow onion, unpeeled, quartered

1 celery stalk, cut into 4 even pieces (use the leaves too)

2 garlic cloves,* smashed

3 parsley stalks

1 bay leaf*

1 thyme sprig

½ tsp black peppercorns

½ tsp coriander seeds

1 tsp kosher salt*

Place all the ingredients in a 7 quart (or larger) stockpot. Bring to a rapid simmer over high heat, then reduce the heat to low and simmer for 2 hours without a lid. It should just be rippling gently—there should not be bubbles popping on the surface. The liquid should reduce by half in this time.

Strain through a fine-mesh strainer, pressing the juices out of the vegetables. You should have 4 cups of broth. If you have much more than this, return the strained liquid to the pot and keep simmering to reduce the broth further. If you have less, top up with water.

Use immediately or cool, then store. (See Note 1 of Chicken Broth on page 349.)

**RECIPES TRULY WORTHY OF MAKING WITH HOMEMADE VEGETABLE BROTH:**

- Saucy Baked Pork Meatballs (page 150)
- Pumpkin Soup (page 183)
- Mushroom Lasagne (page 278)
- Spinach & Ricotta Cannelloni (page 167)

## How to use the homemade broths in this book

Use a ratio of 1:1 in place of store-bought broth in any recipe in this cookbook but add ¼ teaspoon salt per 1 cup homemade broth EXCEPT in Red Wine Sauce (page 327) and Lamb Shanks in Red Wine Sauce (page 260). These recipes use broth in massively concentrated form so, if more salt is added, the sauce will be far too salty!

# BEEF BROTH

**MAKES: APPROXIMATELY 5 CUPS–1¾ QUARTS | PREP: 15 MINUTES | COOK: 4–9 HOURS**

---

5 lb meaty beef bones, preferably back and neck, plus one marrowbone for richness

1 carrot, unpeeled, cut in half

½ yellow onion, peeled, cut in half

2 tomatoes, quartered

1 tbsp apple cider vinegar

½ tbsp coriander seeds

½ tbsp black peppercorns

1 celery stalk, cut into 3 equal pieces (use the leaves too)

2 bay leaves*

2 thyme sprigs

12 parsley sprigs (optional)

3 quarts cold tap water, plus ¾ cup extra

Preheat the oven to 425°F.

Spread the bones across two large baking trays and bake for 1 hour, flipping the bones halfway, until they are browned. Transfer the bones to a 7 quart (or larger) stockpot.

Discard any fat on the trays. Place one tray on the stove over medium heat and add the ¾ cup water. When it comes to a simmer, start scraping the tray to dissolve the drippings (fond) on the tray into the liquid. Once the tray is mostly scraped clean, pour all the liquid into the stockpot. Repeat with other tray.

Add the remaining ingredients to the pot and squish/arrange everything as snugly as possible. Add the cold water—it should just about cover the bones. Add more water if needed. Bring to a boil over medium-high heat, then simmer as follows:

- **8 hours (best)** on your smallest burner on low, uncovered. It should be simmering ever so gently, with only a small bubble popping on the surface every now and then; or
- **3 hours** on medium-low so it's simmering gently, covered with the lid cracked (1¼ inch gap). There should be lazy small bubbles regularly popping on the surface.

Scoop off any surface scum that pools on the surface using a ladle and discard.

Remove and discard most of the bones with tongs. Strain the remaining broth contents out through a fine-mesh strainer set over a large pot.

You should end up with between approximately 5 cups and 1¾ quarts of broth. If it's much more, reduce on the stove, otherwise the flavor will be too weak. If you have less than 5 cups, top up with water.

The broth can be used immediately or stored. To store, measure out the broth into containers. Allow to cool on the counter, then refrigerate. When cooled, scrape off and discard any white fat that rises to the surface and solidifies. Use immediately or cool, then store (see Note 1 of Chicken Broth, opposite).

**RECIPES WORTHY OF MAKING WITH HOMEMADE BEEF BROTH:**

- Lamb Shanks in Red Wine Sauce (page 260)
- Chicken Ragu (yes, I wrote *chicken* ragu!) (page 281)
- Swedish Meatballs (page 30)
- Gravy (page 326)
- Mexican Shredded Beef (page 208)

**RECIPES THAT ONLY WORK WITH HOMEMADE BEEF BROTH:**

Red Wine Sauce (page 327)

# CHICKEN BROTH

 **MAKES: 2 QUARTS | PREP: 5 MINUTES | COOK: 3½ HOURS**

---

4 lb chicken carcasses

1 carrot, unpeeled, cut into 4 equal pieces

½ yellow onion, peeled and halved

1 celery stalk, cut into 4 (use the leaves too)

½ tbsp black peppercorns

1 tbsp apple cider vinegar

2 bay leaves*

2 thyme sprigs

3 parsley sprigs

3 quarts cold tap water

Place all the ingredients into a 7 quart (or larger) stockpot. The water should just about cover the bones. Bring to a boil over medium–high heat. Scoop off and discard any foam that collects on the surface using a ladle (this keeps the broth clear).

Reduce the heat to low and simmer for 3 hours, uncovered. The heat should be low enough so the surface is barely rippling and you just get a gentle bubble every now and then. Too rapid boiling = murky broth.

Using the lid to hold the bones and vegetables in the pot, pour the liquid from the pot through a fine-mesh strainer into another pot. You should end up with 2 quarts (8 cups) of broth. If you have more than about 9 cups, reduce by simmering on low (or the broth will be too weak). If you have less than 2 quarts, top up with water.

The broth can be used immediately or stored. To store, measure out the broth into containers. Allow to cool on the counter, then refrigerate. When cooled, scrape off and discard any white fat that rises to the surface and solidifies. Use immediately or cool, then store[1].

**RECIPES WORTHY OF MAKING WITH HOMEMADE CHICKEN BROTH:**

- Chicken Fricassee (page 178)
- Guinness Stew (page 292)
- French Sausage & Bean Casserole (page 153)
- Mushroom Ragu (see Mushroom Lasagne recipe on page 276)
- Our Secret Family Quick Ramen (page 244)
- Laksa (page 240)
- Moroccan Harira Soup with Lamb (page 164)

**NOTES**

1. *Storage*—All broths can be stored in the fridge for 5 days or freezer for 6 months (thaw before use).
2. *Freezing*—I portion broth into a variety of quantities ranging from 1 cup to 4 cups, for convenience of use after freezing. I prefer using recycled glass jars (be sure to leave ¾ inch head-room) rather than plastic containers, to ensure no freezer odor gets into the broth. Portioning out while warm also helps the broth cool much faster than leaving it in a giant pot!

   To use, thaw frozen broth overnight in the fridge then use in liquid form. To speed up thawing, partially submerge the jar or container in water to thaw enough so the broth can be scraped into a saucepan to melt. Alternatively, gently microwave (be sure to remove any metal lids). Broth that is thawed can be refrozen as long as you bring it back up to a boil for 3 minutes to sterilize it.

# MEASUREMENT CONVERSIONS

*Measuring cups and spoons may vary slightly from one country to another, but the difference is generally not enough to affect a recipe. Below are measurement conversions from imperial to metric, based on the measurements I have used in this book.*

### DRY MEASUREMENTS

The most accurate way to measure dry ingredients is to weigh them. However, if using a cup, add the ingredient loosely to the cup and level with a knife; don't compact the ingredient unless the recipe requests "firmly packed."

| IMPERIAL | METRIC |
|---|---|
| ½ oz | 15 g |
| 1 oz | 30 g |
| 2 oz | 50 g |
| 4 oz (¼ lb) | 120 g |
| 6 oz | 180 g |
| 8 oz (½ lb) | 250 g |
| 12 oz (¾ lb) | 350 g |
| 16 oz (1 lb) | 500 g |
| 32 oz (2 lb) | 1 kg |

### LIQUID MEASUREMENTS

| CUP | IMPERIAL | METRIC |
|---|---|---|
| ¼ cup | 2 fl oz | 60 ml |
| ⅓ cup | 3 fl oz | 85 ml |
| ½ cup | 4 fl oz | 125 ml |
| ⅔ cup | 5 fl oz | 160 ml |
| ¾ cup | 6 fl oz | 180 ml |
| 1 cup | 8 fl oz | 250 ml |
| 1¼ cups | 10 fl oz | 310 ml |
| 1½ cups | 12 fl oz | 375 ml |
| 2 cups | 16 fl oz | 500 ml |
| 2¼ cups | 19 fl oz | 560 ml |
| 2½ cups | 21 fl oz | 625 ml |
| 2¾ cups | 23 fl oz | 685 ml |
| 3 cups | 25 fl oz | 750 ml |
| 3½ cups | 30 fl oz | 875 ml |
| 4 cups | 34 fl oz | 1 litre |
| 5 cups | 42 fl oz | 1.25 litres |
| 6 cups | 51 fl oz | 1.5 litres |

### LENGTH

| IMPERIAL | METRIC |
|---|---|
| ⅛ inch | 3 mm |
| ¼ inch | 5 mm |
| ½ inch | 1 cm |
| ¾ inch | 2 cm |
| 1 inch | 2.5 cm |
| 1¼ inches | 3 cm |
| 1½ inches | 4 cm |
| 2 inches | 5 cm |
| 3 inches | 7 cm |
| 4 inches | 10 cm |
| 6 inches | 15 cm |
| 7 inches | 18 cm |
| 8 inches | 20 cm |
| 9 inches | 23 cm |
| 10 inches | 25 cm |
| 11 inches | 28 cm |
| 12 inches | 30 cm |

### OVEN TEMPERATURES

| FAHRENHEIT | CELSIUS |
|---|---|
| 120°F | 50°C |
| 200°F | 100°C |
| 250°F | 120°C |
| 275°F | 140°C |
| 300°F | 150°C |
| 325°F | 160°C |
| 350°F | 170°C |
| 350°F | 180°C |
| 375°F | 185°C |
| 400°F | 200°C |
| 400°F | 210°C |
| 425°F | 220°C |
| 450°F | 230°C |
| 475°C | 240°C |

| FAHRENHEIT | GAS MARK |
|---|---|
| 200°F | ¼ |
| 250°F | ½ |
| 275°F | 1 |
| 300°F | 2 |
| 325°F | 3 |
| 350°F | 4 |
| 375°F | 5 |
| 400°F | 6 |
| 425°F | 7 |
| 450°F | 8 |
| 475°F | 9 |
| 500°F | 10 |

### OIL TEMPERATURES

| IMPERIAL | METRIC |
|---|---|
| 355°F | 180°C |
| 375°F | 190°C |
| 390°F | 200°C |
| 410°F | 210°C |
| 430°F | 220°C |

# INTERNAL COOKED TEMPERATURES

*The tables below provide the target internal cooked temperatures for varying levels of doneness for proteins used in this cookbook. The* ***pull temperature*** *in the tables below is the target temperature at which the protein should be removed from the heat. The temperature of the protein will continue to rise as it rests (this is called "carry-over cooking") so the final temperature results in the doneness that you want. This is the* ***rested temperature*** *in the tables below.*

| BEEF | RARE | | MEDIUM RARE (RECOMMENDED) | | MEDIUM | | MEDIUM WELL | | WELL DONE | |
|---|---|---|---|---|---|---|---|---|---|---|
| | PULL | RESTED | PULL | RESTED | PULL | RESTED | PULL | RESTED | PULL | RESTED |
| Steak | 120°F | 125°F | 125°F | 135°F | 130°F | 140°F | 140°F | 150°F | 150°F | 160°F |

| LAMB | MEDIUM RARE | | MEDIUM WELL (RECOMMENDED) | | WELL DONE | |
|---|---|---|---|---|---|---|
| | PULL | RESTED | PULL | RESTED | PULL | RESTED |
| Chops | 140°F | 145°F | 140°F | 150°F | 150°F | 160°F |
| Rib chops | 140°F | 145°F | 145°F | 150°F | 155°F | 160°F |

| PORK | MEDIUM (RECOMMENDED) | | MEDIUM WELL | | WELL DONE | |
|---|---|---|---|---|---|---|
| | PULL | RESTED | PULL | RESTED | PULL | RESTED |
| Chops / tenderloin | 140°F | 145°F | 150°F | 155°F | 155°F | 160°F |

| CHICKEN | COOKED INTERNAL TEMPERATURE | |
|---|---|---|
| | PULL | RESTED |
| Breast / tenderloin | 155°F | 160°F |
| Thigh / wings / drumsticks | 160°F | 170°F |

| FISH | MEDIUM (RECOMMENDED) | |
|---|---|---|
| | PULL | RESTED |
| White fish | 130°F | 135°F |

| SALMON | MEDIUM RARE (RECOMMENDED) | | MEDIUM WELL | |
|---|---|---|---|---|
| | PULL | RESTED | PULL | RESTED |
| Salmon & trout | 125°F | 130°F | 140°F | 145°F |

It is recommended to cook white fish to medium where it is at the point of just fully cooked with optimum juiciness. White fish is typically not served medium-rare. Salmon, on the other hand, is at its juiciest when cooked to medium-rare.

# The team!

For many years, *RecipeTin Eats* was a one-gal, one-dog gig. However, for this cookbook I was lucky enough to be supported by a small, talented team. Here's my motley crew!

**JEAN-BAPTISTE ALEXANDRE**
Le chef

**KRISTIN JAGGER**
Everything girl

**GOH MAEHASHI**
Tech bro

**HERRON OH**
Video editor queen

**YUMIKO MAEHASHI**
Mama RecipeTin

**ARWYN TOMAC**
Our ray of sunshine

**KRISTIN JAGGER**
Everything girl

**JEAN-BAPTISTE ALEXANDRE**
Le chef

**STEPHEN FIXTER**
RecipeTin Meals chef boss

**ARWYN TOMAC**
Our ray of sunshine

**DOZER**
CEO

**MEG YONSON**
Wordsmith whiz

**ROB PALMER**
Camera genie

**GOH MAEHASHI**
Tech bro

**YUMIKO MAEHASHI**
Mama RecipeTin

**BARL ROUNDS**
RecipeTin Meals muscle

**EMMA KNOWLES**
Food whisperer (stylist!)

**HEATHER HANCOCK**
Recipe testing fiend

**JENNIFER POGMORE**
Pastry chef extraordinaire

**HERRON OH**
Video editor queen

**INGGRID GISLINGHAM**
Human calculator

**JAIMEE FOLEY**
Recipe testing powerhouse

# Thank you!

## Creating this cookbook has been the hardest project of my life, and I owe many thanks to many people for supporting me through it.

Firstly, to my website readers and social media community. You are the reason RecipeTin is what it is and why I created this cookbook. It certainly wasn't for my family—being such capable cooks themselves, they will never use a single recipe from it!!

Thank you for your messages of support, for the laughter, and your patience during the months of silence as I worked on this cookbook. You make me strive to do the very best I can!

Next, to my team. What a ride it's been! Lots of laughs, lots of dirty dishes, and so . . . Much Good Food!

Jean-Baptiste Alexandre, still the best chef I know. You make me want to be a better cook.

Kristin Jagger, my assistant. What do you mean your job description didn't include "house renovation management" and "cookbook chief-of-staff"? You are a superwoman.

Herron Oh, my video editor. How can someone so young be so good at so many things?

Arwyn Tomac, our team support. Your sunny disposition has lifted me on my most stressful days. We have all fallen in love with you!

To my brother Goh. Tech guru. Walking food encyclopedia. Cracking the code of cult foods. Is there anything you can't do?

Mum, you are still my hero. But next time we're on national TV together, please don't open with "Nagi was a very lazy child"!

To the boys at RecipeTin Meals (my food bank)—Chef Stephen Fixter and Barl Rounds. Thank you for your dedication to your jobs and all the intentional and unintentional amusement you bring the team. There is no dull day with you two around!

To my sister Tamaki. Thank you for listening as I downloaded on you throughout this cookbook-making process. Sometimes it feels like you're the older sis, not me!

And of course, Dozer. This cookbook was such a wonderful opportunity for you to showcase your taste-testing skills. Everything is a 10/10 except raw kale, eh? I can relate!

To the HAGS, how did I get so lucky? Unconditional support, eternal friendship, and so, SO much laughter! The best friends a girl could ever ask for.

I must also thank a number of talented people who assisted my team and me on this cookbook. Heather Hancock and Jaimee Foley, thank you for your hard work and attention to detail with your thorough testing of the recipes. How many times did you re-test that Baked Fried Rice? Jennifer Pogmore, French pastry chef extraordinaire. How cool is it that we developed the Lemon Cheesecake and Blueberry Tart recipes from opposite sides of the world?

Rob Palmer. You laugh when I call you "Australia's best food photographer." But I'm not joking—to me, you are!

Emma Knowles, the Food Whisperer. I have admired your work for years. What an honor it was for this Fan Girl to watch you style my food!

Michelle Mackintosh, who designed this cookbook. Your beautiful interpretations of my hand-drawn scrawls are magnificent.

Meg Yonson. I brought you in "just" to edit my words, but wow, what a creative powerhouse you are! I look forward to working on more projects with you.

Sally Bruce, our stylist. Thank you for making my team look and feel so fabulous. And Dozer is grateful you let him stay naked!

To the Pan Macmillan team, what a wonderful experience it was working with you all! Thank you for believing in me and your patience as I fumbled my way through this world of cookbook creation. Ariane Durkin, Executive Editor, and Ariana Klepac. I can't tell you what a comfort it was knowing two such talented ladies were there to ensure every detail in this book is precisely accurate. Lucinda Thompson, Creative Coordinator. You're going to be running that place in no time! Sally Devenish, for her brilliant navigation of this book through the production process.

Thanks also to Publicity and Marketing Director, Tracey Cheetham, for nutting out big-picture media, Senior Publicist Candice Wyman for media-schedule kneading, Head of Marketing, Charlotte Ree, for rocket-launching my cookbook into the world, and to the Pan Macmillan sales team for cooking recipes from the book as incentives (bribes!) for the booksellers and getting my book all across Australia and New Zealand. And to everyone else in the Pan Mac family for sharing their baking photos and their enthusiasm for this project!

And finally, to Ingrid Ohlsson, my publisher. We did it! Thank you for your unconditional support and your ruthless-yet-coaxing guidance to bring out my best work. I hope this cookbook is everything you dreamed it would be and that I've done us proud.

**—Nagi x**

GLOSSARY*

### Baby corn

Either drained, canned, or fresh can be used. Canned is often found in the Asian section of grocery stores.

### Baking powder testing

Dead (i.e. inactive) baking powder is a more common cause of baking failures than you'd think! It can be dead even if it's not past the best-by date. To check if your baking powder is still active, pour ¼ cup boiling water over ½ teaspoon baking powder. If it bubbles, it's still good. If not, it's no good. Time to get a new one!

### Baking soda

Used as a raising agent for cakes and also for tenderizing meats in stir-fries (for example, see Easy Everyday Chicken Stir-Fry on page 98). I prefer to use baking powder for baking, but sometimes baking soda works better (either by itself, or combined with baking powder).

### Bay leaves

Fresh are preferable, but can be substituted with dried.

### Beef bouillon cubes

Beef stock powder in cube form, sold in the herb and spice aisle of grocery stores. I prefer the cubes to powder as I find the flavor better. However, 1 cube can be substituted with 1 teaspoon beef stock powder.

### Beef broth

For store-bought, use low-sodium. For homemade, see page 348.

### Beurre manié

A softened butter–flour mixture used to thicken sauces by stirring it in toward the end of cooking time. It's a classical French cooking technique, which is sometimes more suitable than other techniques, such as adding flour at the beginning of cooking time. To convert to gluten-free, use cornstarch instead of flour and reduce the quantity by 25%. Mix with equal parts water (instead of butter), then stir that into the sauce.

### Butter, at room temperature

This means at 65°F. The butter is soft enough to indent when pressed with your finger, but will not leave a slick layer of grease on your finger. Butter warmer than 70°F is not recommended to be used in baking recipes where it is beaten until fluffy, as the end result will be adversely affected. For example, cakes may end up greasy or not rise properly.

To bring butter to room temperature quickly, cut it into ½ inch pieces, then spread on a plate. Microwave a 2 cup bowl of tap water for 5 minutes on High. Open the microwave, remove the bowl and put the butter in the microwave on the plate. Close the door and leave for 5 minutes. Do not turn the microwave on! The ambient heat will gently soften the butter to (or around) room temperature.

### Cannelloni or manicotti

Dried pasta tubes around 4 inches long and 1 inch wide, sold in boxes. They do not require pre-cooking before use. Just fill, smother with sauce, and bake! Manicotti tubes are similar to cannelloni but they are ridged and slightly larger. Despite what the package says, there is no need to pre-cook them if you bake them with enough sauce, as we do in Spinach & Ricotta Cannelloni on page 167.

### Cheese, shredded

*See Shredded cheese.*

### Chicken broth

For store-bought, use low-sodium. For homemade, see page 349.

### Chili pepper (fresh)

The general rule of thumb is that the smaller the chili, the spicier it is.

- ***Bird's eye chili***—A small red chili used in Asian cooking, which is pretty spicy!
- ***Long green/red chili***—Such as fresno, cayenne peppers, and jalapeño, which are not too spicy. I mostly use red, for flavor and also for color rather than for spiciness.
- ***Deseeding chili***—The spiciness is in the seeds! To deseed, cut the chlli in half lengthwise, then scrape out the seeds using a teaspoon. As a precaution, use rubber gloves when handling spicy chilis.
- ***Finely mincing chili***—Deseed the chili (as above), then finely chop using a sharp knife.

### Chinese five spice

Readily available these days, this is a blend of five spices, which is used in Chinese cooking. (Yes that's right, I said FIVE spices. Shock horror!)

### Chipotle in adobo

These are chipotles (dried, smoked jalapeños) in a flavored red sauce (adobo), which is quite spicy and a common ingredient in Mexican cooking. Freeze leftovers in small zip-top bags,* flattened, so it's easy to break a bit off to use as needed. Substitution—For every 1 tablespoon of chipotle in adobo called for in a recipe, substitute with 1 teaspoon EACH chipotle powder,* smoked paprika, and sriracha.* (YES, really, it's pretty close to adobo sauce!)

### Chipotle powder

A staple Mexican spice, this is fried, smoked jalapeños in powder form. It has a terrific smoky, earthy flavor with a bit of a spice kick. Substitution—For every 1 teaspoon of chipotle powder called for in a recipe, substitute with ½ teaspoon smoked paprika + ⅛ teaspoon cumin powder + ⅛ teaspoon cayenne pepper (if you want spiciness).

### Coconut cream

As with coconut milk,* better brands have a higher percentage of coconut extract in the ingredients and therefore better coconut flavor.

### Coconut milk

Not all coconut milk is created equal! Better quality is made with at least 80% coconut and has better coconut flavor than more economical brands, which can be as low as 20%. Full-fat is best, for best flavor and mouthfeel. Low-fat is thinner and lacks coconut flavor.

### Cooking sake

Not to be confused with sake for drinking (save that good stuff!), this rice wine is an essential ingredient in Japanese cooking. Find it in the Asian section of grocery stores and Asian grocery stores.

### Cream

The type of cream I use most often is called "heavy cream," which has a higher fat percentage than other types of cream. The equivalent of this in Australia is called "thickened cream."

### Crispy fried shallots

Deep-fried slices of shallots,* which are crunchy and salty. They add great texture and pops of salt into anything you add them to. Readily available in the Asian section of supermarkets these days, but cheaper at Asian grocery stores!

### Cucumbers

Recipes in this cookbook calling for cucumbers are either the regular cucumbers, which are around 6 inches long, or the longer English cucumbers. Use thin-skinned varieties that do not need to be peeled.

### Cutting beef against the grain

This produces the most tender slices for eating, whether slicing before cooking, such as for stir-fries, or after cooking (for things like Thai Beef Salad, page 188). To do this, look at the piece of steak and you will notice that most of the fibers are going in one direction. Turn the steak so the fibers are going left to right directly in front of you. Then cut across the fibers—i.e. 90 degrees perpendicular to the direction of the fibers.

### Dried shiitake mushrooms

Fairly easily accessible these days, sold in the Asian section of large grocery stores and in Asian grocery stores. They have a more intense savory flavor than fresh shiitake mushrooms* and other mushroom varieties. Rehydrate in boiling water first, then squeeze out the excess water before use in cooking.

### Dozer

The large mass of golden fur often found lurking in the kitchen waiting for scraps to "accidentally" fall to the ground. Otherwise known as The Scavenger, the self-appointed RecipeTin Taste Tester spends his days making important contributions to this world, such as eating, sleeping, playing, hoping to eat, and hoping to play. Read more about him on page 10.

### Eggs

- ***Egg yolks***—Yolks are easiest to separate from the whites when the eggs are fridge-cold. I crack the eggs, then pass the yolks back and forth between the shells, allowing the whites to slip out. If you are not confident with this method, simply crack the egg into your hand and allow the egg white to slip through your fingers.
- ***Large eggs***—Eggs that are 2 oz each (in the shell). The egg cartons are usually labeled as "large eggs," as this is an industry standard.
- ***Room-temperature eggs***—Eggs that are not fridge-cold so they incorporate better with other ingredients. To de-chill eggs quickly, place in a bowl of warm tap water for 5 minutes.
- ***Soft-boiled eggs***—Fill a medium saucepan with 4 inches of water. Bring to a boil over medium–high heat, then carefully lower up to four fridge-cold eggs into the water using a slotted spoon. Set the timer for 6½ minutes. Wait until bubbles reappear on the surface of the water, then lower the heat to medium so there are bubbles rising from the base of the saucepan but not so rapidly that the eggs are bouncing around (shells sometimes crack). Transfer the eggs into a large bowl in the sink. Fill with tap water, then leave the eggs for 5 minutes, changing the water as and when it gets warm, until the eggs are cool enough to handle and peel.

### Fish

- ***Firm white fish fillets***—Includes cod, grouper, haddock, halibut, snapper, striped bass, swordfish, Alaskan pollock.

- ***Oily, strong-tasting fish***—Mackerel, mullet, sardines.
- ***Fish that dry out easily when cooked***—Bonito, marlin, swordfish, tuna. Unless you're extremely careful they can become dry inside. I feel these fish are (mostly) better in raw/rare form, such as in ceviche, poke bowls, and tartare.

### Garam masala

Commonly used in Indian cooking, garam masala is like a better version of curry powder! Available in some large grocery stores, Asian, and Indian stores.

### Garlic

The preparation method matters!

- ***Finely grated garlic***—Garlic grated using a Microplane* or similar. It will grate garlic into a juicy paste, which works better for some dishes rather than finely mincing it with a knife. You can also use a garlic crusher.
- ***Minced garlic***—Garlic that is finely chopped using a knife. If a recipe calls for this, do not finely grate it with a Microplane* or garlic crusher as there is a reason for it. For example, garlic that is pressed with a garlic crusher burns and spits on the stove, instead of turning golden.
- ***Smashed garlic (skin on and off)***—Place the flat side of a heavy knife blade on a clove of garlic, then smack down on the flat side of the blade with the palm of your hand to make the garlic clove burst open but mostly hold together. The recipe will specify whether the garlic should have the skin on or have the skin peeled off.
- ***Store-bought garlic paste in jars***—Don't talk to me about that stuff! It bears little resemblance to the real thing.

### Garlic chives

Garlic-flavored chives (wait, did the name give it away?!) that look like grass reeds. They're a secret ingredient in traditional Gyoza (page 237) and Pad Thai (page 114)!

### Ghee

A type of clarified butter used in Indian cooking. It tastes like butter—on steroids!

### Ginger

The preparation method matters!

- ***Finely grated ginger***—Grated using a Microplane* or similar.
- ***Julienned ginger***—Cut into very fine strands using a knife.
- ***Minced ginger***—Finely chopped using a knife.
- ***Peeling ginger skin***—Scrape it off using a teaspoon, or cut a slice approximating the amount you need, then use your knife to cut the skin off.
- ***Store-bought ginger paste***—Don't do it! Fresh is best.

### Green onion

Also called "scallions," these are the long, thin, green-stemmed onion. Not to be confused with shallots* or spring onions (green stems with a white bulb attached to the base). If a recipe calls for "1 green onion," it means the whole green onion including the white base (often with roots attached) and the long green stalks, usually two to three per stem.

### Ground red chili

Ground pure red chili pepper, which is spicy. Substitute with an equal amount of cayenne pepper. Not to be confused with American chili powder, which is a Tex-Mex spice blend that is not very spicy.

### Kaffir (makrut) lime leaves

The leaves of the kaffir (makrut) lime tree, used to add earthy citrus flavors into Asian food. Sold at large grocery stores, independent fresh produce stores, and Asian stores. Dried is an okay substitute (same amount), but I really urge you to try to find fresh if you can because it has a better flavor. Freezes 100% perfectly for 6 months, so I always have a stash!

### Kale leaves

To easily remove kale leaves from the tough stem, grab the base of the kale stem with your nondominant hand, then grasp the stem with your other hand and in one swift motion strip the leaves off the stem away from you. *Voila!* Kale destemmed in 2 seconds!

### Kecap manis

A syrupy Indonesian sweet soy sauce. Fairly accessible these days, found in the Asian section of grocery stores.

### Kewpie mayonnaise

A popular Japanese mayonnaise easily found these days in the Asian section of grocery stores. Famed for its smooth flavor and gentle rice vinegar tang! Substitute with whole-egg mayonnaise. *See also Mayonnaise*.

### Kosher salt

*See Salt*.

### Lemongrass

To prepare for use, trim the woody base off and the reedy green top, leaving around 5 inches of the base of the lemongrass stem. Peel the outer green layers to reveal the softer white and very pale green part that contains the lemongrass flavor—this is the part to use in cooking.

### Mandoline

A handy tool to make short work of finely slicing vegetables.

### Mayonnaise

For Western dishes, I use whole-egg mayonnaise, which has a smoother, richer flavor than ordinary mayonnaise. For Asian dishes, *see also Kewpie mayonnaise*.

### Measuring spoons

I use ½ fluid ounce tablespoons, which is the standard size of measuring spoon in North America. And there are 3 teaspoons per tablespoon. Measuring spoons many vary slightly from one country to another but the difference is generally not enough to affect the outcome of a recipe.

### Microplane

Genuine Microplane graters are (in my opinion) the sharpest and best, most convenient shape for fine grating. I use it for citrus, parmesan, ginger, garlic, making chocolate dust, and grating nutmeg. I particularly love that you can grate garlic and ginger without peeling them. The skin just kind of gets pushed out of the way as you grate and ends up on top, so it's easy to pick off and discard. I'm very passionate and protective about my Microplane—nothing else I've tried comes close to this!

### Mirin

A sweet rice wine that is an essential ingredient in Japanese cooking. Easily found these days in the Asian aisle of grocery stores and Asian grocery stores.

### Molasses

Not to be confused with "blackstrap molasses," which is a different product (bitter and less sweet). Look for bottles labelled "true," "natural," or "light" molasses.

### Mussels (buying, cleaning, and preparation)

These days, cleaned mussels are fairly readily available at seafood stores and even supermarkets. Good mussels should smell like the ocean, and not fishy—even from a vacuum-sealed package, which is how I usually buy them. Even if the packages say they are cleaned, I still recommend you give them a scrub, just to be sure.

To clean mussels, soak them in a large bowl or sink filled with cold tap water for 5 minutes. They will purge themselves of sand and grit. Use a clean brush to scrub the shell of the mussels to remove any debris, such as seaweed, barnacles, mud, or sand. It's okay if you can't remove every speck off the mussel shell, just whatever comes off with a scrub. Remove any "beards" hanging out from the mussels (the hair-like tufts sticking out of the shell). Just pinch the beard between your thumb and forefinger, then gently pull toward the hinge of the mussel shell (the pointy end) until it comes away. Discard any mussels with large chunks of shell missing. (Minor chips are okay.) If there are any open mussels, press the shells together and, if they stay closed, the mussels are still good. If the shells will not stay closed, then it means the mussels are dead and should be discarded. You can also easily tell if a mussel is off just by smelling it! Place cleaned mussels in an empty bowl until ready to cook. Use any water released by the mussels that collects in the bowl—just add it into whatever you are cooking!

### Napa cabbage

A cylindrical-shaped cabbage with a white core and layers of tightly packed, wrinkly green leaves that are softer than standard green cabbage. A great cabbage to use for "slaw-like" Asian salads.

### Oil for deep-frying

- ***Temperature testing*—**It is best to use an instant read thermometer* to check the temperature of the oil. Otherwise, test using a small cube of white bread. For 350°F, it should take 15 seconds for it to turn golden and crispy. For 375°F, it should take 10 seconds.
- ***Oil reuse*—**The number of times oil can be reused depends on what it was used to cook. If it was used for neutral-flavored food fried for a short period of time, the oil should be able to be used three times. Less for seafood or heavily flavored foods. To clean the oil, the easiest way is to strain the oil using a piece of cheesecloth set in a strainer.

### Pandan leaves

Pandan leaves are sold fresh and frozen in Asian stores and some produce stores. To prepare for use, tie the pandan leaves into a knot (like a rope!) to hold them together to fit in the pan and release their flavor.

### Panko bread crumbs

A Japanese bread crumb favored for the extra-crispy coating it gives breaded foods. You can buy it at most large grocery stores these days in the Asian food section and also at Asian grocery stores. Substitute with regular bread crumbs if you can't find it.

### Parmesan

Different recipes call for varying preparation methods.

- ***Finely grated parmesan*—**Finely grated using a Microplane* or similar. This is especially important so the parmesan melts effortlessly into creamy sauces and on bubbling bakes.
- ***Parmesan shavings*—**Use a potato peeler on a block of parmesan to make big, paper-thin shavings.

### Peanut butter, natural unsweetened

This is thinner and with a stronger peanut flavor than the commercial, sweetened spread, which makes it ideal for satay sauces. Commercial peanut butter spread can be substituted but sauces/dressings will be thicker, slightly sweeter, and the peanut flavor is not quite as strong.

### Pine nuts, toasted

Heat a small skillet over medium-high heat (no oil). Add the pine nuts and cook for 3–5 minutes, shaking the pan regularly, until they smell nutty and are kissed with gold. Immediately transfer to a bowl, then use warm or at room temperature, whichever is directed in the recipe.

### Pomegranate

To remove the seeds, cut the pomegranate in half. Over a bowl, turn the cut face downward into the palm of your hand (fingers loosely spread), then use a wooden spoon to (very!) firmly smack the back of the pomegranate. The seeds will fly out through your fingers into the bowl. It's very satisfying! Keep smacking all over the skin until all the seeds are out. Pick out any white pith that falls out, then use the seeds as per the recipe. You will probably get some juices pooling in the bowl; add these to the dressing too.

### Rayu

Japanese chili oil sold in small bottles at Asian grocery stores. Mum claims it is better than other Asian chili oils. Most people can't tell the difference!

### Red curry paste

My favorite store-bought red curry paste is the Maesri brand, which comes in small cans. It has the best, most authentic flavor and also happens to be the cheapest. Find it at Asian grocery stores and online.

### Refried beans

Refried beans look thoroughly unappetizing straight out of the can, but they make a terrific binder for enchilada fillings as well as adding flavor. Trust me on this!

### Salt

The type of salt you use matters!

- ***Kosher salt***—This is the salt I use for cooking. The grains are larger than table salt making it easier to pinch for use in cooking. If you only have table salt, use three-fourths of the amount of kosher salt called for (i.e. 1 teaspoon kosher salt = 3/4 teaspoon table salt), otherwise your dish may be too salty.
- ***Table salt***—Also referred to as fine salt, these fine grains penetrate foods more easily than the larger-grained kosher salt, which is the default salt I use for all my recipes. If you only have table salt, reduce the quantity listed in the ingredients by 25%.

### Sambal oelek

An Indonesian chili paste that is available in some large grocery stores, as well as Asian grocery stores. This can be substituted with sriracha, for most recipes.

### Sesame oil

Comes toasted (brown—stronger sesame flavor) and untoasted (clear yellow). I only use toasted.

### Sesame seeds

To toast white sesame seeds, preheat a small skillet (no oil) over medium heat. Add the sesame seeds, then toast, shaking the pan regularly, until lightly browned and they smell nutty, about 1½–2 minutes. Remove from the skillet immediately when ready. Note: I do not toast black sesame seeds.

### Shallots

Also known as French onions, these look like baby onions but have purple-skinned flesh (once the brown skin is removed). Sweeter and finer than yellow onions, they are great for dishes where you want delicate onion flavor and/or to avoid big lumps of onion. Not to be confused with what some people in Australia call shallots.*

### Shaoxing wine

A type of rice wine for cooking often used in Chinese cuisine. It is widely available these days, sold in the Asian section of grocery stores. It's a secret ingredient that makes recipes truly taste like those you find at Chinese restaurants, adding depth of flavor and complexity with just a small dash. Chinese restaurants use it by the gallon in everything from stir-fry sauces to soup broths, marinades, and wontons!

### Shiitake mushroom

A variety of mushroom native to Asia. It has a more savory flavor than common mushroom varieties, such as button and brown mushrooms. *See also Dried shiitake mushrooms.*

### Shredded cheese

It is is always best to shred your own cheese because it melts better. Store-bought pre-shredded cheese contains anti-caking agents, which make sauces grainy. Also, the cheese tends to be shredded into larger pieces so it doesn't melt as well.

### Shrimp, peeling

To peel shrimp, break the head off, then peel the skin off the body. To devein (i.e. to remove the thin black string/digestive tract running through the shrimp), make a small incision with a small sharp knife down the back of the shrimp to reveal the vein, then lift it out and discard. Alternatively, if you prefer to keep the shrimp whole rather than butterfly the back, here's how I do it: Enclose the body of the peeled shrimp with your fingers so it is held straight. Pinch the end of the black string from the head-end of the shrimp, then carefully pull it out.

### Soy sauce

The type of soy sauce you use matters! Here are the different types used in this cookbook:

- ***All-purpose soy sauce***—Any soy sauce that is not labeled light soy sauce, dark soy sauce, sweet soy sauce, or as another specific type of soy sauce. As the name suggests, it is an all-rounder! Use it as a substitute in recipes calling for light soy sauce.
- ***Dark soy sauce***—A more intense flavor than light soy sauce and all-purpose soy sauce, which stains noodles and proteins a deep mahogany color.
- ***Light soy sauce***—Can be substituted with all-purpose soy sauce. Do not substitute with dark soy sauce, which is much more intense in flavor and color.
- ***Soy sauce***—If a recipe calls for just "soy sauce," you can use either light soy sauce or all-purpose soy sauce but not dark soy sauce.
- *See also Kecap manis.*

### Sriracha

A popular chili sauce that is flavored with other ingredients including garlic and vinegar. Easily found these days in most grocery stores as well as Asian grocery stores.

### Tablespoons

*See Measuring spoons.*

### Tamarind puree

A soft sour paste, made from a tropical Asian fruit, sold in jars. Labeled tamarind puree, concentrate, or paste, find it in the Asian section of large grocery stores or in Asian grocery stores. Use leftovers for Pad Thai (page 114). Although it won't taste quite the same, the best substitute is pomegranate molasses.

### Teaspoons

*See Measuring spoons.*

### Thai basil

Tastes like normal basil with a more pronounced aniseed flavor. Find it some larger grocery stores and Asian grocery stores. As a last resort, substitute with normal basil.

### Thermometer

Used to measure the internal temperature of food and cooking oil for deep-frying. I use a Thermapen, which is an instant read thermometer. It's well-designed, folds up neatly, and declares itself the world's best for speed and accuracy—and I believe it based on my usage! If you like your meat perfectly cooked, this is a worthy investment I highly recommend.

### Tomatoes

To deseed tomatoes, cut them into fourths, then use the knife to cut out the watery center. Don't discard the watery seeds—add them to your morning green smoothie, your bolognese sauce, or sneak it into a salad (it makes a great dressing!).

### Tomato passata

Pureed, strained pure tomatoes found in the pasta aisle of some large grocery stores, and in Italian delicatessens. Passata is excellent for making thick, smooth sauces, rather than slow-cooking crushed or diced tomato until it breaks down into a smooth sauce. Substitute with what is called "Tomato Sauce" in the US.

### Tortillas

Sold in varying sizes depending on intended purpose. I prefer corn over flour tortillas because they have better flavor. I'd use them for everything from tacos to enchiladas, but large corn tortillas are hard to come by where I live. (Yes I know, your heart bleeds for me!) I use 5–6 inch corn tortillas for tacos, 8 inch flour tortillas for enchiladas, and 10 inch jumbo flour tortillas for burritos. See page 225 for how I warm tortillas (and keep them warm).

### Vegetable broth

For store-bought, use low-sodium. For homemade, see page 347.

### Wine

Used in cooking to add and enhance flavors. I especially enjoy using wine to make sauces, whether it be quick pan sauces, such as in Garlic Butter Prawns (page 23) or slow-cooked dishes like Lamb Shanks in Red Wine Sauce (page 260). The two types of wine I always have in stock for cooking are chardonnay (white wine) and pinot noir (red wine)—see below. But in real life, I'm a sauvignon blanc and cab sav gal! *See also Shaoxing cooking wine.*

- ***Chardonnay***—My go-to wine for cooking for the best flavor addition and roundest flavor. Substitute with any dry white wine that is not too woody/oaky, fruity, or sweet. No need to use expensive wine.
- ***Pinot noir***—My most used red wine for cooking, for the smooth, light flavor it adds with richness that is not too heavy or overpowering—meaning it works in just about any dish calling for red wine. It's the traditional wine used in famous

dishes like beef bourguignon and the ideal choice for classic Red Wine Sauce (page 327).

- ***Red wine***—I mostly use pinot noir for cooking. See above. However, you can use other medium-body reds, such as merlot, cabernet sauvignon, or even a light shiraz.
- ***White wine***—Chardonnay is my most used white wine for cooking. However, you can use other moderately dry whites, such as semillon, sauvignon blanc, or pinot gris/grigio.
- ***Wine quality***—It is pretty well documented these days that there's no need to use expensive wine for cooking because, once cooked, you simply can't tell the difference. This is especially the case when something is slow-cooked for hours, and for reducing when deglazing pans. In fact, in some blind testing scenarios, cheaper wine yielded a better result! I use discounted wine from liquor stores, typically $15–20 wines discounted to $5–7.

### Zip-top bag

For some recipes, a zip-top bag is the best way to keep meat well surrounded by the marinade. Used bags can be washed in warm soapy water and reused. Alternatively, you can use a glass container that the meat fits in snugly, then toss the meat a few times during marinating time, or increase the marinade by 50% (no need to turn the meat).

## Pots and Pans

Recipes in this book usually specify type and/or size when it comes to cooking vessels. This is because the size of a pot, for example, can affect how long it takes for sauces to thicken to the desired consistency. Here are the types and sizes of pots and pans called for in my cookbook.

### Cast-iron skillet

The best pan to use for high-heat searing, such as steaks and chops, for the best crust. Develops a natural nonstick coating (seasoning) with repeated use. It is also the ideal pan for stove-to-oven cooking. I have a 10 inch Lodge cast-iron skillet. Note: Nonstick skillets are not recommended for high-heat cooking as this will reduce the life of the nonstick coating.

### Skillet sizes (nonstick)

Small 7–8 inches, medium 9 inches, large 11 inches, large deep 12 inches wide and 2½–3 inches deep.

### Heavy-based pots and pans

This refers to pots and pans that are made of thicker and heavier materials, so they absorb, distribute, and retain heat better than thin, lightweight (cheap!) aluminum pots and pans. A couple of popular examples include cast-iron skillets (see above) and dutch ovens.

### Pot sizes

Small 9 inches, large 10–12 inches, stockpot 7 quarts+ capacity.

### Saucepan sizes

Small 6 inches, medium 7 inches, large 8 inches.

# RECIPE INDEX

## BONUS RECIPE!



## EVERYDAY FOOD



## EFFORTLESS



## STIR-FRIES & NOODLES



## WHAT I DO WITH A PIECE OF . . .



## PASTA & COZY FOOD

## MEAL-WORTHY SALADS



## MEXICAN FOOD



## ASIAN BITES & SOUPS



## BIGGER THINGS



## SWEET ENDINGS



## EVERYTHING ELSE YOU NEED

INDEX

## BACON



## BEANS



## BEEF



## BEEF, GROUND



## CHEESE-FORWARD



## CHICKEN

## FISH *See also* **Salmon**



## GLUTEN-FREE



## LAMB



## MEAT-FREE (VEGETARIAN)

## MUSSELS



## NOODLES & SOBA



## ONE-POT RECIPES



## PASTA



## PORK

## RICE



## SALMON *See also* **Fish**



## SAUSAGE, CHORIZO, & CURED MEATS



## SHRIMP



## SLOW-COOKED



## VEGGIE-LOADED

*See also* **Meat-free (vegetarian)**

中濃ソース

MUTTI
Passata
KIKKOMAN
Soy Sauce
ABC

First published in 2022 by Macmillan, an imprint of Pan Macmillan Australia Pty Limited.


Printed in Canada
First American Edition 2023



Design by Michelle Mackintosh
Edited by Ariana Klepac
Index by Danielle Walker
Typeset by Studio31 Graphics
Prop and food styling by Nagi Maehashi and Emma Knowles
Hair and makeup by Gina Cartwright and Jaclyn Hnitko
Clothing styling by Sally Bruce
Manufacturing by TC Transcontinental

Countryman Press
www.countrymanpress.com

An imprint of W. W. Norton & Company, Inc.
500 Fifth Avenue, New York, NY 10110
www.wwnorton.com

978-1-68268-842-7

10 9 8 7 6 5 4 3 2 1

**Kale. Rejected again!**

Thumbs down! Try again . . .

Smells good, doesn't it, Dozer?

Dozer makes an excellent research assistant!

Queen of Dirty Dishes

Unnatural state—getting dolled up for photos!

Dozer, me, and the cookbook manuscript

Getting my hands dirty